# JUSTIFYING LANGUAGE

STUDIES IN LITERATURE AND RELIGION

General Editor: David Jasper, Director of the Centre for the Study of
Literature and Theology, University of Glasgow

*Studies in Literature and Religion* is a series of interdisciplinary titles, both
monographs and essays, concerned with matters of literature, art and
textuality within religious traditions founded upon texts and textual
study. In a variety of ways they are concerned with the fundamental
issues of the imagination, literary perceptions and theory, and an
understanding of poetics for theology and religious studies.

*Published titles include:*

David Scott Arnold
LIMINAL READINGS
Forms of Otherness in Melville, Joyce and Murdoch

John D. Barbour
THE CONSCIENCE OF THE AUTOBIOGRAPHER
Ethical and Religious Dimensions of Autobiography

Tibor Fabiny
THE LION AND THE LAMB
Figuralism and Fulfilment in the Bible, Art and Literature

Max Harris
THEATRE AND INCARNATION

David Jasper (*editor*)
POSTMODERNISM, LITERATURE AND THE
FUTURE OF THEOLOGY

TRANSLATING RELIGIOUS TEXTS

Ann Loades and Michael McLain (*editors*)
HERMENEUTICS, THE BIBLE AND LITERARY CRITICISM

Irena S. M. Makarushka
RELIGIOUS IMAGINATION AND
LANGUAGE IN EMERSON AND NIETZSCHE

Linda Munk
THE TRIVIAL SUBLIME

George Pattison
KIERKEGAARD: THE AESTHETIC AND THE RELIGIOUS

# Justifying Language

## Paul and Contemporary Literary Theory

Kevin Mills

First published in Great Britain 1995 by
**MACMILLAN PRESS LTD**
Houndmills, Basingstoke, Hampshire RG21 6XS
and London
Companies and representatives
throughout the world

A catalogue record for this book is available
from the British Library.

ISBN 0–333–63374–1

First published in the United States of America 1995 by
**ST. MARTIN'S PRESS, INC.,**
Scholarly and Reference Division,
175 Fifth Avenue,
New York, N.Y. 10010

ISBN 0–312–12989–0

Library of Congress Cataloging-in-Publication Data
Mills, Kevin.
Justifying language : Paul and contemporary literary theory /
Kevin Mills.
p.   cm. — (Studies in literature and religion)
Includes bibliographical references and indexes.
ISBN 0–312–12989–0
1. Bible. N.T. Epistles of Paul—Language, style.   Bible as
literature.   3. Literature, Ancient—History and criticism.
4. Christianity and literature.   I. Title.   II. Series.
BS2655.L3M55   1996
227'.066—dc20                                    95–24537
                                                      CIP



10   9   8   7   6   5   4   3   2   1
04   03   02   01   00   99   98   97   96   95

Printed and bound in Great Britain by
Antony Rowe Ltd, Chippenham, Wiltshire

To
Alma and Isla

# Contents

# General Editor's Preface

The field of literary approaches to the Bible has changed and developed radically in the past few years, and is becoming much more conscious of the place of the Bible in the complex and multidisciplinary arena of critical theory. Generally, however, such study is conducted from a highly sceptical perspective and without the recognition that the Bible and its long literary history within the Judaeo-Christian tradition have profound insights to offer to contemporary critical thought yet remaining within the perspective of faith.

This perspective is powerfully maintained by Dr Mills, who yet sustains a learned and lucid commentary on critical thinking. He uses the thought and writings of Paul to offer a critique of postmodern thought within theological categories that such thought might seem to negate or deconstruct.

This is a demanding book, but one which will be welcomed by those who remain committed to the Christian tradition while recognizing the difficulties of doing so within the critical space of postmodernity. It is a real contribution to the vigorous debate surrounding the problems of 'postmodern theology'.

DAVID JASPER
*General Editor*

# Preface

Two spheres of influence have converged to produce this study. I grew up in a Nonconformist Christian family where the Bible was habitually read and regarded as sacred scripture. With this background informing my approach to literature and interpretation, I discovered critical theory as a mature student. The subsequent confrontation between Truth and discourse, between the Book and textuality, gave rise to a strong desire to follow through its implications for interpretation and belief.

In both of these spheres of influence I owe large debts of thanks. My mum and dad, Edith and (the late) Frank Mills introduced me to the Bible, and have provided me with a living commentary. I am sure that the people of Zion Christian Fellowship will understand if I name Royden Morgan in thanking all of them for their material and moral support over the last few years. Without the technical back-up and largesse of Gordon Hughes this book would never have seen the light of day.

My intellectual debt to Christopher Norris will be evident to anyone who reads this work, but I also owe him a great deal of personal gratitude – he 'never made me fear/ and he didn't trample any hopes/ for he just carried a book . . .'. Despite our profound ideological differences, his generosity of spirit and his critical intelligence have been deeply appreciated. I am very grateful, too, to David Jasper for seeing this work through to publishable form, and for the friendship to which this project has given rise. I also want to thank Elaine Shepherd, John Schad and Roger Pooley for their encouragement, and Charmian Hearne at Macmillan for her help. Thanks also to Daniel Boyarin for being the only person ever to send me a fax.

Of all my debts the greatest are those to my wife Alma and to my daughter Isla. Their charity is boundless. My thanks is partly expressed by dedicating this book to them.

I am grateful to the editors of *Literature and Theology* and *Textual Practice* for permission to reprint material that has appeared in their respective journals.

K. M.

# Textual Note

The Pauline canon is disputed. I work with only those letters which are universally recognized as genuinely the work of Paul: Romans, 1 & 2 Corinthians, Galatians, Philippians, 1 Thessalonians, and Philemon. In Chapter 5 I make reference to Colossians. This is explained in an endnote signalled in the text.

I refer, mainly, to the King James (Authorized) Version of the Bible (1611). All quotations are from that source unless otherwise indicated. I have referred to other versions only for comparison of translation, or, where there seems to be little difference in content, for the sake of providing a coherent quotation with the minimum of ellipsis. Greek references are to the Concordant Version (A. E. Knoch, 1926). Abbreviations of other versions of the Bible used in the text are as follows:

NIV New International Version (International Bible Society, 1973, 1978, 1984).

RSV Revised Standard Version (Division of Christian Education of the National Council of the Churches of Christ in the USA, 1946, 1952).

RV Revised Version (1881).

# 1
# Introduction



Writing about 'Revelation in the Jewish Tradition', Emmanuel Levinas describes what might seem like an anxiety, which is as relevant to Christian thought as to Judaic. He speaks about the questions confronting:

> anyone who may still be responsive to these truths and signs but who is troubled to some degree – as a modern person – by the news of the end of metaphysics, by the triumphs of psychoanalysis, sociology, and political economy; someone who has learnt from linguistics that meaning is produced by signs without signifieds and who, confronted with all these intellectual splendours – or shadows – sometimes wonders if he is not witnessing the magnificent funeral celebrations held in honour of a dead god.[1]

This is where I begin: with a dual responsiveness – to the 'truths and signs' of Christian faith, and to the 'triumphs' of post-Christian discourses which are still celebrating God's magnificent funeral. Today, those who confront what has been called a crisis for theology and belief are characterized as either '[s]uspended between the loss of old certainties and the discovery of new beliefs', or as standing in 'defiant rejection of every critique of foundational beliefs'.[2] This is a false alternative for those to whom such critiques are productive of insights and challenges for Christian faith as well as of questions and problems.

Despite a certain hermeneutical suspicion (learned from Paul Ricoeur), I approach the problems of language and representation from (or towards) what David Jasper has referred to as 'the abyss of fundamentalism'.[3] Even so, I share Jasper's sense of 'boredom' with theology as such; not only its Casaubon-like obscurantism, but also its assumption of the scholarly totalization of religious thought and experience.[4] This disaffection extends to popular versions of 'correctness' in interpretation. *The Lion Handbook to the Bible*, for example (which includes contributions from such notable scholars as David Clines, Donald Guthrie and Howard Marshall), brings Bible interpretation down to a matter of historical context: 'What did the passage mean to the original hearers? How does the same message apply today?'[5] Without any historical relativist axe to grind, it makes little sense to me to inquire after 'original meanings' over such huge temporal and cultural-linguistic gulfs. Even if such meanings were readily available, why should the 'same message' assume such importance? Wouldn't such a message represent a reduction of the text's potential relevance?

These objections have as much to do with Pauline interpretation as with contemporary theory. Paul was rarely concerned with original meanings. What, for example, would today's hermeneutic purists make of his treatment of the law in 1 Corinthians 9: 'For it is written in the law of Moses, Thou shalt not muzzle the mouth of an ox that treadeth out the corn. Doth God take care for the oxen? Or saith he it altogether for our sakes?' (vv. 9–10a).

Luther's sense of the scripture *pro nobis* may have a kind of precedent here. Paul seems to see the law as being 'for us' as much as (if not more than) for the 'original hearers', and he liberates it, unashamedly, from its historical context. This is not to suggest that Paul had no regard for historical meaning. I argue the contrary case, in fact, with regard to his use of allegory (in Chapter 5), as part of the consideration of the letter/spirit polemic. Here, it can be noted that, scholarly as he undoubtedly was, Paul was not averse to exegetical practices alien to the modern inheritors of High Critical seriousness. His techniques include those midrashic, intertextual strategies long despised by western scholars, but now enjoying something of a vogue amongst literary theorists. It is to these theorists that I owe my (very limited) knowledge of midrash and intertextuality, and this knowledge has immeasurably enriched my appreciation and enjoyment of the biblical text. Mine, then, is a restless, critical, suspicious and iconoclastic 'fundamentalism'.

In this book I attempt to restate the case for a radical Christian faith, in a way that attends to the questions raised against it by the long and powerful philosophical assault on its basic principles. I want to affirm the viability of a critical belief which is cognizant of the array of philosophico-linguistic objections to its existence, and yet understands why faith, hope and love are able to remain in the face of this onslaught.

## APPROACHING PAUL

Although this study consists of an approach to Paul, and must therefore, at times, engage with his theological commentators, it is not a theological work in that it is not concerned with Christology, ecclesiology, soteriology, or any other '-ology' in that disciplinary set. Neither am I concerned to produce an alternative interpretation of Paul, which would 'rescue' him from theology in the interests of literary theory. Rather, my approach is from that position outlined by Levinas: a faith which is suspicious (and potentially critical) of the 'triumphs' of contemporary thought, in tension with the recognition – 'as a modern person' – that the intellectual environment in which such a faith arises is also a profound challenge to that faith. What emerges should, perhaps, be understood as a renewed (rediscovered) faith, which is critical of both the secular and the religious discourses that attempt, respectively, to destroy or to totalize it.

I do not wish to offer any definition of faith, hope, or charity, other than those which emerge in the course of the discussion, since their significance for hermeneutic enquiry is precisely the task in hand. Further, no definition would be without remainder, even a definition tailored to certain specific ends. A wide-ranging discussion of Pauline contexts, Greek etymologies, and doctrinal inferences, would constitute at least three separate (book-length) studies, and is beyond both the ambit of the present work and my scholarly competence. There are, no doubt, inconsistencies and blind spots in my deployment of these terms, but translation was ever an imprecise art, and it can never be overlooked that the Bible, in all its parts, is, *par excellence*, a text in translation. The strains and tensions evident in Paul's work are themselves products of cultural exchange, of a multi-layered translation: from Judaism to Christianity, from Jew to Gentile, from Hebrew to Greek, from the Christian emergence out of the Hebrew/Greek dichotomy to the cosmopolitan cultures of Rome, and from Christianized Jew to Judaized Christian.

In the maelstrom of these cultural interchanges, Paul forged a hermeneutic of deference, centred on the kenosis of incarnation and crucifixion. As Gerd Theissen says:

> Paul occupied a special place in this (i.e. Roman–Hellenistic) pluralism, for he stood on the boundary of two cultures. According to his origin, he is a Jew; but according to his task, missionary to the Gentiles.[6]

The originary Jewgreek/Greekjew, Paul is neither one nor the other without remainder. There is, it seems, no complete approach to his text, either within or outside of theology. Even his first-century readers were hard pressed to give an adequate account of his letters, as the author of 2 Peter admits: 'our beloved brother Paul . . . hath written unto you . . . some things hard to be understood' (2 Peter 3:15–16). His is a hermeneutic of the borderland, of travel, of exile, and of persecution. It has long since been traduced, reconstructed as an orthodox, dominant, monological, and frequently repressive ideology, but the rise of pluralism and the fall of theism has begun to return it to the margins. It is this new exile which enables it to be re-read, which demands its re-reading, not to shore up crumbling institutions, but to de-institutionalize the text in a new phase of dissent.

It is also in the interests of a de-institutionalized reading of Paul's text that I do not use the appellation 'saint' in front of his name. To do so is to categorize him according to an established nomenclature, produced by the ossification of a hierarchy in the post-Constantinian Church – an institution to which he did not belong.


## THE REMAINDER

This study could be read as an extended meditation on Paul's statement of remainder: 'And now abideth faith, hope, charity, these three; but the greatest of these is charity' (1 Corinthians 13:13).

Every linguistic utterance begins with the remainder, with the question, 'What is there left to be said on this matter?' It can never completely fill the requirement. It leaves a remainder, which is the possibility of further utterances.

Every linguistic utterance requires interpretation, and each interpretation has its own presuppositions, its own agenda, its own blindspots and insights – effectively a pre-formed remainder. Since interpretation must exclude certain possibilities if it is to be meaningful, and since each interpretation is also an utterance in need of interpretation, it leaves a further remainder, which is the possibility of further interpretations.

An introduction is an attempt to think the remainder, to make up the ground not covered in the main body of the text. It is an interpretation of what the unsaid of that text might contain. Since it is both utterance and interpretation, it cannot fill the gap, but, by means of this double insufficiency, serves only to widen it, leaving a greater remainder, which is the possibility of exchange and debate.

What would it mean to think the remainder? It will always be beyond the grasp of thought, eluding every strategem of discourse, always forming precisely that which is not said in the attempt to capture it: the future of language. Perhaps it requires that we attend to the logic of supplementarity which Jacques Derrida outlines.[7] The remainder, as supplement, supplies a lack in the text, but also supplants the text, appearing to be both a part of it and apart from it, questioning its borders. But even after the supplement, what remains?

The question has appeared in other contexts, in other terms. When, for example, Rudolf Bultmann sought to interpret the message of the New Testament for a post-mythological era, there remained a double surplus: was the mythic sublime reducible to scientifically acceptable categories? and could the scientific world-view 'perceive the whole reality of the world and of human life?'[8] The current distaste for totalization is outraged by the very idea of perceiving the 'whole reality of the world and of human life'. The last attempt to unite knowledge in an encyclopaedic gesture, structuralism, was stillborn. It gave birth to its own death, as its centre, or heart, the linguistic sign, was ruptured by deconstruction. Derrida's reading of Saussure did no violence to the sign, but exposed it to its own logic.[9] If, as Jacques Lacan says, 'there is no structure except of language',[10] then this deconstruction is not just the demise of structuralism; it is the undoing of structure itself, of the 'structurality of structure'.[11] The very possibility of conceiving reality as a whole is in doubt.

What this brings into view is the closure of metaphysics, its self-representation as closed circle.[12] Is there a remainder after metaphysics has closed itself off? Is there anywhere a trace of an other-than-metaphysics within the language it employs? If there were no such traces, then would it even be possible to ask after them within our inherited conceptuality? I believe the remainder itself to be such a trace. If every linguistic act and every interpretative discourse attests to its own open-endedness, so that there is no last word in hermeneutics, then even the most up-to-date encyclopaedia, or the most exhaustive dictionary, would require its supplements; and the supplements themselves open onto infinity, so that 'I suppose that even the world itself could not contain the books that should be written' (John 21:25b), nor could such a

Borgesian library contain the world.[13] Perhaps language and the world are constituted as remainders, each of the other?

At a time when the remainder has assumed more importance than its preludes, and when every interpretative act can be construed only as a prelude to what remains unsaid, what does it mean to view the remainder in terms of faith, hope and charity (love) – theologically determined categories? Isn't deconstruction, in its de-centring of the structurality of structure, also the death knell of all such explanatory 'grand narratives'?[14] On my account, faith disrupts the deconstructive account of signification, while hope questions assumptions about the relation between faith and closure, and love turns language away from structure. In this light, Paul's hermeneutic demands a certain critical orientation to the modes of contemporary literary theory, whether deconstruction or postmodernism.

Again, it might be objected, the notion of critique has also been subjected to deconstruction. Critique presupposes that which, Derrida tells us, does not exist: an outside to the text.[15] He writes:

> [D]econstruction is neither an analysis nor a critique. . . . It is not an analysis in particular because the dismantling of a structure is not a regression toward a *simple element*, towards an *indissoluble origin*. These values, like that of analysis, are themselves philo-sophemes subject to deconstruction. No more is it critique, in a general sense or in a Kantian sense. The instance of *krinein* or of *krisis* (decision, choice, judgement, discernment) is itself, as is all the apparatus of transcendental critique, one of the essential 'themes' or 'objects' of deconstruction.[16]

In Chapter 2, I attempt to establish a response to deconstruction which neither breaks with it nor remains within it. This argument involves seeing deconstruction as both analysis and critique. It is analytic because predicated upon a critique of the Saussurean sign. It is certainly the case that it does not effect a regression toward the sign as a simple element; contrarily, it shows that the sign is mani-festly *not* a simple element. But in order to de-stabilize this axial point in the structuralist project, it must begin at the semiotic level. This is already an analytic gesture: a reduction of language to its 'elemental' state. I contrast this to Paul Ricoeur's synthesis of the semiotic, the semantic and the hermeneutic levels of language.

Ricoeur's work informs much of the subsequent discussion, par-ticularly his early essays on hermeneutics in *The Conflict of Interpreta-tions*, which represent, for me, a starting point in thinking through the problems of language, associated with poststructuralism. Deconstruction can also be seen as critique, because it will always involve some kind of choice or judgement, if only in the selection of texts to be read. Christopher Norris made the point in 1982, that 'Derrida's virtual silence in regard to Marx can only be construed as a prolonged postponement'.[17] Kevin Hart noted the continued prolonging of this postponement in 1990, asking 'at what level the issue of choice takes root in deconstruction'.[18]

At this stage, faith is the paradigm of what remains: it is what remains of language after every shaking of concepts, whether under the sign of deconstruction, or the postmodern. That is to say, language works because its tokens are accepted in exchange, not for the world, but for relations, for community, for exchange itself. This faith is explored as the historical relationship between words and the Word, between the text and the Book, in order to show that Paul's insistence that 'faith cometh by hearing, and hearing by the word of God' (Romans 10:17) is, potentially, and in the context of an approach to contemporary literary theory, the key to a hermeneutical resistance to the ideology of interpretative freeplay.

Chapter 3, continuing the exploration of faith as a hermeneutical principle, discusses its relationship to ideology in some recent works, and to the postmodern suspicion of all 'metanarratives', religious or otherwise. If faith is intrinsic to the linguistic process, then it cannot be equated with ideology, which is a product of language. The question then arises of the specificity of the faith under consideration. There is a critical choice involved, which I do not want to disguise. I am considering the potentialities of faith as it appears in the writings of Paul. I see this particular, Christian faith, as encoded by, or encrypted within language, so that every utterance is fiduciary. Paul's writing, when read in tandem with contemporary literary theory, yields this understanding in a double movement, which is both within and against a certain theoretical matrix. This does not involve claiming that this 'language' is universal. It may be that it only refers to languages associated with the Christian interpretative tradition of western Europe. However limiting that may seem, it is also the limit of 'logocentrism', of deconstruction, of all critical approaches to the centripetal force of the *logos*.[19] In the words of Ariel: 'Where the bee sucks, there suck I'.

Where faith is, hope will be. Chapters 4 and 5 develop the implications (for interpretation) of faith in its manifestation as hope-in-belief. If the remainder is the future of writing, then hope must inform every linguistic utterance: the hope of communication, of understanding, of exchange. It is outlined as the opening of the hermeneutic circle in the direction of resistance to received interpretation, breaking with a diversity of perceived constraints, such as the epistemological derivations of Platonic *anamnesis*, Nietzsche's notion of 'eternal recurrence', Gadamer's 'tradition' etc.[20] This hope is then related to Kantian postulation, and Hamann's hermeneutical vision. In this light, Hamann's conversion is an eighteenth century linguistic turn, which gives prominence to hope as an interpretative imperative entwined with Kant's epistemological turn.

The theme of conversion, in its renewal of interpretative procedures for Paul, Augustine and Hamann, is taken up as of crucial importance to hermeneutics guided by hope. But an interpretative hope derived from Paul's text is confronted with an apparent reduction in the opposition of the spirit and the letter. If 'the letter killeth, but the spirit giveth life' (2 Corinthians 3:6b), as Paul says, then is it not the case that the deconstruction of such oppositions as speech versus writing, presence versus absence, intelligible versus sensible, is also the demise of Pauline interpretation? In Chapter 5, I set out to explore this problem. Finding a series of fractures or slippages in Paul's texts, which de-stabilize the letter/spirit distinction, but retain the explanatory force of the gesture as a limit-situation of interpretation, I trace the historical durability of this distinction, concluding that it is criterial to any interpretative act.

Far from finally undermining it, the advent of deconstruction actually enables a new understanding of Paul's distinction, and of its tenacity. It reappears, heavily disguised, in Simon Critchley's recent account of *The Ethics of Deconstruction*. For Critchley, a deconstructive reading is a double reading which consists of:

> [F]irst . . . a patient and scholarly commentary following the main lines of the text's dominant interpretation, and second, . . . locating an interruption or alterity within that dominant interpretation where reading discovers insights within a text to which that text is blind.[21]

I do not want to claim that this double reading sets up two categories of interpretation which exactly correspond to a 'literal' sense and a 'spiritual' sense, but that there has always been, at least since Paul, a double demand in interpretation, and that the 'patient and scholarly commentary' of Critchley's first reading has, for centuries of interpreters in the Christian tradition, constituted the 'literal' sense. On the other hand, the blindness of the text to its own insight suggests an enlightening irruption within the text, an alterity which could be strategically named as the 'spritual' sense, provided that the latter is understood in the context of the proposed instability of oppositions: the reciprocal constitution of different senses which occupy the same textual space.

The latter part of Chapter 5, and much of Chapter 6, is concerned with two key themes: *deference* and *kenosis*. Deference is the enlightening irruption within the text of deconstruction, discovered in the interior of Derridean *différance*. It opens deconstruction up to the third term of Paul's abiding trinity: charity or love, recalling it to responsibility. The trajectory of hope-in-belief then passes on towards an ethical concern that interpretation should not be guided by personal, individualized norms, but should be understood as a demand from the realm of intersubjectivity, from the realm of language itself. Kenosis names the ascetical moment when the subject recognizes itself as constituted by its other, and divests itself of the right to determine either its own meaning or that of its other. It is also the trope of referentiality, of language dying to itself in order to name the world. Meaning, then, is seen as the product of a double ascesis: the acknowledgement that I am only myself by virtue of a shared investment in language, and that language is enabled by my self-divestment in the face of the other.

Together, the five chapters (2–6) progress through Paul's three key terms, faith, hope and charity, as principles of language and interpretation. These should not be understood as hypostases of language, nor as discrete levels or regions of temporality within interpretation. Paul says that charity 'believeth all things, hopeth all things' (1 Corinthians 13:7), so the first and second terms inhere in the third. Also, if language constitutes the subject-in-relation, then the fiduciary character of language is already a charitable gesture, made in the hope of exchange. But Paul characterizes faith, hope and charity as 'abiding', they are characteristic of the remainder. As I discuss in Chapter 6, Paul gives them this abiding status in 1 Corinthians 13, at the end of his hymn to love, which is, in turn, set into a discourse on glossolalia (speaking in unknown tongues). He is concerned with a certain use (or mis-use) of language, and with the demand for interpretation. The remainder that opens up beyond every utterance, which is the unknowable possibility of renewed discourse, is hedged around, bordered, or enclosed by the conditions of entry into language: the other-involving criteria which Paul names as faith, hope and charity.


My thesis can be summarized, then, as a claim that contemporary literary theory, for all its rhetorical sophistication, has not progressed beyond Paul's first-century hermeneutic. His categories of faith, hope and charity still govern interpretation, and where they are transgressed, language goes into freefall, prey to the kind of abuses that legitimate oppressive political forces as well as libertarian causes. I argue that Paul's writings offer an understanding of language and interpretation which has not yet been extrapolated from them, but which has been hidden under centuries of theologically determined readings. I attempt to situate this Pauline hermeneutic within the history of ideas, and to elucidate it in (and against) the theoretical context of deconstruction and poststructuralism.

# 2

# Language, Faith, Understanding

Faith cometh by hearing, and hearing by the word of God. (Romans 10:17)

[T]o understand the text, it is necessary to believe in what the text announces to me; but what the text announces to me is given nowhere but in the text. This is why it is necessary to understand the text in order to believe.[1]

## INTRODUCTION

The Christian literary theorist lives on what Robert Browning called 'the dangerous edge of things', amongst 'the honest thieves, the tender murderers, the superstitious atheists', having to balance a commitment to a supra-linguistic reality with a seemingly inescapable textuality, a life-changing faith with a critical suspicion.[2] Like Bishop Blougram, I imagine a chorus of 'He may believe; and yet, and yet/ How can he?' Earlier in his monologue, Blougram likens this region of paradoxical affinities to a chessboard which might represent either a 'life of doubt diversified by faith' or 'one of faith diversified by doubt:/ We called the chess-board white, – we call it black'. Faith and doubt define each other in this metaphor, in a way which illustrates Ferdinand de Saussure's claim that linguistic meaning is a product of difference. Each word in a given language derives its value from other (contrasted) words.

Saussure (1857–1913) used the game of chess to illustrate some of the fundamental notions of structural linguistics, in his *Course in General Linguistics* (English edition 1966). The state of the game at any given time corresponds to an historically specific moment in the development of a language; the value of each piece is dependent upon its relative position as well as its assigned pattern of movement; each move has repercussions for the whole system.[3] Similarly, linguistic signs derive their value from the difference between one 'piece' and another, and this value is not permanently fixed. There is a kind of faith involved in this, which can be recognized by comparison with acceptance of the rules of the game. If the rules are not agreed, or if the players cannot be trusted to keep to the rules, then there is no game. I must accept the relative value of the pieces, and keep to the limited movement of each piece within the grid of the chequerboard. If I want to engage with my antagonist, I must see the marked-out black and white squares as the ground on which the contest will take place. Within the restrictions of the game, I am not free to disregard any of these rules. This faith is a kind of criterion for the game. I will return to Saussure later in this chapter.

## Faith and Language

Given its celebration of the theological *logos*, and its emphasis on 'the word made flesh', it is not surprising that Christian faith is frequently, and without question, associated with 'logocentrism' and the 'metaphysics of presence'. What is meant by these terms will become clearer as the discussion proceeds. The deconstruction of that metaphysics goes by way of Saussure's semiology (study of signs), with its privileging of self-present speech (spoken and heard simultaneously by the speaker) over written language (from which the author is absent). Taken together, these two facts more than suggest that Saussure's game of chess is played out on Bishop Blougram's board. The issue of faith is a crucial one in this context, because the structure of the board itself already demands that a prior 'faith' has accepted the rules of engagement. It begins to appear that even before faith and doubt mark out the grid of Blougram's chessboard, and prior to the consideration of linguistic difference, some kind of faith must already be in place. A radical faith, which deconstruction, poststructuralism and postmodernism overlook, must subtend the appearance of the network. The bringing to light of this prevenient faith is the task which I have set myself here.

## Paul

Over the last two decades, literary studies have focused, with increasing assiduousness, upon the issues surrounding linguistic theory and the concomitant problems of representation. As a result, the language of biblical texts has come under closer scrutiny, particularly their suasive, rhetorical, and (under the influence of structuralist thought) narrative language. Comparatively little of this work has centred on the Pauline canon, as against the amount of attention paid to the Gospels, and none of it has actually considered, in any depth, the relationship between current hermeneutic theory and Paul's interpretative practice.

There is, perhaps, little need to argue the central importance of Paul's writing in the development of hermeneutics. His work inaugurates the (still current) task of interpreting biblical texts in the Christian era. A cursory perusal of recent issues of scholarly journals, or a quick browse through publication lists, would serve to show that the Bible is still very much under scrutiny in the field of literary theory. Paul's place in this ongoing enterprise is unique inasmuch as his letters not only interpret scripture but have themselves become part of the canon, part of what the Christian tradition accepts as biblical. This may be said of any or all of the New Testament writers, but since Paul's work forms a comparatively large percentage of the specifically Christian canon, and since it contains such a high proportion of directly interpretative material, it is of particular significance in the history and development of Bible interpretation and its descendent discipline – literary theory.

Reading Paul's letters without a specific concern as to their implications for modern theories of text interpretation, or for the impact of such theories upon our reading of these ancient writings, it would be easy to miss the many references to language and interpretation, and the complexity of many rhetorical gestures which, when scrutinized alongside modern theoretical works, yield surprising hermeneutical insights and ramifications. Despite a certain perceived silence, the absence of a detailed search, Paul has a great deal to say about language, representation and the questions that interest critical theorists.

## LANGUAGE ACQUISITION

One famous Pauline dictum (from Romans 10:17) serves to open the discussion, since it raises questions about both language and that traditional prerequisite of Christian interpretation, faith: 'Faith cometh by hearing, and hearing by the word of God'. Psychologists of language hold various opinions about its acquisition: how a new speaker comes to understand a language. All models of the acquisition process, however, require that the infant is exposed to a competent user of the language to be learned.[4] Debates about the innateness of linguistic potential have no bearing on the process itself only on its psychological significance, and even those as convinced as Noam Chomsky (born 1928) that 'the idea of "structure dependent operations" is part of the innate schematism applied by the mind to the data of experience', have no doubt that language 'cometh by hearing', just like faith.[5] In both cases 'hearing' must be a perceptual paradigm since those deprived of that particular sense are capable of coming to terms with language and with faith.[6] In fact, relatively little is known about the factors involved in acquiring language, and the process remains (to a great extent) mysterious. If the model of reading is applicable, *mutatis mutandis*, to the psychology of language then Paul Ricoeur's formulation of the hermeneutic circle (quoted above) may point towards a Chomskian view, since the circle seems to be devoid of empirical access. In terms of the current argument this is simply to focus attention on the fact that psycholinguistics can no more elucidate the problem of how we gain our linguistic competence than can hermeneutics. It also suggests that the latter, in its concern with understanding, has relevance beyond the realms of Bible interpretation and literary criticism. It is clear that the structure of the problem of understanding is the same at the level of acquisition as it is at the level of interpretation. Indeed, for Friedrich Schleiermacher, a key figure in the development of modern interpretation theory, acquisition was a hermeneutic process since 'every child arrives at the meaning of a word only through hermeneutics'.[7]

The question here is one of the grounding of understanding. Tracing it back to acquisition simply begs the same question and elicits a response which might explain the psychodynamics of language use (the mental processes involved), but cannot clarify the processes internal to language itself. The psychological model proposed by Chomsky is of no value in illuminating the hermeneutic circle as Ricoeur states it, because the discourse of psycholinguistics takes place at a different level of analysis than hermeneutics. What needs to be noted before those levels of analysis are explicitly differentiated is that the dialectic of belief and understanding (suggested both by the chess metaphor and by the quotations from Paul and from Ricoeur), seems to offer no transcendental principle of the order of Chomsky's 'innate schematism'. Is there even a possibility of identifying such a principle without psychologizing or appealing to some pre-determined order of things – offering a theological explanation, for example? Can language itself be understood as offering such a principle? This question is fundamental to any hermeneutic venture cognizant of theories of language which shape the intellectual debates of our age: structuralism, poststructuralism, deconstruction.

In the remainder of this chapter, I open a discussion of Ricoeur's formulation of the hermeneutic circle and its relation to Paul's insistence that 'faith cometh by hearing, and hearing by the Word of God', with the aim of uncovering the role of faith in language and understanding. Before the discussion, 'faith' names the possibility of understanding, a still hidden (or at least unclear) principle. The chapter heading already gives an indication of the work of faith, coming as it does between language and understanding. At the end of the chapter I offer a reading of Romans 10 in order to trace this movement in the work of Paul.

## RICOEUR AND DERRIDA

### The 'Tension' Theory of Metaphor

Paul Ricoeur (born 1913) has done a great deal to re-establish the importance of hermeneutics in philosophy. Developing aspects of the work of earlier thinkers such as Friedrich Schleiermacher (1768–1834). Wilhelm Dilthey (1833–1911) and Martin Heidegger (1889–1976), he has focused critical attention on the problems of understanding, especially on the questions associated with the interpretation of written texts. His study of the creation of meaning through metaphor is of great significance in any consideration of modern theories of linguistic representation.[8]

In *The Rule of Metaphor* (English edition 1977), Ricoeur structures his treatment of the subject according to three levels of linguistic analysis. The rhetoric of metaphor, particularly in Aristotelian terms, takes the word as its unit of reference, considering metaphor as a single-word figure of speech defined as a trope of resemblance. Demonstrating the inadeqacy of this model, the discussion moves via the distinction between semiotics (in which the word is the minimum level of complete meaning), and semantics (in which meaning is carried by sentences), to the level of hermeneutics (interpretation of discourse). In considering metaphor as a function of discourse rather than sentence, Ricoeur proposes an opposition between a 'tension' theory of metaphor and a 'substitution' theory.[9] The tension theory uncovers 'a tension between identity and difference' within the work of resemblance. This tension is held in the role of the copula of metaphor: the 'is' which both equates and differentiates between the two terms so linked, rather than substituting the one for the other. The 'x is y' structure of metaphor maintains the distinction between x and y, whilst asserting their identity. It cannot be applied to single words since it affects both terms: If I say 'Love is the star to every wandering bark', then I say something about love and also about the pole star. The effects of metaphor do not stop there: '[t]o affect just one word, the metaphor has to disturb a whole network by means of an aberrant attribution'. So metaphor is a 'discursive phenomenon'.[10]

## 'Use' and Discourse

If such an important aspect of meaning is located at the level of discourse then there must be implications for those critical projects based in versions of semiotic (sign-based) theories of language. Jacques Derrida's *Of Grammatology* (English edition 1976) set up deconstruction as just such an approach. Deconstruction actually works as a kind of anti-semiotics, undoing the structure of the sign, but it is nevertheless a sign-based discourse. I will return to this shortly. In an important engagement with Derrida's essay on the role of metaphor in philosophical texts, 'White Mythology',[11] Ricoeur argues that a tension theory of metaphor, operating at the semantic level, works against the Platonic affinity between a substitution theory of metaphor and the transfer of the sensible to the intelligible in philosophical discourse. So contrary to Derrida's assertion that philosophy gains a force from its metaphors that is unsustainable once it is realized that 'figures are reduced to modes of "expression" of the idea' by philosophical texts, Ricoeur claims:

> No philosophical discourse would be possible, not even a discourse of deconstruction, if we ceased to assume what Derrida justly holds to be 'the sole thesis of philosophy', namely, 'that the

meaning aimed at through these figures is an essence rigorously independent of that which carries it over.'[12]

The role of metaphor in the texts of philosophy is not the issue here. The current significance of the exchange between Ricoeur and Derrida is that, in Ricoeur's analysis, 'metaphor presents itself as a strategy of discourse that, while preserving and developing the creative power of language, preserves and develops the *heuristic* power wielded by *fiction*'.[13]

Metaphor as discourse, rather than single-word figure, is aligned against an etymologizing tendency at work in texts like 'White Mythology', which implies a semiotics rather than a hermeneutics. Recalling 'dead' metaphors (i.e. showing the figurality of words that are used as conceptual) appeals to some notion of 'proper' meaning at the level of 'word' or 'sign', as distinct from 'figurative' meaning. What sustains the difference between literality and figurality, Ricoeur insists, is use in *discourse*. The distinction is not available at the semiotic level.

In 'The *Retrait* of Metaphor' Derrida counters Ricoeur's objections on two fronts. He says that Ricoeur is wrong to conclude that the argument of 'White Mythology' theorizes the interpretation of metaphor as a transfer from the sensible to the intelligible. It is precisely this kind of formulation that Derrida wishes to put in question, since it privileges this particular trope in metaphysical discourse. Secondly, Ricoeur is seen to fail to take full account of the play on 'use' as both 'wear and tear' and 'usury'. He sees this as a 'diversionary tactic' whereas Derrida's text shows it to be inherent in the 'intractable structure' of metaphoricity. Derrida does not reduce metaphor to the process of becoming-worn-out, which determines Ricoeur's distinction between 'live' and 'dead' metaphor, but allows the play between 'use' (or 'currency') and 'usury' to disrupt the unitary understanding of metaphoricity.[14] When Ricoeur then sees the difference between literality and figurality as a matter of 'use', his text falls back within the 'intractable structure' which he is seeking to elucidate.

Derrida, then, does not disagree with Ricoeur's treatment of metaphor, but shows that his reading of 'White Mythology' attributes to that text assertions which Derrida is at pains to deconstruct, and that in doing so it reveals its own investment in the very trope that it defines. This does not altogether abrogate the effectiveness of Ricoeur's move in shifting the focus of meaning from semiotics to hermeneutics, but it does necessitate a renegotiation of the move from sign to discourse. Such a detour demands that the debate be taken back to Saussure's linguistics and the founding texts of modern semiotics.

## SAUSSURE

It will be useful to quote Ricoeur's *The Rule of Metaphor* again: 'To say with de Saussure that language is a system of signs is to characterize language in just one of its aspects and not in its total reality'.[15] Saussure's linguistics and the structural model of language deriving from Louis Hjelmslev's highly theorized form of it, is a linguistics of the sign. Language, on this analysis, is a system of signs which derive their value from one another by means of significant contrast. A sign has value only as part of the system in which it functions. There can be no positive terms, then, only relations of interdependence. In his *Prologomena to a Theory of Language* (1969), Hjelmslev establishes an opposition between 'process' and 'system', asserting: '*A priori* it would seem to be a generally valid thesis that for every process there is a corresponding system, by which the process can be analyzed and described by means of a limited number of premises'.[16] This is a formalization of Saussure's maxim insisting upon the synchronic approach to language study (which 'freezes' it at a given point in time in order to discover its structure) as opposed to the diachronic (historical) approach. If language as a system is to be brought into view, the historical, developmental axis must be ignored. In Hjelmslev this is modified into a dialectic of process and system in which 'the process determines the system', and yet the system 'governs and determines' the process.[17] He concludes (paradoxically, to my mind) that, whereas a process is unimaginable without an underlying system, 'a system does not presuppose the existence of a process'. Translated into specifically linguistic terms: 'It is thus impossible to have a text without a language lying behind it. On the other hand, one can have a language without a text constructed in that language'.[18]

The abstract possibility of language existing as a pre-textual structure is a direct development of the closing of the system of signs. In this view language is sealed off from the world of act and event. As Ricoeur observes in 'Structure, Word, Event', the definition of the sign in line with these assertions cannot allow it to stand for a thing.[19] Saussure, of course, is explicit about this: 'The linguistic sign unites, not a thing and a name, but a concept and a sound-image . . . the two elements are intimately united, and each recalls the other'.[20] Language is thus objectified in a way that makes possible an approach to its study which can understand itself as scientific. What Hans-Georg Gadamer (born 1900) refers to as 'distanciation' takes place: a process that problematizes the issues of interpretation and re-orients them as structuralism. Gadamer sees this objectifying tendency as a loss of the truth of our participation in language to technical method.[21]

Ricoeur expressly rejects the 'truth or method' alternative by appeal to what he calls the 'dominant problematic' i.e. that of the text. I have already spoken of the levels of analysis through which he pursues his discussion of metaphor. Proceeding from semiotics through semantics to hermeneutics, he moves from consideration of the word, through sentence to discourse. The linguistics of discourse provides his response to the problem of meaning. He claims that Saussure's definition of language ('a system of signs') is not wrong but simply inadequate. He then sets out to synthesize the descriptions of language as semiotic and semantic. In *Hermeneutics and the Human Sciences* (English edition 1981) he takes up some of the pairs of traits of discourse, identified in *The Rule of Metaphor*, to show the relevance of distanciation to hermeneutics. The movement that synthesizes language as word-oriented and as discourse-oriented is the same as that which overcomes the alternative of truth or method. When 'discourse is realised as an event' it is also 'understood as meaning'.[22] As 'event' discourse is temporal as against the atemporality of the system, it is historically particularized and has an intentionality which is 'something completely different from the meaning of an isolated sign'. Signification takes place at the semiotic level, intentionality at the level of semantics:

> Just as language, by being actualised in discourse, surpasses itself as system and realises itself as event, so too discourse, by entering the process of understanding, surpasses itself as event and becomes meaning. The surpassing of the event by the meaning is characteristic of discourse as such. It attests to the intentionality of language . . .[23]

Appealing to intentionality is not an instance of the 'intentional fallacy' resurrected to reclaim language for 'common sense' usage.[24]

Writing the text renders it autonomous. This is another moment of distanciation which cannot be reduced to a question of method, but which becomes the very condition of interpretation. Interpretation cannot be a process of looking behind or beyond the text to find authorial meaning; it is 'to understand oneself in front of the text'.[25] Ricoeur's term for the recovery of meaning 'in front of the text', as self-understanding, rather than 'behind the text', as authorial meaning, is 'appropriation'. This is not to return interpretation to a pure subjectivity, but to revise the whole question of subjectivity in terms of the text and its meaning as ideal object (having neither mental nor physical reality). Following the 'arrow of meaning' in the text involves the reader in a 'divestment' of self. I want, eventually, to move away from Ricoeur's notion of interpretation as a revision of self-understanding, and to develop the theme of self-divestment. For now, I will let his argument run its course, with just the observation that there is a tension between 'appropriation' and 'divestment' which needs to be explored.


## SENSE AND REFERENCE


By means of Gottlob Frege's well know distinction between 'sense' and 'reference', Ricoeur is able to make the distancing effect achieved by discourse a condition of meaning. Sense (as the thought expressed by a sentence) is only distinguishable from reference (as its truth value) at the semantic level. Language as semiotic has no referential function: its values are purely differential. That this leaves an aspect of language unaccounted for is made clear by Frege's example of the planet Venus, also known as both 'the Morning star' and 'the Evening star'. The reference of the latter two phrases is the same, but not their sense. To assert that they have the same reference is meaningful only in so far as the difference between senses is also asserted. The thought that is expressed by each phrase is different but the truth value is the same: they both depend upon a condition of the real-world situation, i.e. the existence of the planet Venus and its perceptibility to the human eye.[26]

Reference, then, is a direction of discourse; an intentionality which, as a function of distanciation, relates the problem of truth and method to that of semiotics and semantics. Once the question of meaning is related to discourse, intentionality is brought into play. As Sollace Mitchell observes with regard to the most autonomous of discursive forms, 'no sense can be made of writing except as the mark of an intentional activity'.[27] A linguistics of signs, arranged in an a-temporal system, is inadequate to cope with the effectiveness of language as event. The material historicality of the instance of discourse causes language to transcend itself as system, even if the system has a *bona fide* heuristic function.

This referential power of discourse has implications for the structural model found in Hjelmslev. If the very function of language is only discovered in text (whether written or spoken) then it is not possible, as Hjelmslev claims to 'have a language without a text constructed in that language'. If structure is simply held to be prior to usage, and the synchronic emphasis gives rise to a model of language that is ahistorical, and so excludes discourse as event, then the attack upon language launched under the sign of deconstruction is allowed to undo referentiality and leave language 'hanging, unanchored to anything that would lend determinate semantic value to words'.[28] This is clearly not what Derridean deconstruction is seeking to achieve. That language works with a kind of intentionality, only available at the semantic level, is acknowledged by Derrida as an 'indispensable guardrail'. Such a claim is seen, admittedly, as 'protecting' rather than 'opening' readings of particular texts so that appeal to intentionality is seen to make of interpretation a doubling of the text:

> Yet if reading must not be content with doubling the text, it cannot legitimately transgress the text toward something other than it, toward a referent (a reality that is metaphysical, historical, psychobiographical, etc.) or toward a signified outside of the text whose content could take place, could have taken place outside of language, that is to say, in the sense that we give here to that word, outside of writing in general.[29]

In *Of Grammatology*, one of the founding texts of deconstruction and poststructuralism, Derrida reads the 'structure' of Saussure's linguistics as a kind of writing before the letter. This move deconstructs the opposition of speech and writing everywhere at work in Saussure's text, in that it enables speech, privileged by the text, to be read as a determined modification of writing. 'Writing in general' is a description of language that holds this deconstruction in place, but as the prevenient *structure*, 'writing in general' must have already fallen into question. That is to say that the hermeneutic power of discourse, which can give rise to the synchronic structure (elaborated in metalinguistic *discourse*), actually shifts the linguistic centre of gravity so that the speech/writing deconstruction leaves that hermeneutic power intact. Since (contrary to Hjelmslev's contention) it is not possible to conceive of a system without a process, 'writing in general' is a belated discovery, already testifying to the power of discourse. So, the distanciation of writing is nothing other than the condition of interpretation, not of a kind which transgresses the text in search of a controlling authorial intention, but which ranges across the text as an intentional phenomenon. The possibilities of this hermeneutic venture will occupy subsequent chapters.

## THE PROBLEM OF THE LINGUISTIC SIGN: DECONSTRUCTION

### Signifier and Signified

The problem that determines the relationship between hermeneutics and deconstruction here, is not the question of intentionality, but that of where meaning is located. Language, according to *Of Grammatology*, is that which a linguistics of language cannot totalize. In engaging with Saussurean linguistics the problems of semantics and of a linguistics of discourse are never approached, because the linguistic sign dominates the discussion:

> From the moment that there is meaning there are nothing but signs. We *think only in signs*. Which amounts to ruining the notion of the sign at the very moment when, as in Nietzsche, its exigency is recognized in the absoluteness of its right.[30]

In his discussion of linguistic value Saussure replaced what he had earlier referred to as 'concept' and 'sound image' with 'signifier' and 'signified' as components of the sign. He wrote of the signified as a 'psychological imprint', another kind of signifier. So a chain of signification is set up which equates the signified of language with a kind of writing ('psychological imprint'). Writing, for Saussure, is simply a sign of a sign: 'Language and writing are two distinct systems of signs; the second exists for the sole purpose of representing the first'.[31] Thus, 'representation', Derrida says, 'mingles with what it represents to the point where ... one thinks as if the represented were nothing more than the shadow or reflection of the representer. . . . In this play of representation, the point of origin becomes ungraspable'.[32] The notion of the sign is ruined because its exigency enforces itself even at the level of the signified, which will always be in the position of a signifier, so the two 'faces' of the sign cannot be held apart. The opposition signifier/signified which is the structure of the sign, and the key distinction around which Saussure's entire system is built, is unsustainable.

This is not a simple inversion of Saussurean semiology which perversely reorders the privileging of speech over writing. Derrida's concern is to show the work of what he sees as 'the metaphysics of presence' in what looks like scientific distanciation in the study of language. Speech is valued over writing because of its self-presence: the simultaneity of speaking and hearing, and the presence of the addressee which enables meaning to be controlled and delimited. If such control is possible in speech it is not so in writing. Writing is autonomous because of the absence of the author. So speech *versus* writing is a version of the Platonic (or, more particularly, Plotinian) oppositions between presence and absence, immediacy and mediation. When Derrida shows such a metaphysics of presence at work in Saussure, and also exposes the unsustainability of its founding opposition in the *Course in General Linguistics*, he not only calls into question the presumed scientificization of language study, but also the very possibility of a 'pure' scientific discourse. The distanciation which marks Saussure's method also signals its participation in a metaphysical project going back as least as far as Plato. This is not an isolated or insignificant quirk of Saussure's text but the linguistic predicament of all scientific discourse.

## Participation and Distanciation

There is a sense in which the exigency of the sign is the triumph of method over truth, of distanciation over participation. When Derrida writes *'There is nothing outside of the text'* (*'Il n'y a pas de hors-texte'*) he is approaching a 'Question of Method', and the immanentist approach to the text (reading it without reference to any external constraints) holds it at a remove from the phenomenology of reading evident in Ricoeur.[33] In Ricoeur's approach to Saussure and Gadamer there is a hermeneutic that refuses the exigency of the sign and the choice between truth and method which it enforces. Abandoning the linguistics of discourse and the historicality of the language-event strips language not only of its ability to function meaningfully but

also of its materiality. Derrida's notion of intentionality as an 'indispensable guardrail' is extremely problematical as long as the insistence on semiotics excludes semantics. It becomes fully viable only
at the level of discourse, and at this level hermeneutics operates.

Ricoeur, in fact, sees the tension between truth and method as an
antinomy:

> [B]ecause it establishes an untenable alternative: on the one hand,
> alienating distanciation is the attitude that renders possible the
> objectification which reigns in the human sciences; but on the other
> hand, this distanciation, which is the condition of the scientific
> status of the sciences, is at the same time the fall that destroys the
> fundamental and primordial relation whereby we belong to and
> participate in the historical reality which we claim to construct as
> an object.[34]

It is clear that the problem of distanciation in its relation to this antinomy takes place at the level of the sign, and not at that of discourse,
in Saussure's text. The movement of science is analytic (breaking its
objects down into their constituent parts) not synthetic (bringing
parts together to form wholes). To what extent can the problems of
the sign be overcome by a synthetic movement from sign to text?
This question underlies *The Rule of Metaphor* and much of Ricoeur's
work. I have already argued that this movement represents a polemical break between deconstruction and hermeneutics. Deconstruction
is seen to be an effective attack on the project of hermeneutics only
if the analytic movement which breaks up language into compon-
ent parts is logically prior to the synthesis which produces texts.
That is to say that if language is primarily a system of signs, and if
semiotics therefore grounds semantics, then deconstruction undoes
interpretation at every turn, because the locus of meaning, the sign,
is capable only of infinite deferral, exigent difference, what Derrida
calls *différance*. Ironically, Sollace Mitchell, in an argument aimed
against what he calls 'significationism', turns language away from
discourse towards the sign:

> A theory addressed to the meaning of words as they function in
> texts is at best incomplete without an account of the meanings
> those words carry into the text, for the textual work a word does
> must derive from a standard meaning that it bears in the lan-
> guage at large, outside of any one text.[35]

The problem with this is that 'outside of any one text' is also inside another text. There is always the double movement that Ricoeur has identified at work in language – participation and distanciation. A language will always work by cultural agreement of terms with which the subject of language must keep faith in order to communicate and interpret. That agreement is the work of practice, of textual production. So the meaning of a word is always within a text and between texts which allude to one another, cite one another, feed off one another. Hjelmslev's unsynthesized dialectic of process and system is at work here. The resolution towards the objectification of language that is structuralism, or towards the de-objectification that is poststructuralism, is one which Ricoeur is unwilling to make. He sees the work of hermeneutics as maintaining the levels of analysis made available by different discourses, and moving towards meaning as something made possible by the intentionality of the text as 'work'.[36] Whereas Derrida uses writing to unsettle the metaphysical sediment in metalinguistic texts, Ricoeur uses it to wrest text away from authorial intention, opening the possibility of interpretation: a kind of distancing process that, far from opposing participation, actually demands it. As a consequence of the 'autonomy of the text', the distanciation effected by writing cannot be seen as the product of a particular methodology, or as some kind of eisegetical technique; 'rather it is constitutive of the phenomenon of the text as writing. At the same time, it is the condition of interpretation.'[37]

Infinite signification, the play of signifiers detached from any other reality, is the consequence of structural linguistics and of its deconstruction. If, however, as Derrida claims, the point of origin of representation is ungraspable, then priority cannot be established for the sign nor for the text, and some kind of hermeneutic becomes inevitable. Language presents itself as always already text, discourse, context and intertext. The analytic movement demands and entails the hermeneutic.

Linguistic faith, the trust we place in a language we do not choose and cannot control, but which binds us to its other users in a joint investment, is what places us inside the hermeneutic circle. We 'believe', in Ricoeur's terms, 'in what the text announces' because it is inseparable from our understanding. Outside of the text of language we have no understanding, or at least no shared understanding. 'Faith cometh by hearing' so is irreducibly linguistic, and language, because it is always already there, requires faith. Here again there is no graspable point of origin, but faith and language constitute each other, ground each other, and will not be parted.

## WORD OF GOD

It is not my intention to claim for Paul a linguistic awareness that makes him the precursor to modern critical theorists, but simply to show that his work can be read as offering a rich and complex view of language and its relation to faith; one that is not altogether reducible to theological categories, but institutes its own hermeneutic. I have argued that his insistence that 'faith cometh by hearing' is borne out by contemporary theory; that is only half of the claim made by Romans 10:17: 'faith cometh by hearing and hearing by the word of God'. In fact this rendering (that of the King James version) is based on textual sources that are no longer in favour. The now-accepted sources read: *rhematos christou*: 'word of Christ'. The *christou* is an objective genitive: it is the word spoken about Christ rather than by him. Even so, the conjunction of faith and the word is richly suggestive.

In terms of traditional biblical hermeneutics, Pauline faith is theologically determined, and the formulation of Romans 10:17 is undialectical. There is no evidence, in a great deal of Christian theology, that the bearing of faith to the hearer of the word of God is in any sense problematical. The King James text, even if its version is obsolete, requires that the idea of 'the word of God' be examined. It is possible to understand this without appeal to specifically theological language, but in the language of theologians who, following Heidegger, have attempted to establish a hermeneutic based on awareness of the problematics of language – the so-called 'New Hermeneutic'. Associated mainly with the work of theologians influenced by Rudolf Bultmann, especially Ernst Fuchs and Gerhard Ebeling, the New Hermeneutic stressed the importance of relating the New Testament to today's world, asking, in the words of Anthony Thiselton, '[h]ow does language, especially the language of the Bible, strike home to the modern hearer?'[38]

### Bultmann

The approach of Bultmann (1844–1976) to the problems of theology and contemporary society is crucial to this undertaking. For him it is not the Bible *per se* which is the word of God, it is its kerygmatic core, that is, the essential proclamation set free of the mythological terms in which it is couched. For the word of God to find the understanding of contemporary readers it must be 'demythologized'. It is no coincidence that the opening quotation from Ricoeur is culled from an essay entitled 'Preface to Bultmann'. In that same essay he writes:

> To abandon this mythic wrapping is quite simply to discover the distance that separates our culture from the culture in which the good news is expressed. In this sense, demythologization cuts to the letter itself. It consists in a new use of hermeneutics, which is no longer *edification*, the construction of a spiritual meaning on the literal meaning, but a boring under the literal meaning, a *de-struction*, that is to say, a deconstruction, of the letter itself.[39]

A hermeneutic suspicion here is not content with any notion of 'literal' meaning, since it is in itself an interpretation, and a text requiring further interpretation. I am not as convinced as Ricoeur seems to be that this approach to the text is not 'the construction of a spiritual meaning', and my reasons for saying so will become clear in Chapter 5. The demythologizing process is inseparable from the difficulty of negotiating the hermeneutic circle. The *kerygma* is only there in interpretation, which is why Ricoeur insists that it is necessary 'to enter the hermeneutic circle'.[40]

He sees three levels of demythologization. The first level is, as already discussed, the process of interpreting from an older world-view into contemporary terms. Demythologization must also interpret myth itself, relating it to 'the self-understanding which is both shown and concealed in it', so that we who interpret follow the 'intention' of the myth. The third level is the work of the kerygma itself, and here is a return to Paul who, for Ricoeur, 'begins the movement of demythologization' by exposing concepts from older mythologies ('world', 'flesh', 'sin') to an anthropological interpretation. These three levels Ricoeur associates with Bultmann as modern man, existential philosopher and believer, respectively. The latter's existentialism stems not only from his personal association with Heidegger, but also from his conviction that there is no interpretation possible without presuppositions, and '[e]very interpreter is inescapably dependent on conceptions from a tradition, consciously or unconsciously, and every tradition is dependent on some philosophy or other'. It then becomes a matter of seeing in existentialism a philosophical school which has human existence as its direct object of attention.[41] This makes it a convenient ally for religious discourse, and a ready source of conceptual schemata which can be brought to bear in the interpretation of scripture.

Ricoeur characterizes Bultmann as less than rigorous in his deployment of Heideggerian language because he fails to attend to the 'questioning of being' to which the anthropology that he adopts is attached, leaving the 'radical revision of the question of language which it allows' out of the frame.[42] Bultmann, in fact, fails to carry the project of demythologization through, in that where the believer takes over from the existentialist philosopher the language of faith is allowed to go free in a way that is unacceptable to Ricoeurian suspicion. The notion of the word of God is therefore, as a term of faith, insufficiently scrutinized. It remains the kerygmatic core, 'not having its origin in human considerations and human intention; it comes from God'.[43] Bultmann's view of language, then, is insufficiently critical. What is significant for the present discussion is the constitutive role of faith in understanding.

In an essay in *Faith and Understanding I* (1969), Bultmann places the New Testament idea of the word of God in the context of its Jewish and Greek backgrounds. This combines God's word as act and event with *logos* as principle of reason and thought. In Judaism, he claims, 'God's word is not directed to the intellect but to the will. It is not seen but heard'. This is the background to Jesus' emphasis on 'hearing' the word as a summons to decision for obedience: 'everyone who hears these words of mine and puts them into practice is like a wise man' (NIV) as Matthew puts it (Matthew 7:24). Bultmann sees this formulation as decisive for the New Testament, over against the Greek concept of *logos* as reasonable content originating wisdom. The main difference here between the Old Testament word of God and the New Testament word of God is that 'the concept of the word of God in the New Testament is almost exclusively described as spoken in human speech to men'.[44] What E. P. Sanders has called Bultmann's 'anthropocentrism'[45] is evident here. Its influence can be detected in Günther Bornkamm's assessment of 'God's word and man's word in the New Testament': the two are not fully distinguishable because in Jesus they become one: 'the primary and intrinsic secret to which the New Testament message directs us is that God's word has become *one* with man's word, that it has come to us and become understandable in a human word'.[46]

The task of kerygmatic interpretation in this light is assessed clearly by Ricoeur in his 'Preface to Bultmann':

The kerygma is not first of all the interpretation of a text; it is the announcement of a person. In this sense, the word of God is, not the Bible, but Jesus Christ. But a problem arises continually from the fact that this kerygma is itself expressed in a witness, in the stories, and soon after in the texts that contain the very first confession of faith of the community. These texts conceal a first level of interpretation.[47]

The hermeneutic circle is manifest for those seeking to arrive at the *kerygma*. We come to faith only by hearing, but what we hear as the word of God depends upon a prior faith. So Paul's theorem of faith is intimately connected with the hermeneutic circle, and with the identification of the word of God with Jesus. The difference between saying that the word of God is Jesus Christ, and saying that it is *rhematos christou* is not as significant as it might seem, precisely because of the effect of the hermeneutic circle. The distance that necessitates (in Bultmann's view) demythologization, and the distance that is writing, bind Jesus to his word so that, even at this textual level, faith comes by hearing. The person of Jesus as object of faith is, firstly, a text in need of interpretation by faith.

Bultmann proposes five theses for the exegesis of biblical writing: 1) interpretation must be unprejudiced (in the sense that it should not presuppose its findings), and yet 2) it is not possible without pre-suppositions (Heideggerian pre-understanding); 3) a 'life-relation' of the exegete to the subject matter combines with pre-understanding which, nevertheless 4) is not 'closed' but open to revision by the text itself; 5) the understanding of the text remains open to future interpretation.[48] Gadamer describes a similar interpretative process when summarizing Heidegger's hermeneutic:

> A person who is trying to understand a text is always performing an act of projecting. He projects before himself a meaning for the text as a whole as soon as some initial meaning emerges in the text. Again, the latter emerges only because he is reading the text with particular expectations in regard to a certain meaning. The working out of this fore-project, which is constantly revised in terms of what emerges as he penetrates into the meaning, is understanding what is there.[49]

This amounts to the breaking down of the Cartesian subject/object dichotomy in the realm of interpretation. There is not a clear division between the reading subject and the read object. Understanding arises between text and reader. Even this understanding is not originary, but an intertext with pre-understanding and 'life-relation'. Such a phenomenology of reading is directed toward a self-understanding which undoes immediate consciousness, false consciousness, ideology. The relation between reading and ideology is clearly identified in the historical dimension of the discussion about the word of God. I will come back to this shortly, and then go on to examine the problem of faith and ideology in Chapter 3.

Bultmann's work, whilst insufficiently language-oriented to provide material support for the current argument, gains this direction for it: it clarifies the role of participation in understanding, not as antithetical to distanciation but as entwined with it, just as faith and language themselves entwine. His claim that 'God's word has no authentication; it demands recognition. From a neutral standpoint it cannot be understood as God's word', must be held in check by his assertion that there is no interpretation without presuppositions. There is no 'neutral standpoint'.

## The New Hermeneutic: Ebeling

For Gerhard Ebeling (born 1912), interpretation is the removal of obstacles to understanding, 'in order to let the word perform its own hermeneutic function'. Hermeneutics cannot step outside of language in order to provide this aid, but it represents 'a deeper penetration into the linguistic realm in order to understand by means of language'.[50] There is an assumption in this that language has a 'depth', and the removal of hindrances suggests the availability of an ultimate perspicuity. This is checked by a return to the text in the recognition that interpretation itself is language, but the motion is sustained by the requirement of a 'deeper penetration'. It is somewhat paradoxical to speak of 'understanding by means of language', as Ebeling does, where language is also perceived as that which is itself a hindrance to understanding, and is to be overcome if understanding is to be attained. Ebeling's hermeneutic does not take adequate account of the circularity of understanding which places faith and meaning in dialectical tension: understanding requires faith, belief in what the text announces, but what the text announces is only available by understanding the text. Ebeling's formulation is less complex: 'the proclaimed word seeks to effect faith, but does not presuppose faith as a necessary preliminary.'[51] Yet he is concerned with what grounds understanding, and how the hermeneutic enterprise affects the concept of the word of God. He thinks of language as bearing meaning, as perspicuous, opening onto a realm of understanding which 'is not understanding OF language, but understanding THROUGH language . . . the word is what opens up and mediates understanding, i.e. brings something to understanding'.[52]

In order for understanding to arise, a pre-understanding must already have occurred, and 'only where word has already taken place can word take place'.[53] This Heideggerian formulation develops a metaphysics of presence, with its now familiar privileging of speech over writing, in a semiotics of word that ignores the distancing effect of writing, and the hermeneutics of discourse. Quoting Luther's insistence upon the orality of the gospel, Ebeling revealingly comments:

> It is symptomatic of the impoverishment of the understanding of the word in orthodoxy that those insights were lost from sight. It was no longer borne in mind that to the essence of the Word belongs its oral character, i.e. its character of an event in personal relationship, that the Word is thus no isolated bearer of meanings, but an event that effects something and aims at something.[54]

It is the word as event that governs Ebeling's understanding of the word of God, stressing the orality of proclamation. This stems from the rejection of the orthodox doctrine that scripture is the word of God, in favour of the teaching that scripture contains or witnesses to the word of God. Scripture is writing, authorial absence, distance, whereas the word of God demands participation and communication. The word event is a promise for Ebeling, referring to the absent but 'in such a way that in the promise the absent thing so to speak presents itself.'[55] The 'so to speak' marks the unconquered absence as the writer is confronted by the figurality which cannot be diminished or overcome because this is a kind of writing about speaking. Ebeling encounters a distance that cannot be made up, even at the point of 'speaking' about promise. Faith, it is claimed, is awakened by this calling to presence, and so it depends upon a view of language that I have already argued against. Faith cannot be the product of language in any straightforward undialectical way because it is constitutive of it. At this point it may be objected that in order to think faith as constitutive of language, and as a product of it, it is only necessary to distinguish between linguistic faith and religious faith. It is just this distinction which is in question. With regard to the Bible as a whole the argument is at least partly historical. David Lawton's *Faith, Text and History* (1990) traces this relationship.


## FAITH'S HISTORICAL TEXT

The central observation of Lawton's book, that 'different people have different Bibles',[56] is not just a claim about the radical subjectivity of reading or the impossibility of finally fixing meaning; it is also an historical narrative. As the subtitle (*The Bible in English*) might suggest, he pays a great deal of attention to translation: its political dimensions and its symbiotic relationship with interpretation. The Bible (whatever that might be!) is, as already observed, an increasingly popular text upon which to rehearse modern reading techniques, and *Faith, Text and History* goes some way to explaining why this should be. The biblical text is self-allusive, many-authored, contradictory, self-authorizing, multi-valent and frequently obscure. It is a text in need of interpretation, itself representing manifold interpretation, and a source of interpretation theory. There is no authoritative originary text for its many versions; it exists, as Stephen Prickett has pointed out, always already in translation.[57] It has no common language. It *is* language, Lawton affirms,[58] and as such it carries the condition of its own possibility in its accounts of creation by the word, Adamic naming, the fall of language at Babel and its renewal at Pentecost. There is also a traditional division, a breach, a cleavage, or hinge that separates/joins the Jewish and Christian scriptures. What then can be called 'The Bible'?

Lawton draws on diverse strains of contemporary theory as he sets out to explore this question. The book of Job is seen as a kind of precursor to Michel Foucault in its equation of power and knowledge. Derrida and Roland Barthes make occasional appearances; the former, in unfamiliar guise, is characterized as 'a new Origen': an unexplained claim which involves placing him as 'a lineal descendant from early allegorists'[59] – a view that is challenged by my readings of work by Daniel Boyarin (Chapter 3) and Susan Handelman (Chapter 5). A more telling point in his use of Derrida is made by asking the long overdue question of whether Derrida 'can be right to claim that the Graeco-Christian tradition privileges speech over writing', given the extent to which 'Christianity is *par excellence* the religion of the book'.[60]

This question is a crucial one for deconstruction, not in the way that it is framed here, but in the way that it might be framed if a term like 'the Graeco-Christian tradition' were to be explored rather than swallowed whole. This is a task to which I will return. The point can be made against the question as Lawton writes it, that Christianity is the religion of the Book and not of the text. There is a commitment to an other-than-text, to a beyond-text that canonizes and institutes texts into the Bible. It is this that Derridean deconstruction sets its face against, and it is the vicissitudes of this process of canonization and institution that Lawton traces here. The focus of the study is an attempt 'to read the text as the history of its possible readings'. Treating of the history of interpretation alerts the reader to this as an interpretation of that history, and Lawton, aware of the implication, seeks to declare his interest (albeit somewhat negatively). 'The question of the Bible's truth is a crucial one', he confesses, 'but it requires a book to deal with it, not a paragraph'. It has, of course engendered many hundreds of books, and continues to do so. Lawton continues to stake out his ground: 'If I had an easily labelled position on the question – as militant atheist, say, or fundamentalist Christian – I should now declare it'.[61] He makes no declaration. 'Easily labelled' he is not. 'Militant atheist' and 'fundamentalist Christian' seem to pose two extremes between which he takes his stand.

This somewhat coy interpretative elusiveness is slightly disquieting in the light of other assertions about reading position, for example, the insistence that 'the history of reading is the history of parties'. The politics of reading plays a crucial role here, not only because the Bible itself, particularly the Bible in English, has a history that is shot through with political determinations, but also because writing such a history must also be a political act given the material in question.

The careful negative which defines Lawton's position as *neither* militant atheist *nor* fundamentalist Christian is replaced by a veiled positive as the paradigm shifts from religious categories to interpretative practices. All ways of reading are named as sub-species of hermeneutics: that most Bible-oriented of approaches. Reading is directed back towards the Bible (and the history of its interpretation in the reading being offered).

In reading Ruth, Job, the Gospels and other biblical texts, he evinces an acquaintance with phonetics, narratology and semiotic analysis. A synchronic perspective is thus allowed to interpret the diachronic survey of translation, interpretation and canon-formation. The links that this fusion of history, theory and critical practice is able to establish present an interpretative imperative based on the momentum of a continuing history, arrested by a structural analysis. It is precisely this analytical arrest, already questioned in the consideration of Saussure and deconstruction (above), which masks the historical necessity of faith. In order to make this clear, the political aspects of the work need to be brought into sharper focus.

The political forces that Lawton uncovers at work around the biblical text are of particular moment with regard to a text that has been so authoritatively read and held in such regulatory regard. The conflict of interpretations, which is the history of the English translations of the Bible, demonstrates how interpretation, translation, and canon-formation interweave. The institutional demands that informed the production of translations, from their complete ban (sustained by a death penalty in the fifteenth century) to the royal authorizing of a version in 1611, are exposed. The observation that there is very little distance, at times, between political opposition and reading, seems entirely justified in context.[62] Lawton sees the pressure for English translations of the Bible growing when the burgeoning middle classes of the late fourteenth century, largely illiterate as far as Latin was concerned, wanted an increased political say and a literature in their own language. The Church opposed it because its institutional authority was threatened by a greatly extended access to the closely-guarded text which legitimated its power. John Wycliff's followers ('Lollards') were branded heretics by a statute passed in 1401, and were to be burned at the stake. Proof of guilt, Lawton says, was possession of the English Wycliffite Bible.

The harsh politics of reading outlined in this history run out in Lawton's own predilections about current attitudes to the way that the Bible is to be read. In the final chapter, under the sub-heading 'Apocalypse and closure' he shapes a response to the latter-day apocalypticism that purports to interpret events of our own age in terms of the books of Daniel and Revelation. Commenting on a pamphlet pushed into his letter-box, he writes against its claim of biblical authority: 'No, actually, it is *not* in my own Bible. It is in your own minds. I hope . . . that this book may help to foster a real respect for that maligned and traduced Bible through knowledge, by seeing it again as new'.[63] But different people have different Bibles.

Lawton has insisted on this and made it a central tenet of the book. Further, interpretation is preceded, in the historical narrative of the development of the Bible in English, by faith. This is faith, text and history, with faith coming first. Canon-formation, dependent as it was upon interpretative concerns, was a process governed by faith: 'Such readers begin not with the Book, but with the Faith, and admit into that book only what strengthens the faith. That is what the early Christians did, quite self-consciously'.[64]

There is no Book prior to the act of faith, only texts. Faith is in place, underpinning the canon, as a tradition of belief that is potent enough to be normative for interpretation and provide criteria for entry into that canon. With this historical given in mind it is hard to understand Lawton's closing pages. The historical process that led to the unitary existence of the Bible was authorized by an appeal to faith as something more fundamental than the texts which it engenders (and by which it is engendered), so that it seems problematical to read the Bible without acknowledging that it exists only by an act of faith, an act inconsistent with reading it as 'the history of its possible readings'.[65] To do so simply begs the same question as the refutation of apocalyptic Armageddon rhetoric: What Bible is being read? Or, more precisely, Whose Bible? As I have already suggested, this historical, diachronic perspective is subjected to a synchronic technique.

The religious positions (from militant atheism to Christian fundamentalism) cannot be calibrated with the theoretical (from reader-response theory to deconstruction), but the hermeneutic at work here is seen as prior to both, and, since interpretation and its discourses descend from biblical models, is faith-engendered. This faith-interpretation is the difference between the Book and the text; between the Word and words. Despite this historical precedence of faith, Lawton's own interpretation wants to be outside of faith: to posit a hermeneutic of hermeneutics: a place of suspicion opened up by the simple rejection of extremes. His position is never asserted in terms of meaning but only of possibility. This possibility is encoded in the Apocalypse as two possible futures: Armageddon or the New Jerusalem. A choice of reading. But to make this relevant Lawton has to forgo the hermeneutic of suspicion and re-enter the discourse of faith:

Are fundamentalist readers of the Bible then entirely wrong? Is the Bible no longer to be valued, a text without the power of prophecy? On the contrary, the Bible is intensely relevant to our reading of our past and our possible futures. As a book radically at odds with itself, the Bible is one of the greatest aids we possess to understanding the extremes, the moral obscenity and the idealism, of our subjectivity and our time.[66]

In a discussion that ranges generously from words from the mouth of God in Genesis to the Book of Life in Revelation Lawton would have done well to heed the letter that is a citation of the Word in Revelation 3:15–16: 'I know thy works, that thou art neither cold nor hot: I would thou wert cold or hot. So then because thou art luke-warm, and neither cold nor hot, I will spew thee out of my mouth.' Bearing this in mind might have prevented the tepidity of the closing paragraph: 'It will need all manner of people to produce careful readings of all manner of texts if we are to avoid destruction. I should argue that one of those texts should be the Bible, provided only that we are able to read it.'[67] Anybody, he seems to say (except militant atheists and fundamentalist Christians!), should read anything, so long as they are able to do it carefully.

The critical issue is again one of participation and distanciation, of believing and understanding. As the quotation from Revelation (above) indicates, commitment is required. The point has already been made with regard to Bultmann. E. P. Sanders makes participation a Pauline soteriological principle as one of what he calls 'transfer terms' in Paul's work. Participation in Christ's death is a transfer from one lordship to another. The language of participation is distinguished from juridical language as that which gives depth to his thought, whilst the latter prevents it from lapsing into antinomianism. Participation is closely linked with 'justification' – a term used to translate the problematic Greek term *dikaiosyne*. Since English has no cognate verb for righteousness it is usually translated as 'justify', so the noun is sometimes translated as 'justification'.[68] The importance of this will become clearer when justification is discussed as a hermeneutic principle (in Chapter 3). Participation is an act of faith, of joining a discourse in what Ernst Fuchs calls 'empathy' (*das Einverständnis*).[69]

What Lawton's work brings into view is the historical connection between the translation and interpretation of the Bible and modern paradigms of interpretative practice. The question is one of authority. 'Which texts are authored by God and which are not?' canonizers must ask. Only faith or unfaith can answer. Modern concern with the issues of interpretation (or what have come to be perceived as alternatives to it) are approaches to just this question, as Roland Barthes' famous essay 'The Death of the Author' indicates:

> Once the Author is removed, the claim to decipher a text becomes quite futile. To give a text an Author is to impose a limit on that text, to furnish it with a final signified, to close the writing ... to refuse to fix meaning is, in the end, to refuse God and his hypostases – reason, science, law.[70]

Leaving aside the peculiarly un-Pauline theology that sees reason, science and law as hypostases of God (or acknowledges the possibility of such hypostases), the point moves in two directions. If refusal to fix meaning is to refuse God, then to interpret is to approach a theology. Thus, not only does the history of interpretation relate linguistic faith to religious faith, but contemporary critical theory offers a negative support for the same conclusion. This is why a certain parallel has been drawn between deconstruction and negative theology, a comparison which Derrida has expressly acknowledged.[71] To enter the hermeneutic circle is to keep faith, to refuse it is to return language to a closed system of signs, or a process of endlessly deferred signification. Again, Lawton's rhetoric refuses participation and yet enjoins it, not in a Ricoeurian tension but in a failure to think through the implications of the role of faith in the history of the text and its interpreters. It remains to read in Paul's work the path I have been tracing: a dialectic of language, faith and understanding.


## READING PAUL (1)

In reading texts from the Pauline canon, I am not setting out to 'explain' them in any theological or devotional sense, nor even to contribute to scholarly debate on Paul. My interest is in what happens when the modern questions of meaning and representation are put to this ancient work, and in the possibility of allowing its rhetorical force to come into dialogue with contemporary modes of interpretation. At this point, my concern is to follow through the exploration of 'faith', 'hearing' and 'the word of God' by examining it in its Pauline context.

In one sense, the very work of showing the constitutive role of faith in the concept of the word of God has done the job of illuminating the dialectical nature of Paul's formulation, but this may still be seen as an eisegesis which simply replaces a fideist acceptance of an unproblematic concept with a modern suspicion. Short of resorting to the non-explanations of naïve intentionalism, it is not possible to state simply that there is or is not a question, for Paul, about what 'word of God' may signify when applied to text(s). 'The word about Christ' and its alternative in the sources used by the King James Version, 'the word of God', may not be as different as they appear at first. As the already quoted passage from Ricoeur suggests, 'the word of God', for Paul, 'is not the Bible, but Jesus Christ'. There is, then, no escaping the role of faith, whether in the recognition to which history, theory and even theology attest: that the difference between words and the Word is faith, or in an acceptance of the word about Christ.

Even if it is maintained that Romans 10 simply proclaims that there can be no faith in Christ unless the word about Christ is heard (an assertion with which I would, in a sense, be in sympathy), the interweaving of faith and proclamation in the text makes the relationship between them one of interdependence. That is, it establishes a reciprocity between faith and language that is not fully expressed by a formulation which keeps faith and proclamation apart, making of them discrete stages of a process.

## Paul's Intertextual Strategy

By means of an adroit interlacing of allusion and quotation, Paul's writing, which announces that 'faith cometh by hearing', works itself into the fabric of the faith-engendering text, which the faith thus engendered interprets as the word of God. 'Hearing' the word of God is thus structurally related to faith, which becomes, by this movement, a material process akin to, and epistemologically identical with, language acquisition, still unclear but discernible as a history of reading; not known in its origin, but observed as the trace of what is always already taking place. Faith is revealed as the *sine qua non* of language itself.

The intertextual strategy, employed in Romans 10 for mapping the relationship between law and faith, offers a means of access to this question of faith and language. The Law is the paradigm of the word of God. Given in a face-to-face encounter between God and Moses, it represents a total presence forgone by writing. The account of the Sinaitic revelation in Exodus records the mark of that presence as 'tables of stone, written with the finger of God'. That writing, witness to God's presence, is also, for the people of Israel, the mark of his absence, of his non-appearance to all but Moses. On my reading, Paul does not substitute a simple presence for a simple absence but opens what might be called a hermeneutic of modified absence – absence modified by faith's dialectical entwining with language. This modified absence cannot be reduced to an undifferentiated interpretative category because it is revealed and concealed simultaneously in the movement that discloses faith as linguistic, and language as fiduciary.

In a rich weave of texts from Leviticus, Deuteronomy, Isaiah, Joel and the Psalms, Paul includes twelve (possibly thirteen) allusions in a relatively small textual space. In terms of its division into verses, twelve out of twenty-one contain quotation. A text from Leviticus is interpreted by one from Deuteronomy (vv. 5–8), and the exchange possibly alludes to Psalm 107. Isaiah is used to ratify the interpretation and take the argument on to its subsequent stages. The crucial assertion of verse 17 is itself an interpretation of Isaiah 53:1a: 'Lord, who hath believed our report?' The collocation of believing and report gives Paul the opportunity to connect faith with hearing, but he does so in such a way that a tension is created between the quotation from Isaiah and his own formulation. Isaiah's question asks about a faith that is in place to receive a message, so the message is distinct from the faith that could receive it. Paul's interpretation insists that faith is not prior to the 'report'. Between the quotation from Isaiah and his interpretation of it he places a sign of logical entailment: 'consequently', 'so then' (or even 'aha!'). So the two verses (16 and 17) run thus: 'But they have not all obeyed the Gospel. For Esias saith, Lord, who hath believed our report? So then, faith cometh by hearing, and hearing by the word of God'.

Isaiah's question has already been answered negatively by Paul: 'they have not all obeyed the Gospel'. So faith does not always accompany hearing and cannot precede it. This leaves only some kind of dialectical possibility for understanding the relation between faith and 'report', once it is insisted that 'faith cometh by hearing'. If the rhetorical force of the 'so then' at the beginning of verse 17 is to carry through, there must be a connection between the existential possibility of the word of God as choice and the irreducible dialectic of faith and word.

Traditionally, Christian theology has identified the breach between accepting the Gospel and rejecting it in terms of a soteriology of free will or predestination: an opposition which Paul seems to hold in dialectical tension. Faith, here, cannot be reduced to a radical subjectivity which grounds choice in an undifferentiated free will, because its approach is already mediated by language and further exteriorized as written text. Paul quotes multiple written texts, citing them intertextually (that is, he allows them to interpret one another). The epistle itself, this very passage under scrutiny, weaves itself into the fabric of the text that exteriorizes faith, and yet heralds and effects its approach in the word of God. Thus it canonizes itself, insists upon its own role in bringing faith to light. But neither can faith be excluded from the subjective realm. It cannot be totally objectified or all would have believed the report and obeyed the Gospel as soon as they heard it. This comes close to what Ricoeur identifies as the the subjective-objective dialectic at work in meaning.[72]

A phenomenology of reading is implied which places faith as a moment of determined understanding, constituted by and constituting the 'report', the instance of discourse. The force of this phenomenological understanding is located in the reflexive character of the intertextual strategy which Paul employs. It is by assembling texts from an authoritative tradition (the acceptance of which already implies faith), to work toward the faith which confesses 'Jesus is Lord' (v. 9), that Paul is able to assert that 'faith cometh by hearing'. It is just this reflexivity which enables the dialectic of faith and hearing, which is also a dialectic of faith and text, and will become a dialectic of faith and confession. At each turn faith is a criterion of the linguistic process.

## Confessing Jesus

The pieces of text that Paul selects to work into his own serve to question his own discourse as originary text in a new faith. The confession of Jesus becomes the dominant strand in a historical text that begins with Moses and continues through Isaiah, the Psalms and Joel to Paul, in the unbroken appeal to language that calls forth faith: in Deuteronomy 30:14 it is that 'the word is nigh thee' (v. 8); in Isaiah 28:16 it is that 'he who believes in him will not be disappointed' (v. 11); in Joel 2:32 it is that 'everyone who calls on the name of the Lord will be saved' (v. 13); in Isaiah 52:7 'the feet of those who bring good news' are said to be 'beautiful' (v. 15); in Psalm 19:4 it is that 'their voice has gone out into all the earth, their words to the end of the world' (v. 18).

When the question of the failure of this multiple witness to call all to obedience to the Gospel is raised, Paul shifts the paradigm from language and faith to understanding. Quoting Deuteronomy again, he writes: 'I will provoke you to jealousy by them that are no people, and by a foolish (*asunetos*) nation I will anger you' (v. 19, quoting Deut. 32:21). The word translated as 'foolish' in the King James Bible means 'without understanding'. Paul is not neatly sidestepping the issue here. He relates the dialectic of faith and language to interpretation as understanding, by means of the intertext he has already established.

For reasons which will quickly become clear, 'understanding' can be taken here in the sense derived from Wilhelm Dilthey's distinction between explanation and understanding, defining the latter as the recovery of authorial intention as the original addressees perceived it in the original context of discourse.[73] In Paul's text a midrashic juxtaposition twists older texts free of their original situation, and sets up an understanding of understanding as a negative principle: the word of God is to be heard by those who are 'without understanding'. Understanding becomes detached from its linguistic mooring, becoming other than either language or faith. What replaces it in the movement of the intertext is revelation (*emphaneis*), in a quotation from Isaiah 65:1: 'I was found by those who did not seek me; I revealed myself to those who did not ask for me' (NIV). Revelation is the dialectic of language and faith stripped of the 'understanding' that would enable 'Israel' (Paul's term in v. 19) to read the privileged texts of their heritage with an access to something like authorial intention, based on cultural and linguistic proximity. Thus, a breach appears in the tradition of biblical interpretation which doubles that between the 'Old' and 'New' Testaments, and it appears here, where the 'Old' is taken into the 'New' and the two become one text. This is breach like Derrida's 'la brisure' as join and severance.[74] Paul does not make the confession of Jesus the end of the Old Testament as the word of God. The whole question of allegorical interpretation in Paul which this claim evokes is examined in Chapter 5. At this point, the breach can be identified in the citations of Moses as well the process of revelation.

## Moses *verus* Moses

Moses is accredited with an insistence upon the relevance of the legal code which is in apparent opposition to Paul's claim that 'Christ is the end of the law' (v. 4): 'For Moses describeth the righteousness which is of the law, that the man which doeth those things shall live by them' (v. 5, quoting Leviticus 18:5). Against this, Paul does not place a theological argument of his own devising, but another text from the Pentateuch:

> But the righteousness which is of faith, speaketh on this wise: Say not in thine heart, Who shall ascend into heaven? That is to bring Christ down from above. Or, Who shall descend into the deep? That is to bring Christ up again from the dead. But what saith it? The word is nigh thee, even in thy mouth, and in thy heart, that is the word of faith which we preach . . . (vv. 6–8)

Carefully interspersing quotation with interpretative gloss, Paul creates an intertext which, whilst it makes Christ's resurrection a theme of the law, also makes the law a matter of faith and confession in a way that leads into the claim about confessing Jesus as Lord (v. 9) with consummate rhetorical ease. In verse 19, Moses is cited by name again, this time as the source of a quotation from Deuteronomy 32:21 (quoted above). When it is realized that the above rejoinder to the Mosaic 'righteousness which is of the law' is drawn from a passage some two chapters earlier in Deuteronomy, then it becomes clear that Paul believes Moses to be the author of both of these texts: that which requires adherence to the law, and that which fore-ordains 'the righteousness which is of faith'.

There is no direct rejection of Moses. Rather, Paul attempts to read the reciprocity of the word of God and faith back into the founding moment of the Word as text, i.e. the Sinaitic theophany; the moment when an absolute presence issued not in self-present speech, but in the distanciation of written text 'inscribed by the finger of God'. It is this very distance that gives rise to Paul's text, in that the writtenness of the Mosaic work is the condition of its re-iterability. Paul can quote and re-contextualize it. He can juxtapose texts so that they interpret one another in a kind of midrashic proximity, so that Moses is used to unsettle Moses, and a synthesis emerges in the direction of the reciprocal constitution of faith and language. This represents a profound opposition to an understanding of Paul as conducting a kind of hermeneutic of attrition against the Pentateuch. Ernst Käsemann, for example, uses Romans 10 to suggest that 'large parts of the Old Testament have become meaningless for

Paul'.[75] In fact, Paul's use of the Pentateuch represents a renewed attempt to find meaning there, meaning which goes beyond the original context, and not to render it obsolete.

Just as Moses told the Exodus generation, 'the word is nigh thee', so Paul proclaims the nearness of the word in the work of confession and belief:

> The word is nigh thee, even in thy mouth, and in thy heart, that is the word of faith which we preach, That if thou shalt confess with thy mouth the Lord Jesus, and shalt believe in thine heart that God hath raised him from the dead, thou shalt be saved. (vv. 8 & 9)

What was, for the Exodus generation, a consolation for the absence of God, that is, the nearness of the word, is, for Paul, not only consolation, but the very possibility of his hermeneutic. In verses 8 and 9, the assertion that 'faith cometh by hearing, and hearing by the word of God', is prepared for by observing the dialectic of confession and belief.

Confession can be understood as the other side of hearing. Faith and hearing produce belief and confession. I do not intend an absolute distinction between faith and belief here. Faith reappears as belief in the act of confession. But belief and confession do not have an undialectical relationship, since confession is a kind of performative utterance, the perlocutionary force of which is constitutive of the salvific event, but not without the belief that it is so. No performative, in fact, can take effect unless it is believed to do so. The belief *is* the effect.[76] This is expressed in a chiasmatic structure in verses 9 and 10. Following on from the above quotation the text reads: 'For with the heart man believeth unto righteousness, and with the mouth confession is made unto salvation.' In verse 9 confession precedes belief, whereas in verse 10, belief precedes confession. This is also a dialectic of speech and writing, with confession related to the mouth, and belief to the heart. As 2 Corinthians 3:3 makes plain, the heart is the Spirit's writing table: 'written not with ink, but with the Spirit of the living God; not in tables of stone, but in fleshy tables of the heart.' Taking up Jeremiah's promise of a new covenant, which will be marked by the writing of the law on human hearts, rather than on tablets of stone (Jeremiah 31:31–3), Paul relates the prophecy to Jesus.

## Faith is a Kind of Writing

In Romans 10, then, faith must be a kind of writing, in contradistinction to the confessing mouth, and that faith is profoundly associated with Jesus. The written prophetic witness is made to call forth the spoken confession of 'the Lord Jesus', and so becomes identical with the belief written on 'fleshy tables of the heart'. As I have already noted, belief is not undialectically prior to confession, so the prophetic witness, though historically prior to Jesus, comes into a new dialogical relation with the Jesus of Paul's text. Thus Jesus is not only the focus of Paul's soteriology, but also the linchpin of his hermeneutic. That hermeneutic is not directed against the law, nor the other writings of the Hebrew canon, but towards a new understanding of understanding. How, it asks, can the understanding of the Hebrew scriptures within a tradition of interpretation, culturally continuous with the originary text, be understood by a new community of readers?

Paul sees Jesus as the point of departure for this new understanding, announcing a teleology of absence that modifies the mark of divine absence in the law, by means of an eschatology realized in Jesus: 'For Christ is the end of the law for righteousness to every one that believeth' (v. 4). Christ is the *telos* of the law, its goal or consummation, its fulfilment and its result. Yet, another absence takes place, that Paul marks by appeal to Deuteronomy (the second law!), and the nearness of the word of faith. As he says in 2 Corinthians 5:6: 'whilst we are at home in the body, we are absent from the Lord'. The writings of Paul continually assert that this absence is modified by faith as it gives rise to hope. The hermeneutic function of hope will occupy the third and fourth chapters. Here, it is only necessary to point to it as the principle, identified in this passage as the nearness of the word, appearing in the dialectical movement of belief and confession. The apparently total closure of the law and its sub-texts is not allowed to rest. It is returned to the requirement for belief: 'to every one that believeth'. This belief is the work of the word of God, which, as Paul wrote to the Thessalonians, 'effectually worketh . . . in you that believe' (1 Thess. 2:13).

# 3

# Justification of Faith

... being justified by faith ... (Romans 5:1)

The discipline of interpretation is founded ... on a logic of validation.[1]

Where, after the metanarratives, can legitimacy reside?[2]

## INSTITUTION

### 'The abdication of Belief'

'The abdication of Belief', wrote Emily Dickinson, 'Makes the Behaviour small'. Hermeneutics, whether from the point of view of belief or not, asks a question so large as to appear unanswerable: How is interpretation possible? Perhaps there can never be an answer that will satisfy the long search for validity in interpretation, running (according to a possible narrative account) from the first-century re-reading of the Hebrew Scriptures, under the Christian imperative, to the hermeneutics of Gadamer and Ricoeur. But faith has a way of giving rise to hope, and the faith which produces linguistic meaning brings along with it a hope that such meanings are justified. How real a hope is it? The Dickinson poem continues: 'Better an ignis fatuus/ Than no illume at all'.[3] This chapter sets out to reveal faith (emerging from the intra-linguistic process) as a hermeneutic principle at the level of the text, and to relate it to the orientation of hermeneutics in hope, taken up in subsequent chapters. Inquiring into the justification of meaning requires that the role of faith (as it is found already at work in language) is taken into account in the process of interpretation, not as an external constraint which protects rather than opens a reading,[4] but as the possibility of reading itself. To abdicate belief is to attenuate language, to deprive it of the very hopefulness which drives the speaking subject on towards communication. These intimations of faith and hope may seem slight and tenuous, appearing as an 'ignis fatuus', but they come to us from language itself. 'The abdication of Belief' has made language small, not indeed in terms of critical attention, but in terms of its human function, its importance as characteristic of all human 'Behaviour'. If, as I have already argued, faith is involved in the very process of understanding language, then 'abdication' (which suggests wilful action) is an appropriate term for describing the renunciation of faith by the subject of language.

## Defining 'Faith'

Accounts of the relationship between faith and interpretation have been limited to the development (or destruction) of a technique that allows certain readings and disallows others – an effective ideology of reading. In the previous chapter, I attempted to show that faith operates on language from the inside. To understand it simply in terms of a code of practice, or as a set of normative prescriptions which limit or control meaning according to certain institutional demands, is to mistake faith for the institutions which have sought to maintain a hegemonic discourse, ostensibly under its aegis. Such a claim reveals the problem of definition, within which this study takes place: What does faith mean? Against the totalizations of faith, both by the institutions that purport to dispense it, and by its detractors, this is an act of re-appropriation. The definition of faith here, can only be the work as a whole. It is a reading *of* faith that acknowledges the ambiguity in the 'of' – that faith is read, and that reading is an effect of faith.

At this point it will be helpful to pursue the question of definition through Anthony Thiselton's remarks about faith as a Wittgensteinian 'polymorphous concept'. In his rejection of the 'craving for generality', the later Wittgenstein showed how changes of context affect concepts. Appropriately (for present purposes) he exemplified this with the concept of 'belief': 'If there were a verb meaning "to believe falsely", it would not have any significant first person present indicative. . . . My relation to my own words is wholly different from other people's'.[5]

This emphasis on particularity gave rise to the formulation of the notion of 'polymorphous concepts', i.e. concepts which divide into different, local, contextual or situational variants. Such variants share a 'family resemblance'. Thiselton applies this model to elements of the theological vocabulary of the New Testament: specifically, 'faith', 'flesh', 'fleshly', and 'truth'. He attempts to show how the various usages of 'faith', for example, in the New Testament, undo claims to isolate its 'essence': 'For what faith *is* is only answered by the New Testament writers, including Paul, in relation to what is *the issue at stake*.'[6] Faith is never an abstract generality, but is always applied to some specific concern, so that in Romans 4:5 'faith' is the disposition of Abraham in giving up his own activity as a means to salvation, whilst in Romans 10:9 'faith entails an intellectual conviction'.[7] If, however, faith is taken back into language, then it becomes a determining factor in such re-contextualizations, and the local nuances of its deployment do not amount to changes of concept. Faith becomes the interpretative principle employed by Abraham; not an attitude or disposition, but that which gives rise to these affective states in the process of understanding God's word. Language, whether word of God or any other, involves a trust, a belief, a faith, without which it could have no currency. I must believe in order to understand, and understand in order to believe. Language and faith are not separate. If faith is held to be just a religious category, then re-contextualization will re-function it, but that also returns it to the level of ideological constraint.

## Tradition

The consequences of limiting faith to an ideological level include the effective disenfranchising of the hermeneutical project. If it is seen as a tradition which forms part of a pre-understanding, effectively limiting the possibilities for reading against received ideas, then there may be good reason why a certain version of the hermeneutic circle should be challenged. Christopher Norris mounts this criticism in his *Spinoza and the Origins of Modern Critical Theory* (1991). Coming out against hermeneutics on just this basis, he sees the hermeneutic circle, as described by Heidegger and Gadamer, closing off interpretation from the work of questioning the tradition in which it is placed:

> On this view it is strictly inconceivable that a text could put up the kind of stubborn resistance to consensus values – or provoke the kind of stubbornly resistant reading – that would constitute a genuine challenge to prevailing institutional norms. There could thus be no question of criticizing consensus-values from an alternative (more rational or enlightened) standpoint, since this would

entail the impossible claim that thinking can achieve an order of knowledge ideally independent of the beliefs, meanings, or presuppositions that make up a given cultural 'form of life'.[8]

What Norris objects to here is not the claim that no reading is presuppositionless; he acknowledges the correctness of such a position, so long as it is not used to support an argument for excluding 'oppositional critique'.[9] What is required is that the hermeneutic circle be formulated as other than vicious, and, with this in mind, the work of hope in relation to hermeneutics is explored in Chapters 4 and 5. It is at this point that faith has to be seen as other than ideological. Spinoza's work was directed against 'interpretation', which he saw as an approach to texts from the point of view of already existing beliefs imposed upon the text to be interpreted, preventing reasoned argument from questioning the truth-claims of an institutional authority. A circularity exists where authority is based on a particular interpretation, which also authorizes that very interpretation. This is indeed a vicious circle, but is not really analogous to the hermeneutic circle as already discussed. Faith is interpreted as the proprietor of a closed hermeneutic by those who, like Norris, want to mount an oppositional critique against various forms of institutional power. Removing faith from this frame is not to oppose this kind of critique, but to restore a radical hermeneutic of faith, that questions both the institutional interpretation that has totalized it, robbing it of its power of resistance, and those who oppose the hermeneutic venture as a mode of conservatism.

The role of pre-understanding can be seen as other than an advance interpretation. It is in place as a 'horizon' (in Gadamer's term) within which understanding is enabled. It must be revised by what the text brings to light. Such a revision may be radical, for understanding is not 'confined' to the hermeneutic circle as a round of 'endless interpretive visions and revisions'.[10] It sets up its own resistances, and can actually reveal the very role of pre-understanding in the process of interpretation, allowing a questioning to take place, effectively raising consciousness.

## Truth and Meaning

There is another point at which Norris on Spinoza is relevant to the present argument: that of the the distinction between truth and meaning. Norris criticizes Frank Kermode for his use of Spinoza's distinction in *The Genesis of Secrecy* (1979).[11] According to Norris, Kermode fails to recognize that 'truth', in Spinoza, is of two kinds. On the one hand there is revealed religious truth; on the other, 'the highest object of all philosophical enquiry'.[12] For Kermode, truth is 'very firmly on the side of authority, tradition and vested institutional power', while meaning is a matter of 'interpretive codes and conventions', which resist closure and multiply happily.[13] The conventions of poststructuralism demand that meaning is prolix and unrestrained. Norris resists this poststructuralist discourse of interpretative freeplay by appeal to a species of Enlightenment reasoning – one of Spinoza's two kinds of truth. Truth here is roughly equated with Kant's 'ideas of reason' – not necessarily available, but in place as a regulative possibility which orients interpretation. I would argue that resisting the freefall of interpretation is part of any hermeneutic concern, not in the interests of totalization, but for the sake of communication, that is, for love of the other, which is the goal of meaning, its orientation, its truth.

I want to go on to examine the possibility of a ground for meaning as a determined mode of such truth, a direction which will have emerged through the reading of Romans 4. Three movements are traced: validation, as Ricoeur adapts it from E. D. Hirsch; legitimation in Lyotard's *The Postmodern Condition*,[14] and justification in the work of Paul. Before doing so, it is important to reinforce the claim that faith is not necessarily an ideological constraint upon meaning. There are some recent works in which current modes of construing the relation between faith and interpretative practice can be identified, and these can now be usefully examined.


## FAITH AND IDEOLOGY

### Midrash and Criticism

The history of hermeneutics in the West relates contemporary theory to its sources in pre-Christian interpretative practice, specifically, to the Jewish practice of midrash.[15] The publication (under the title *Midrash and Literature*),[16] in 1986, of a collection of essays dealing with the relevance of Rabbinic exegesis to current modes of reading, did much to alert contemporary criticism to this relationship. In fact, Susan Handelman had already prepared the ground with the publication of her book *The Slayers of Moses* in 1982.[17] Jewish scholars such as Derrida, Geoffrey Hartman and Harold Bloom had been working with derivatives of these techniques (frowned upon by Western practitioners of the Higher Criticism and its later cognates) for more than a decade. Handelman effectively supplied deconstruction with a context and a history, and at the same time placed literary theory outside of the Christian framework in which it first emerged as a distinct discipline. One consequence of this re-emergence of pre-Christian interpretation is that it has seemed to justify an opposition between a Graeco-Christian tradition and a Jewish one, with Christianity appearing as a species of Platonism, now faced, in deconstruction, with the return of an anti-metaphysical, anti-Platonic, Hebraic critical practice. This needs to be questioned, and, to this end, I will return to it in Chapter 5, where Handelman's work will also be subjected to certain related criticisms.

The work of Daniel Boyarin is germane to the relation between midrash and contemporary theory, as well as to that between faith and interpretation. In his excellent book *Intertextuality and the Reading of Midrash* (1990), he aims to delineate a new theory of midrash which will reveal it to be an interpretative discourse working within certain constraints. These constraints are not imported, but are seen to be set up by the interpreted text itself. The Hebrew Bible is read as a 'self-glossing text', a heterogeneous fabric, the intertextuality of which provides rich possibilities for the production of meaning. Meaning is preserved from a freeplay which would render it untenable by ideology: 'the majority of the community which holds cultural hegemony controls interpretation. To put it another way: correctness of interpretation is a function of the ideology of the interpretive community.'[18] Both the production of meaning by intertextuality, and its preservation by ideology are problematical as Boyarin writes them. Taking first the problem of ideology as an interpretative safeguard, what Boyarin contends is that the consensus ruled midrashic interpretation. This consensus must refer to a majority within the interpreting community (itself a restricted body). Within this community there is a political expedient which not only democratizes the processes of reading, but also textualizes politics:

Our story is the story of a community in which interpretation was the central, definitive act of religion and therefore of culture. Misinterpretation (from the perspective of that culture's practice) was perhaps analogous to the violation of ritual and taboo in other cultures and led therefore to the removal of the misinter-preter from the society.[19]

The cultural hegemony of consensus interpretation is seen here to be a kind of totalizing of the text, both of the Bible and of the culture in which interpretation took place as the 'central definitive act'. Interpretation becomes a political shibboleth which, far from showing midrash to be the 'liberating force from the tyranny of "correct interpretation"' that Boyarin claims, gives it a potentially oppressive force.[20] Nor is this force disarmed by the inversion of authorial intention as controlling voice in interpretation, as the case of R. Eliezer shows. He was 'excommunicated and exiled for his insistence that the Author controls the reading of his text'.[21] Boyarin's claim here is that the Torah's survival depended upon its being 'renewed' by interpretative practice, and kept free from final state-ments of Authorial intent. Such appeals to intent would threaten the continuing of interpretation, which, as 'central, definitive act of religion and therefore of culture', must be perpetuated for that reli-gion and culture to survive. Where the Author is God, the affirma-tion of consensus rule in matters of meaning must involve the defeat of God by his text, and this is exactly what Boyarin shows in the Mekilta.[22] But the removal (or bracketing) of one author(ity) is not necessarily a liberating move, as many coups and revolutions have shown.

The problem is one of limiting freeplay. Where authorial inten-tion is disallowed, interpretative hegemony, however 'democratic', takes its place and excludes the misreader. Ideology becomes a sub-stitute theology. Boyarin describes a dialectic of interpretation and ideology in which midrashic readings are both constrained by and formative of the cultural practice. This does not loosen the hold of the dominant, but legitimizes its claim, renders it inexorable. The constraint upon meaning has been given political force, but Boyarin does not allow the political expedient to keep unchecked control. If God has been defeated by his own text, that text is called upon to regulate itself by means of intertextual strategies.

The book of Exodus is interpreted in the Mekilta by a thematiz-ing of its interpretation in the 'prophets and writings' (i.e. the non-Pentateuchal books of the Hebrew Bible). In some brilliant and *jouissant* close-readings, Boyarin builds a convincing case for under-standing the Bible intertextually. Indeed, the midrashic technique, as exemplified by the Mekilta, is claimed to be a doubling of the heterogeneity of the Biblical text, and a revelation of its 'self-glossing' qualities. The midrash is compared to the Higher Criticism as a way of reading more amenable to postmodern sensibilities, and is claimed to 'provide support for the project of deconstructing (that) metaphysics'.[23] In his introduction, Boyarin places his work as undertaken in 'the theoretical context' of what he calls 'the philosophical project of Jacques Derrida.'[24] It is not clear how Boyarin perceives the relation between midrash and deconstruction, or in what way intertextual strategies can be used to unsettle metaphysics. If it is simply that midrash offers '[a]n alternative tradition to the of Europe's metaphysics',[25] then the binary opposition between Judaic and Graeco-Christian thought is being made to bear the weight of deconstruction entirely. It seems implausible that Derridean deconstruction should acknowledge '[a]n alternative tradition', which is a reification of the process that produced 'European metaphysics' out of Judeo-Christian-Greek thought. It can never be feasible to oppose Judaic thought to Graeco-Christian thought as if there were two entirely separate traditions. Christian hermeneutics emerged as much from Jewish as from Greek antecedents. This is evident, on Boyarin's own terms, from the intertextual strategies already identified in Paul's writing.

There is no midrashic escape from the 'logocentrism' that Boyarin ascribes to metaphysical interpretation of texts. This is manifest in his own formulation of rabbinic hermeneutics as 'ideally a practice in which the original moments of the unmediated vision of God's presence can be recovered'.[26] The recovery of presence, especially of God's presence, is the very appeal to a transcendental signified that deconstruction disavows. Thus Derrida: 'I have identified logocentrism and the metaphysics of presence as the exigent, powerful, systematic, and irrepressible desire for such a signified'.[27] Boyarin, in seeking to describe a theory of midrash which will place it among postmodern theories of reading, has located the question of meaning and freeplay in the realm of ideology. Attempting to limit the damage of this agonistic he has turned back towards a metaphysics, and re-instituted the claim of 'logocentrism' at the heart of the non-Greek, non-Christian, alternative hermeneutic. Midrash, it seems, offers a plurivocal and heterogeneous discourse, but only within the limits of an ideology. Justifying those limits returns the interpreter to a theology of the text.

## Theology and the Limits of Deconstruction

What are the possibilities open to theological determinations of meaning that keep within the rule of deconstruction? Is it not the case that the deconstructive turn is a forsaking of all such determinations, precisely *their* deconstruction? Kevin Hart expressly takes on this issue in his *The Trespass of the Sign* (1990). His aim amounts to the transgression of a perceived limit and the justification of its replacement. The limit in question is the circle drawn around deconstruction to keep it from theology. More particularly, Hart is concerned to 'bring deconstruction into conversation with Christian theology'.[28] He argues that deconstruction is not anti-Christian, despite its framing in Gayatri Spivak's 'Translator's preface' to the English translation of Derrida's *Of Grammatology*, and insists that 'deconstruction's target is metaphysics, not theology as such'.[29] The three parts which constitute Hart's book involve three stages of an argument towards a 'non-metaphysical theology'. The work begins by confronting the atheism of the majority of deconstructive writing, while the subsequent parts involve examinations of the scope and status of deconstruction, and the delineation of what is dubbed 'the economy of mysticism' (i.e. the desire, traced in commentaries on mysticism, to establish a connection between negative theology, mystical experience and allegorical hermeneutics).

The question of deconstruction's relation to atheism is the site of a continuing dilemma for the practitioners of poststructuralist theory: does deconstruction involve any such commitment? Hart's answer, predictably, is 'no'. He states unequivocally: 'Upon my reading deconstruction possesses no assertive power; it is, quite simply, a way of seeing how a particular edifice, a general theory or a specific text, is constituted and deconstituted'.[30] This establishes and, simultaneously, calls into question the project of overstepping the boundaries of what has, so far, passed for 'deconstruction'. Derrida has issued the caveat that 'All sentences of the type "deconstruction is x" or "deconstruction is not x", *a priori* miss the point'.[31] (It might be added, that to say 'deconstruction is *quite simply* x' is to miss the point by an even wider margin!)

Hart's argument is directed against the totalizing of deconstruction by Derrida's deployment of it. Such uses are neither here nor there in terms of its structural potentialities: 'A theory of supplementation, deconstruction is itself always open to be supplemented:

it cannot be formalised without remainder'.[32] There can be, then, no reassuring restrictions on the practice; no extrapolations from Derrida's work can be formalized to serve as limits or constraints. But Hart is keen to disclaim any presumption that he is advocating a free-for-all of signifying practices under the aegis of deconstructive discourse. He wants to disarm the charge that, in liberating deconstruction for his purposes he is also doing so for all sorts of other, less licit ones. It should not be concluded, he says, 'that deconstruction can be pressed into the service of any position'.[33] What could keep misappropriation at bay, however, is less than clear. Appeal is made to Paul de Man's complaint about the misrepresentation of deconstruction, and what he refers to as 'aberrations', but this is not sufficient to set up an exclusion zone around it. Resorting to a distinction between the 'word' deconstruction and the 'concept' involved, Hart concludes: 'the word "deconstruction" at once *describes* a particular process of self-subversion within an interpretation of a text and *names* the philosophical position which seeks to identify and trace this process.'[34] This simply begs the question: What can this 'philosophical position' be if such a critique can be successfully lodged against any interpretant of any text?

The political dimension of deconstructive practice restates the question as one of choice. Hart has argued that deconstruction is not totalized by Derrida's deployment of it, and cannot be said to be structurally atheistic. He admits that Derrida's practice can be read as atheistic, but also connects this orientation with the latter's selection of the texts subjected to close-reading.:

> [I]f Derrida deliberately elects to exempt Marxism from deconstruction at the present time for local reasons of French politics, he is engaging in a choice of some sort and is plainly not attending to the apparent necessity of the 'lines of force' which doubtless occur in the text of Marx and in the Leninist reading of Marx. What interests me here is not so much the choice that Derrida makes . . . but at what level the issue of choice takes root in deconstruction.[35]

What is in question here is the framing of deconstruction. Hart is concerned to unsettle the sediment of a certain chosen reaction, or set of reactions, by pointing out that the experimentation with intertextuality has not been exhaustive. Joyce has been made to unsettle Husserl, and Nietzsche Rousseau, but, 'we could examine the following couples: St. Augustine and St. Gregory Nazianzus; Aquinas and Eckhart; Descartes and Pascal; Kant and Hamann; Hegel and Kierkegaard'.[36] The choice is tactical and, Hart claims, depends upon one's understanding of philosophy: 'Derrida's deconstruction is in terms of the oppositions philosophy/literature and philosophy/politics; ours, however, is by way of philosophy/theology'.[37]

Some of the theological uses to which deconstruction has been put are successfully criticized as Hart attempts to show that it is not open to arbitrary appropriation, but what actually emerges from this is not deconstruction as a philosophical position so much as deconstruction as a particular methodology which has been much misunderstood. This, however, does not limit its usage when 'properly' understood, even if it is granted, for argument's sake, that a 'proper' understanding of deconstruction is a legitimate possibility. It is difficult to do other than de Man did (according to Hart's reading), in conflating the views that deconstruction is identified by its various usages, and that all usages are equally valid. Hart tries to keep these views apart by legitimating a deconstruction along the philosophy/theology axis. He wishes, in doing so, to remove a tactical, perceived constraint, and justify re-closing the borders around his own project, without allowing a damaging haemorrhage of power from deconstructive practice.

Working with the 'economy of mysticism' Hart attempts to locate a blindspot in Derrida's reading of Bataille on Hegel.[38] Bataille understands Hegel as restricting the scope of negativity by failing to see it as a general as well as a restricted economy, but falls back within the dialectic through a failure to think the relation that holds between what Hegel excludes and what enables the dialectic – he simply overturns its values. Just as Bataille wants to convict Hegel, so Derrida wants to convict Bataille, and Hart Derrida, in that he sees the latter as reading Pseudo-Dionysius through Aquinas – a reading which, it is argued, is inadequate precisely in terms of the distinction between positive and negative theologies. Negative theology, for Hart, is not just a restricted economy framed by positive theology, which is how, he claims, Derrida sees it. It is also a general economy which underwrites positive theology. So, negative theology 'performs the deconstruction of positive theology'. One could take this as an example of a deconstructive discourse, in that a binary opposition between negative and positive theologies is shown to be undone by demonstrating that the positive term is a modification of a prior, radical negative. It can be agreed that Hart has shown, in this limited sense, that negative theology takes place as a kind of deconstruction, but this does not really illuminate the relationship between theology, philosophy and deconstruction. Nor does it answer the problem of interpretation raised by deconstruction: Where does meaning reside after the replacing of the signified with another signifier? Or, how can it be legitimated in the epoch of irreducible textuality? The question has conveniently disappeared, vanishing into the realm of mysticism as the pursuit of a 'non-metaphysical theology' slips into the abyss of non-explanation.

Richard Rorty, in an exchange with Christopher Norris, observes: 'Practically anything can be seen, with a bit of imagination and contrivance, as a special case of practically anything else'.[39] It would be wrong, therefore, to set too much store by the deconstruction of positive theology by negative. But the Norris/Rorty exchange is of further relevance here, because their contestation of the status of argument in deconstruction is evoked specifically by Hart in his examination of the status and scope of deconstruction. He sees Norris as maintaining that it proceeds 'by more or less agreed rules of argumentation', and Rorty as claiming the opposite.[40] Between these two, 'Derrida understands both modes of criticism, the grounded and the groundless, to be irreducibly entwined'.[41] Despite Hart's insistence that this is contrary to both Norris and Rorty, there must be a sense in which the force of a critical imperative confronts the question of 'ungrounded' discourse, and will not 'entwine' with it. That an exchange takes place at all presupposes some kind of ground, and Rorty takes on Norris 'by more or less agreed rules of argumentation'. Moreover, in the outlining of radical negativity Hart further problematizes Rorty's view of Derridean deconstruction. Thus Rorty:

> A philosopher cannot, as Derrida does, set his face against totalization, insist that the possibilities of recontextualization are boundless, and nonetheless offer transcendental arguments. For how could he hope to grasp *the conditions of possibility of all possible contexts*? What context would he be putting the potential infinity of contexts in when he did so? How can Derrida's 'trace', 'différance', and the rest of what Gasché calls 'infrastructures' be *more* than the vacuous nonexplanations characteristic of a negative theology?[42]

The so-called 'vacuous nonexplanations' are precisely what Hart is calling upon to place a non-metaphysical theology in relation to deconstruction, and in order to do so he is mounting a kind of transcendental argument: What are the conditions of possibility for a theology that 'can resist the illusions of metaphysics?' Those conditions are inescapably bound up with the justifying of a new boundary around deconstructive practice, which enfolds that theology without erasing it or being erased by it. If negative theology really does perform the deconstruction of positive theology then deconstruction itself operates as a hermeneutic of 'nonexplanation', with 'nonexplanation' as a negative transcendental principle, a radical negative which underwrites positive hermeneutics. The alternative is already encoded in Hart's text, in the title *The Trespass of the Sign*.

Hart explains his title with reference to Dante's Adam, who trespassed the sign of his obedience to God. In Paradise, Adam understands Dante without language. Both this immediacy and the onomathesia of his pre-lapsarian state are denied his descendants because of his trespass, and 'although Adam's trespass was chiefly moral in character it was also a trespass of the linguistic sign – a desire for unmediated knowledge'.[43] But trespassing beyond the borders of the sign is not necessarily questing for unmediated knowledge. It may also be a Ricoeurian progression from semiological to hermeneutical focus.

For both Boyarin and Hart deconstruction seems to represent the trace of a new orthodoxy. Discourses of faith are struggling for access to its privileged places as if, historically, the moment of their exclusion is a vanishing point without eschatological fulfilment. The desire for a share of the text, for a handhold on the sliding surface of poststructuralist debate, is forcing a re-reading of the Book, a translation into text. This is not without a sense of loss. A displacement of theological discourse by means of the techniques of intertextuality, or under the sign of a radical negativity, will not shift poststructuralism into calibration with the economies of faith. Nor will those economies be shifted. The agonistic of textual practices, arising out of the exigent pluralism of multiplying theoretical models, has given rise to the opportunity to play for appropriation, an opportunity that is calling forth these justifications of faith. The frequently used monetary metaphor is apposite. As Derrida observes in 'White Mythology',[44] the process of effacement which erases the conventional imprint (from metaphorical uses of language as from well-used coinage), simultaneously effects their devaluation as tokens and their revaluation as objects. It allows a process of dissimulation which disguises the fact that linguistic material is of value only within a given semiological economy, and its value derives not from itself, but from the faith which accepts it in each exchange. This mask changes the appearance of linguistic faith from a matter of deliberate and willed acceptance for the sake of communication, to the violence of ideology. Being aware of the process is one thing, expending the currency in the kind of linguistic potlatch that annihilates meaning is quite another. What Boyarin and Hart do is to join their discourses of faith to the theoretical unveiling of the need to keep faith with language, forgetting, it seems, that faith is not that which is in need of such justification, but that which justifies; itself.

## HERMENEUTICAL JUSTIFICATION

### Explanation and Understanding

Strategies of interpretation, and the theories that underlie them, relate to their originary texts in different ways. The current predilection for immanentist critiques, which call upon texts to interpret themselves through their own intertextual relations and intratextual tensions, is the consequence of theories of language that, as we have seen, derive their orientation from Saussurean linguistics. So far, a suspicion with regard to the linguistic sign has been evident, one that leads deconstructionist critics to pay ever closer attention to the fine workings of texts, revealing their investment in tropes and figures which perpetuate the movement of signification, never coming to rest in the dependable concepts that they 'intend'. The same suspicion leads hermeneutic theorists to disavow the totalization of language by semiosis, and to propose a synthesizing of linguistic levels which locates meaning at the level of the text rather than at the level of the sign. This is still problematical because it depends upon the maintenance of semiotics as one stage of the 'hermeneutical arc'.[45] Derrida's critique of the sign cuts into any hermeneutical theory at this point, undermining 'appropriation' by severing its link with pre-understanding at the intermediary stage of validation. The terms in question here are drawn from Ricoeur's re-working of E. D. Hirsch's hermeneutic in *Interpretation Theory*.

The difficulty that has to be addressed is that of whether or not
the force of deconstruction is sufficient to invalidate (to render
untenable at the level of validation) the 'hermeneutical arc'. I have
already argued that hermeneutics cannot be effected by deconstruction, but neither can it avoid engaging with it.[46] This becomes
especially evident when the issue of validation is explored. Again,
it is the work of Paul Ricoeur which seems to me to deal with this
issue most effectively. In the fourth chapter of his *Interpretation Theory*
(1976), he formulates a response to the question of how we make
sense of written discourse. He proposes a model of the interpretation
process which has affinities with Heideggerian hermeneutics in its
exposition by Gadamer in his *Truth and Method*. The process begins
with a 'guess', and moves, via validation of that guess, towards
appropriation:

> The first time, understanding will be a naive grasping of the
> meaning of the text as a whole. The second time, comprehen-
> sion will be a sophisticated mode of understanding, supported
> by explanatory procedures. In the beginning, understanding is a
> guess. At the end, it satisfies the concept of appropriation . . .[47]

Explanation and understanding are re-defined in terms of this pro-
cedure, and the Romantic model of understanding as a divinatory
recovery of authorial intention is rejected. Interpretation is no longer
a particular form of understanding (as in Dilthey), but names the
whole dialectical process. Understanding becomes the first phase in
the arc, appropriation, the third, with explanation as a mediating
term. This nomenclature has its sources in the Romantic version of
hermeneutics for which 'explanation' was applicable in the natural
sciences, 'understanding' in the humane sciences. Ricoeur writes of
Romantic 'explanation': 'When there are external facts to observe,
hypotheses to be submitted to empirical verification . . . and subor-
dination of empirical generalizations to hypothetic-deductive procedures, then we may say that we "explain" '.[48]
The motivation for placing 'explanation' between 'guess' and
'appropriation' (i.e. at the level of validation), becomes clear when
validation turns out to be more-or-less equated with structural analysis. The distanciation that seeks to render the study of language scientific thus comes to play a key role in hermeneutic theory. Derridean
deconstruction is a critique of precisely this kind of distanciation,

revealing its participation in a metaphysics of presence. More ser-
iously for hermeneutic theory, Derrida effectively calls into question
the very notion of structure that enables the project of structuralism, when he shows the collapse of the signifier/signified opposition. The centre of the notion of structure is jeopardized, '[a]nd
even today the notion of a structure lacking any centre represents
the unthinkable itself'.[49] The structuralist project is not rendered
completely invalid by the questioning of its centring in the sign, but
is made to represent the beginning of a thinking of the 'structurality
of structure':

> Henceforth, it became necessary to think both the law which
> somehow governed the desire for a center in the constitution
> of structure, and the process of signification which orders the
> displacements and substitutions for this law of central presence
> – but a central presence which has never been itself, has always
> already been exiled from itself into its own substitute.[50]

Without a critical appreciation of the limitations of the structural
model, structuralist practice becomes just another instance of the
metaphysical project of explanatory-system building, and falls prey
to its own best insight – the exigency of the sign. The creation of
empty structures, devoid of any awareness of their own structura-
tion, is a meaningless gesture. Derrida likens such structures to a
'deserted city, reduced to its skeleton by some catastrophe of nature
or art'.[51] Where this sort of structuralist enterprise loses force is the
point at which it diverges from phenomenology, abandoning the
whole question of language as as intentional phenomenon. Derrida
characterizes Husserl as negotiating the straits between the Scylla
and Charybdis of subjectivism and objectivism – facing an impossible
choice between 'genesis' and 'structure', and striving 'to reconcile
the *structuralist* demand . . . with the *genetic* demand'. He adds that,
arguably, 'the phenomenological project itself is born of an initial
failure of this attempt'.[52] The outcome of this is a re-thinking of the
question of structure in terms of phenomenology, and a re-working
of phenomenology in terms of structural analysis. Structuralism and
phenomenology seem to demand and yet oppose each other. They
are, as Christopher Norris observes, 'locked in a reciprocal *aporia*
from which neither can emerge with its principles intact'.[53]

   Returning to Ricoeur, it is possible to see a fruitful re-aligning of
phenomenology and structuralism in his re-working of Hirsch. By

moving from pre-understanding to appropriation via a validation based on structural analysis, the apparent exigency of the sign is bracketed. In other words structure is placed, but not as a 'deserted city'. It is re-inhabited by the creation of 'a new ostensive reference thanks to the kind of "execution" that the act of reading implies'.[54] Validation is not conceived here as verification but as 'a logic of uncertainty and of qualitative probability'. I agree with Stephen Clark that Ricoeur is 'over-sanguine' about the possibility of 'criteria of relative superiority for resolving [this] conflict, which can easily be derived from the logic of subjective probability'.[55] Structural analysis may be capable of fielding an immanent critique which opens the way for appropriation, but there is no guarantee that any criteria of relevance can be introduced which might be capable of arbitrating in the conflict of interpretations. This does not invalidate Ricoeur's gesture but leaves room for the logic of validation to be questioned.

## Validation

For E. D. Hirsch, the logic of validation *is* the hermeneutic enterprise. He presupposes understanding rather than theorizes it.[56] According to his argument in *Validity in Interpretation* (1967), the meaning of a text is reproducible and changeless; what changes is the significance of that meaning. The meaning is and remains the one intended by the author. Against the inaccessibility of authorial meaning Hirsch asserts:

> It is far more likely that an author and an interpreter can entertain identical meanings than that they cannot. The faith that speakers have in the possibility of communication has been built up in the very process of learning a language, particularly in those instances when the actions of the interpreter have confirmed to the author that he has understood.[57]

The possibility of author and interpreter entertaining identical meanings is questionable on epistemological grounds. How could the intepreter recognize his or her own meaning as that intended by the author? What could 'identity' possibly mean in this context? Even if the author's meaning could be recovered intact, its re-contextualization in the experience of the interpreter would alter it by means of a distance that could never be made up. Hirsch would see this as an alteration in the significance of the meaning rather than in the meaning itself, but such a distinction presupposes the kind of objectified meaning that the argument seeks to establish. Further, the belief in the possibility of recovering authorial intent does not guarantee its being actualized in any particular case.

The model of speech is clearly in view in what Hirsch writes, even when he is considering written discourse, and the question of the distanciation effected by writing is resolved by appeal to the 'presence' of the interlocutor in speech. Understanding is a given for Hirsch, and so interpretation is simply a matter of validation, and validation is a matter of informed probablity judgements. These work by narrowing the class, or genre, of the utterance by increasing the number of traits by which the class is defined. The kind of decision that has to be made in narrowing the class, however, must itself be subject to another, prior 'logic'. The very notion of genre is an interpretative device which requires some kind of validation. To propose (or impose) a logic of validation conceals the issue of its own validity – how is validation to be validated? Richard Palmer poses the question with reference to Paul:

> [W]as he trying to convey new self-understanding, or what? Can the norms for judging this be found in Paul himself? If such norms were allegedly found, on what basis would we decide whether these were valid? We are back in the present again ... even the standards for, and of, objectivity are manufactured out of today's historical fabric.[58]

Given such objections, it seems necessary to look for a way of renewing the Ricoeurian hermeneutic along other lines; pursuing an alternative to validation. It is not that Ricoeur swallows Hirschean validation whole, he certainly does not. He rejects the appeal to an immutable and recoverable authorial intention altogether, arguing that it is not the original context of the utterance that has to be understood, but 'what points towards a possible world, thanks to the non-ostensive reference of the text. Understanding has less than ever to do with the author and his situation.'[59] This aim requires something other than Hirschean validation, since the latter is designed to establish a contrary mode of interpretant. It is to the very function of the distanciation of writing, which Hirsch seeks to mitigate, that Ricoeur appeals as the possibility of interpretation and 'the condition of understanding'.

## Postmodern Non-explanation

The question of validity in interpretation has been foregrounded
in contemporary debate by the so-called 'postmodern' rejection of
all large-scale theories of meaning. Jean-François Lyotard's *The
Postmodern Condition* (first published in French, 1979) has been an
important influence in the development of subsequent postmodern
thought. In that work Lyotard takes up the Wittgensteinian notion
of language games, and proposes an extreme form of localized
legitimation based on what he calls 'little narratives' (*petit récit*), as
against 'grand' or 'meta-' narratives. The 'postmodern' is defined as
'incredulity toward metanarratives'.[60] The metanarratives themselves are the explanatory discourses (philosophical, theological,
economic, political etc.) that ground the sciences, legitimating the
knowledge they produce. These metanarratives, it is claimed, only
give rise to 'local determinism', but are managed as if they were
commensurable (or could be calibrated) with one another, in a way
that makes the whole work of knowledge graspable as such. The
legitimation of power to manage 'these clouds of sociality', Lyotard
sees as 'based on its optimizing the system's performance – effi-
ciency'.[61] Once the metanarratives have been questioned, on what
can cognitive legitimacy be founded?

Knowledge, he claims, can no longer be legitimated as a whole.
Only localized 'little narratives' are now available, which ground or
legitimate restricted areas or regions of knowledge. This is, though,
unintelligible on the basis of its own standpoint. Firstly, it is the
case that this critique is directed against the Enlightenment project (the age of the construction of such metanarratives as Kant's
critiques), whilst unavoidably operating within the epistemological paradigm that finds its most powerful expression in Kant and
the thinkers of Enlightenment reason. Legitimation would not be a
question at all other than by appeal to such a metanarrative. Secondly, to look for some kind of legitimation, however restricted or
localized, is to appeal to meaning, to be engaged in an interpretative
venture which would be strictly impossible if no hermeneutical
grand narrative were available.

A further objection to Lyotard's method in *The Postmodern Condition* should also be noted as contributing to the confusion of his
proposals. The work proceeds by the setting up of oppositions, establishing networks of positive and negative terms. This is a familiar
kind of criticism, and one which has produced large numbers of

'deconstructive' readings of all manner of texts, but it has a peculiar force here, since the notion of the 'postmodern' is the thinking of radical heterogeneity (the non-correspondence of different kinds of knowledge). It is not feasible to construct a legitimation based on heterogeneous language games and yet oppose science to narrative, homology to paralogy, expert to philosopher, modern to postmodern, consensus to dissensus etc., as Lyotard does. The terms in each pair cannot be commensurable if they really belong to radically different language games. They cannot engage one another in opposition.

This problem also plagues the line of thought he follows in *The Differend* (1988). There, he is concerned to detail the consequences of the heterogeneous character of what he calls 'phrase regimens': the rules governing the construction of phrases. 'There are', he says, 'a number of phrase regimens: reasoning, knowing, describing, recounting, questioning, showing, ordering etc. Phrases from heterogeneous regimens cannot be translated from one into another.'[62] To what kind of phrase regimen does such an assertion belong? How can it communicate anything meaningful about those other regimens, if, as Lyotard insists, each regimen is hermetically sealed from the others? If the postmodern is an 'incredulity toward metanarratives' then it is also a metanarrative itself: the legitimation of de-legitimation.

Eventually, in *The Postmodern Condition*, Lyotard resorts to asking if a legitimation by paralogy is possible. Is it possible to ground meaning in non-meaning, or reason in unreason? He includes, under the term 'paralogy', 'the study of open systems, local determinism, antimethod'.[63] It is not at all clear how such legitimation would work, nor can it be made clear unless the radical heterogeneity of the postmodern condition is suspended – an impossibility if that condition really prevails. Paralogy is the seizure of reason, the negation of the only faculty that could possibly define paralogy. This is the condition of Lyotard's critique (or of any of the current modes of unreason). It falls prey to the movement of difference in that, just as difference presupposes its opposite, paralogy presupposes a definitive reason.

What is to be made then, of Lyotard's claim that 'the hermeneutics of meaning' is a metanarrative which legitimates, presumably, the humane sciences? Hermeneutics would be, in that case, a discourse on method elaborating norms for interpretation. That this is not now the case is manifest. The history of hermeneutics, on a certain account, may in fact be seen in terms of an 'incredulity toward metanarratives' in its suspicion of literal meaning, its suspicion of figural meaning, its suspicion of authorial meaning etc., but it is not thus allied with Lyotard's postmodernism. As was observed in the case of metaphoricity, being aware of the processes at work in interpretation, and regarding them with suspicion, is not the same as discounting them and purposing to do without them. The hermeneutics of suspicion must involve a certain comportment towards its own metanarrative status, aware of itself as a form of discourse, but must avoid the excesses of the postmodern malaise. This is not to make a programmatic statement, but to recognize that hermeneutics is simply not amenable to the kind of treatment to which Lyotard wants to subject it, because it informs his own text in its interpretation of narrativity. It cannot be rejected as an outmoded metanarrative because to interpret it as such is a self-defeating hermeneutic act akin the Cretan liar's paradox. The kind of genre distinction that enables a categorization like 'narrative' is a profoundly hermeneutic notion.

## The Epistemological Problem

The problem of establishing legitimacy in interpretation is also the founding problem of epistemology. With the work of Immanuel Kant (1724–1804), the question of cognitive legitimacy was shifted from things-in-themselves, which are unknowable, to the process of knowing itself – a paradigm shift which places epistemology (the theory of knowledge) at the centre of philosophical enquiry. Whatever is known must pass through the mind's cognition-process, so knowledge of the world can never be direct or un-mediated. This movement is taken up again by the linguistic turn which has affected philosophy in the wake of Nietzsche and Heidegger. If knowledge of the world is mediated by the mind's cognitive faculties, it must also be recognized that those cognitive faculties are irreducibly linguistic. The linguist Benjamin Lee Whorf (1897–1941) worked this into a language-specific episteme that he considered inescapable. In a much-quoted essay, he writes:

> We dissect nature along lines laid down by our native languages ... We cut nature up, organize it into concepts, and ascribe significances as we do, largely because we are parties to an agreement to organize it in this way – an agreement that holds throughout

our speech community and is codified in the patterns of our language.[64]

So, according to Whorf, our way of knowing is governed by a specific language, which imposes a grid upon the world, through which,
and by means of which, we divide nature up. The grid imposed by
other languages may be similar to that of our own, but often they
cannot be 'calibrated' (that is, they cannot be made to match up so
that their categories correspond). His conclusion is that the same
evidence will produce different pictures of the universe in users of
different languages. This 'new principle of relativity' is a matter of
hermeneutics, in that what is at stake is what governs interpretation.

The plausibility of Whorf's theory depends upon the unprovability
of radical translation from one language into another. A translator
will relate differently to the two languages with which he or she is
working, especially if one is his or her native tongue. No matter how
fluent one becomes in a second language, the relation between the
languages known will never allow them to open onto one another in
complete, reciprocal perspicuity. It is thus never fully ascertainable
that parity between phrases in different languages has been established. That notion of parity will itself be conceived in either one of
the languages, or in both, separately. There is no non-linguistic site
from where the languages in question can be compared. But this
very condition of the plausibility of Whorf's theory is also an aporia
within it. If there is no Archimedean point outside of language
from which it can be observed, then it is meaningless to insist that
'the same evidence' will produce different pictures of the universe.
How could it possibly be asserted that the evidence was the same
in each case? How could this identity be known? In other words, to
what could the word 'nature' refer in the passage quoted? The very
relativism that Whorf's theory propounds makes nonsense of its
own presuppositions.[65] This is, essentially, Hirsch's point about the
interpretation of texts. If meaning is not always the same, then how
can it be possible to speak of different constructions of it? The very
difference at issue has no meaning but by reference to the selfsame
text. But an order of words is not a meaning. I could recite or copy
a text, even a text in a language with which I was not familiar, without ever understanding it. Whorf and Hirsch, in effect, made opposite errors: the former constructed a theory of interpretation upon
an epistemological ground which that theory then denied, whilst
the latter's interpretation made its epistemological ground both a

premise and a result of its argument. Is it possible to navigate a hermeneutic path between them?

Certainly this problem goes very deep in contemporary literary theory, not least because it is predicated upon linguistic difference. Difference itself is a product of its own movement: it is only possible to understand difference in its difference from sameness – a sameness which contemporary theory seems to rule inadmissable on the grounds that meaning is irreproducible. A change of language game, the claim is made, is also a change of concepts. This, presumably, is what leads Lyotard to write off 'the hermeneutics of meaning' as 'some grand narrative' of legitimation.[66] Hermeneutics requires meaning as, at least, a kind of Kantian postulate. I have already argued that Ricoeur's hermeneutic does not require a Hirschean return to authorial intention, but does posit the possibility of meaning as a kind of limit situation of the act of appropriation. This is in stark contrast to thinkers like Lyotard who are willing to do without meaning in the interests of heterogeneity.

Other versions of postmodernism are equally problematical. The French sociologist Jean Baudrillard, for example, following Nietzsche's genealogical tracing of the emergence of truth out of metaphors (mistaken for concepts), offers an elusive account of postmodernity. Simulation replaces the 'real' and the 'true', for Baudrillard, so that there is no getting beyond appearance to any underlying reality, and any attempt to do so falls prey to the delusion that 'truth' was ever more than a convenient fiction. The postmodern age, then, is characterized by the 'hyperreal': the mass-media production of 'public opinion'; the rhetoric of political campaigns; the 'reality' of Disneyland (which is there, Baudrillard says, 'to conceal the fact that it is the "real" country').[67] Watergate, he claims, played a similar role, in that it served as a palliative against the unmasking of the 'incomprehensible ferocity' and 'fundamental immorality' of the capitalist system. The episode was characterized as 'scandalous' in order to reinforce belief in the system that could expose and purge such aberrations.[68]

Whilst it might be observed that Baudrillard's acute perception of the epistemic implications of media saturation have an alarming validity, his rejection of reality and truth as worn-out metaphors needs to be questioned. It is difficult to mount any argument against his texts since he never occupies any stable position; to do so would be to assert its correctness or (perish the thought), its truth! This difficulty, of course, is very much the desired effect. The charge of inconsistency, which will be levelled against the text by the reader who resists the sophistical rhetoric, and judges the argument according to rational (Enlightenment) values, is neatly side-stepped since it is precisely these values which are being challenged. Such a reader is forced to accept that what might be read as inconsistency in the text constitutes an exposure and rejection of the valorization of such notions as 'consistency', 'clarity' etc. There is, then, a sense in which reasoned engagement with such material is futile, as there can be no basic agreement on what should count as a valid criticism if reason is subject to the same vanishing trick as truth and reality. This ducking and weaving technique, however, is no postmodern coup. It is a rhetorical strategem for evading the difficulty of making certain assertions about the impossibility of asserting anything.

There are very telling moments of rhetorical aporia in Baudrillard's text, as in Lyotard's, which can be exploited in critique. One such flaw is detectable in 'Simulacra and Simulations', when a reality which subtends appearance is smuggled into the argument. In the above quotation about Disneyland, he refers to *concealed fact*. This suggests a deceptive appearance covering over an accessible truth. What status can possibly be attributed to 'facts' as distinct from appearance, if, as Baudrillard claims, 'only simulacra exist'?[69] This reveals the extent to which the process of describing the 'hyperreal' is self-defeating, since it involves interpreting the effects of our media-saturated society. Interpretation involves arranging the evidence according to certain strategies, or towards a certain end: every act of interpretation involves an exchange of the apparent for the discernible. If 'hyperreality' had any validity, then it would be utterly beyond diagnosis from within the 'hyperreal', just as the postmodern condition requires that we suspend its characteristic epistemology in order to recognize the inevitability of that very epistemology. Baudrillard should not be able to identify the facts which are said to be concealed by appearances; as far as inhabitants of the 'hyper-real' are concerned, the appearance is all there is.

The same rhetorical gesture occurs later in the essay when he discusses Watergate. Claiming that the scandal was a dissimulation, he adds: 'today, the task is to conceal the fact that there is none'.[70] That there is no scandal, that the underlying system is corrupt, is a 'fact' concealed by the official subterfuge which labels revealed corruption as 'scandalous'. But, if fact and appearance are equated in the 'hyperreal', then 'concealed fact' is an oxymoron: fact is precisely that which appears, which cannot be concealed. The truth is that it is impossible to make any claims at all, even that there is a 'postmodern condition', or a 'hyperreality', without some notion of *fact* as opposed to *appearance*. The very idea of a 'condition' demands a recognition that certain defining characteristics correspond with what is really the case, and that interpreting those characteristics depends upon finding some hermeneutic criteria.

The problem is not just one of the local difficulties associated here with Hirsch, Lyotard and Baudrillard, it is that the whole venture is, in a certain sense too late. The logic of validation, and the non-logic of postmodern legitimation, are launched only as supplementary discourses. Derrida has alerted us to the strange logic of the supplement which both 'supplies' and 'supplants' simultaneously, filling a lack and adding to a whole that cannot be whole because of the lack to be filled.[71] Bringing to bear some kind of validating process has been a secondary move that is also a precondition of meaning, but only of meaning as refined understanding. What seems to have taken place is that the kind of stratification of interpretative levels observed in Ricoeur's hermeneutic, has ossified into an epistemological model, so that validation (or its equivalent) has its ordained place.[72] Models of the hermeneutic process are explanatory devices with external resemblances to the processes that they purport to explain. A degree of reification is inevitable in proposing a 'model' of a 'process', and this is why validation or legitimation is always 'too late'. Once such a process has its particular place in the model of the overall process, its interweaving with other processes, which also have their particular place, in complex and recondite interrelationships, is reduced. Tracing the work of faith back into language helps to offset this reductive effect by its refusal to separate the understanding of language and the understanding of discourse, or, in Saussurean terms, refusing the rigidity of the distinction between *langue* and *parole* (i.e. language as system and as discursive event). This is also to disavow the structuralist moment in Ricoeur's interpretative dialectic, and to seek an alternative to that validation, which holds this deconstruction in place: justification of faith. I am, in fact, approximating what Ernest Gellner calls a 'critical monism', which he defines as 'the attempt to restore intellectual order by the sustained application of simple, delimited, lucid principles . . . an attempt which is mandatory in conditions of intellectual chaos . . .'[73] I believe the paralogical non-explanations of postmodernist anti-hermeneutics to be such a mandate. Admitting that my principles are not as simple, delimited and lucid as I would like them to be,

I want to maintain a suspicion with regard to such principles whilst not discarding them completely.


## READING PAUL (2)

### Faith as the Ground of Signification

Reading the 'of' in 'justification of faith' allows two possibilities, already suggested in the criticism of Boyarin and Hart. The one leads in the direction of apologetics, and this broadly defines the approach which attempts to supplement interpretation with reference to some current, accepted philosophical discourse. This is to justify faith. By acknowledging a theological tone it is possible to hear the 'of' as 'by', so that faith is not that which is justified, but that which justifies (Romans 3:28; 5.1; Galatians 2:16; 3:24). Neither of these possibilities is denied here. That faith justifies is faith's justification.

I do not want, in this discussion, to offer a soteriological argument, but neither is such a disclaimer a denial of Paul's soteriological concern. A type of salvation cannot be neglected here: saving the text, saving language. A contention of this study is that language bears the imprint of the work of faith, and that Paul is the primary proponent of this fiduciary language. His soteriology is also a linguistics and a grammatology.

At this stage faith begins to take on a logic: *logos* and *logizomai*. It becomes accountable, or, rather, it accounts or is accounted. To account for this logic is also to take into account a soteriology of language which is accredited in Romans 4. Here, Paul speaks of justification as a 'crediting' or 'accounting' (*logizomai*) of righteousness as a register of faith. Abraham is the paradigm case:

> For we say that faith was reckoned to Abraham for righteousness. How was it then reckoned? when he was in circumcision, or in uncircumcision? not in circumcision, but in uncircumcision. And he received the sign of circumcision, a seal of the righteousness of the faith which he had yet being uncircumcised . . . (vv. 9b–11a)

Faith is not exchanged for righteousness, but becomes, by interpretation, righteousness itself. By interpretation, because Paul is reading Genesis 15. An interpretation informed by faith – the belief that quotes Genesis 15 as authoritative with regard to the life of Abraham and the status of faith. The confidence that Paul has in the text is related to the order of things that he expounds. Faith, he says, was equal to righteousness *before* the act of circumcision. At one level, Paul's point is about the priority of belief over the acts that it engenders, but it also establishes a ground for signification. In Paul's interpretation of Genesis 15, there is the already mentioned belief in the text. It is possible to read this as an ideological constraint, but it is not necessarily so. I have argued that faith is already at work in the very currency of language, as that principle of acceptance which makes a term valid within its economy. This cannot be held apart from the kind of faith which attributes the biblical text with an axial authority, due not only to the position that the Bible holds in the history of interpretative practice, but also to the fact that the search for a ground for meaning leads back to a theology. Conversely, the negation of stability in meaning, whether in Nietzsche or in Derrida, leads to claims about the 'death of God'. God's fate seems to be ineluctably linked to that of meaning and the text. If this is so, then faith is prior to any ideological discourse which takes place in language. Faith has already arrived when I come to language.

The priority of faith is evident at the level of cultural signification in Romans 4. Circumcision is a 'sign' (*semeion*) (v. 11), that is, it has a culturally-agreed value based on the story of its initiation with the Abrahamic covenant (Genesis 17). Abraham received it as a sign (a kind of writing, an inscription in the flesh). The sign itself has no value, for Paul, other than within the economy of faith. Righteousness comes before the sign, and the sign is received as the mark of a prior faith: 'and he received the sign of circumcision, a seal of the righteousness of the faith which he had yet being uncircumcised' (v. 11). The sign comes as a 'seal' (*sphagis*) in recognition or confirmation of a prior faith which underlies it and gives it meaning. What prevails as the circumstance of accreditation is a moment of meaning prior to the cultural manifestation of its possibility. Righteousness is that validity which interpretation seeks, and is therefore a condition of the possibility of meaning. The 'sign', for Paul (as a 'seal'), is a guarantee, a mark of authorization, a delimitation of access. The play of signification is limited by this double action of the sign, which, as a mark of its prior possibility in faith, also marks a limit for meaning, sealing it.

Rediscovering this work of faith provides a means of access to meaning as it operates within the movement of signification. That is, faith calls the sign to account (*logizomai*), and accounts for its cultural effectiveness, by the process of accreditation, the making current of its currency. This is why Thiselton's notion of faith as a 'polymorphous concept' is inadequate. Context may contribute to the understanding of the deployment of 'faith', but those contexts are determined by a prior faith that, for example, accounts for Abraham's 'disposition . . . in giving up his own activity as a means to salvation'.[74] What but faith can have informed his interpretation of the world, and of God's relation to it and to him, in a way that made such a disposition necessary or desirable? Faith must be prior to that disposition as well as to the acts prompted by that disposition. Faith, on this account, determines 'context' because the latter will always be an effect of discourse. This effect is part of Paul's ongoing argument:

> [T]hat he might be the father of all them that believe, though they be not circumcised; that righteousness might be imputed unto them also: And the father of circumcision, to them who are not of the circumcision only, but also walk in the steps of that faith of our father Abraham, which he had being yet uncircumcised. (vv. 11b–12)

Abraham's pre-circumcision faith gives circumcision its significance, hence he becomes the 'father' of the circumcised – the delimiting context of the sign's meaning. The taking up of the sign of circumcision by his successors will dislodge the sign from its ground unless its use-community 'also walk in the steps of that faith'. Faith is not just the ground of signification, but also a constant of the practice of meaningful discourse. Without it the sign slips its moorings, and becomes ineffective as a means of righteousness. When the practice of discourse seeks to operate without faith (and seeks, paradoxically, to efface it), the discourses of faith appear to be ideologically determined modes of understanding. Once faith is recognized within language, the ideology of un-faith is manifest, and the approaches to  language from within this ideology rob it of the possibility of meaning.

## Between Promise and Fulfilment

Paul's argument continues by showing faith to be prior to the law since God's promise to Abraham pre-dates the law (by four hundred and thirty years, according to Galatians 3:17), and 'the promise comes by faith' (v. 16 – NIV). If the promise is appropriated through observing the law, then Abraham's faith was valueless, and the promise void. Faith must have been effective before the law or the whole of Israel's history is mitigated. Again, the point can be made in terms of language and meaning. The law, in place as a cultural norm, acts to control social meanings, and to define the terms of social existence. It has, then, cultural-agreement which is only in place after the appropriation of the promise by faith. Historically, the law comes after both the promise and its fulfilment. This fulfilment is the birth of the society into which the law comes as a norm: the promise is that of descendent nations (v. 17).

Paul further specifies the role of faith by placing it in a theological framework, and in the material process of human fertility and its temporal limitations. In verses 16–21, he offers a radical version of faith which is theologically irreverent, yet motivated by a theological concern – the soteriology of justification. Abraham is called 'the father of us all' (v. 16), to indicate that the promise of paternity has been fulfilled. The impossibility of the promise is then stressed in order to make faith appear as a material process, and not just an unidentified principle. The promise is that of 'exalted fatherhood'. That 'he is the father of us all' is appropriated by faith – Paul's faith, and, by interpretation, Abraham's faith. This fatherhood becomes the delimiting context for Judaism and for Christianity – Abraham's faith is the possibility of their existence:

> And being not weak in faith, he considered not his own body now dead, when he was about an hundred years old, neither yet the deadness of Sarah's womb. He staggered not at the promise of God through unbelief; but was strong in faith, giving glory to God . . . (vv. 19 & 20)

But for this faith the nation of Israel could not have come about, and the lineage of Jesus vanishes: no Judaism, no Christianity. So, faith is seen to effect the possibility of sexual reproduction in Abraham and Sarah, and, by extension, that of succeeding generations. But this material process did not originate in Abraham. The whole argument is re-contextualized by a theology of faith. Before introducing the impossibility of the promise, Paul traces it to 'God, who quickeneth the dead, and calleth those things which be not as though they were' (v. 17). Again, this is a return to the hermeneutic circle associated with the word of God in Chapter 2. Faith is already in place in the attribution 'word of God', and yet is engendered by 'hearing' that word as the 'word of God'. Here, in 4:17, the tension creates a statement of faith as a theological paradox. God's word engenders faith in non-faith by identifying the two in calling the 'things which be not as though they were'. The 'as though' marks, in the word of God itself, the temporal break between promise and fulfilment. This break is the space that is the necessity of faith. Rather than resolving the dialectical tension, this places faith in much the same role as Derrida's notion of *différance* – differing and deferral – the possibility of meaning.[75] It might be objected that *différance* is the putting off of meaning, the denial of its presence. That is also the condition of faith as occupying the space between promise and fulfilment. Fulfilment is faith's other; not a negation, but a temporal limit to its effect. 1 Corinthians 13:12 also offers the possibility of understanding faith in this way: 'For now we see through a glass, darkly: but then face to face: now I know in part; but then shall I know even as also I am known.' Clearly, this is an un-Derridean formulation in that it avows a future presence in the 'now . . . then' opposition. It is not my intention to claim that faith and *différance* are identical, but that faith springs up in the place of *différance*, disrupting the assumption of its exigence, resisting its semblance of force. I return to the question of *différance* in Chapter 5.

The future orientation of Paul's hermeneutic is evident in the role of hope. Chapters 4 and 5 take up this theme, but its role in Romans 4 can be assessed briefly at this point. Hope (*helpis*), as expectation, is not altogether detached from faith. To expect something is also to believe in its possibility and its temporal approach. The linguistic principle of faith precedes expectation and allows it to appear. Paul divides hope thus: 'Who against hope, believed in hope' (v. 18). The two versions of hope are held apart by faith. Abraham's hope for the fulfilment of the promise is 'in belief', but this hope-in-belief is also 'against' hope. What might be expected of 'his own body now dead', and 'the deadness of Sarah's womb' is the empirical version of hope. Abraham's hope-in-belief is opposed to, and divided from, hope as an empirical response, by faith. This is exactly the state of affairs that raises the questions of validation and legitimation. Faith is neither an empiricism nor a rationalism. It is neither verifiable nor falsifiable, but is itself a cognitive principle which verifies or falsifies, not by guaranteeing the immediate validity of an interpretation, but by being realized as hope-in-belief toward a different kind of knowledge: 'I shall know even as I am known.' Thus, in Romans 4, Paul splits the difference with observable phenomena, opening an alternative to empiricism that is not rationalism. Interpretation is not verified, falsified, validated or legitimated for Paul, but heeds the necessity of the principle already at work in language, making of justification by faith a mode of understanding, as well as a soteriological imperative.

Romans 4 shows, then, the role of faith at different stages of realization. It appears as the mediation between God's word and the world – God promised; Abraham had faith; the promise was fulfilled. It also appears as a gap between promise and fulfilment in the temporal grasp of God's word which 'calleth those things that be not as though they were'. Again, it appears as a principle of hope, dividing it from the appearance of the world. In all of these manifestations, faith remains within the dialectical understanding: engendering the word of God and engendered by it.

# 4

# Pressing On

For we are saved by hope: but hope that is seen, is not hope: for what a man seeth, why doth he yet hope for?
(Romans 8:24)

... [H]ope which does not want to be just as far at any end as it was at the beginning, does away with the sharp cycle.[1]

## OPENING THE CIRCLE

Hope is divided. It is never itself. Or, it may be that when I hope time is not quite itself. Already, the logic of hope demands that this too must be questioned because of its tense: because of a presence and an identity in the 'is', beyond which hope has already progressed. To speak of a time 'when I hope' is also to compromise its strange temporality. In its refusal to be confined to any temporal dimension, hope puts the time-handling linguistic device of 'tense' under pressure. It is not possible to hope without a history and a futurity, so hope cannot be grasped by a purported present. It has to be traced as a trajectory through time.

Hope, in its relation to the future, draws close to the text and to the work of hermeneutics. Reading begins with hope towards understanding: it is part of what hermeneutic thinkers call 'pre-understanding' in that it springs up before (in the face of and in anticipation of) the text. In pre-understanding, the 'pre' marks an expectation that full understanding may follow. The linear progression of reading is the trajectory of hope, and 'writing rewrites the world in the interest of hope', as Michael Edwards says.[2] The specific role of this hope in a hermeneutic that acknowledges the version of the hermeneutic circle discussed in Chapter 2, is to ensure that this circle is not a vicious one. If, as Norris claims, the model of interpretation found in theorists of hermeneutic circularity precludes the possibility of breaking with received ideas and the *doxa* of 'common sense', then hope, as the possibility of critique and the orientation towards a postulated truth, is in question.[3] The unmitigated hopelessness of historical momentum then seems possessed of an unchecked force, unresponsive to any kind of reasoned discourse. Such a hermeneutic results in a situation akin to that proffered by Lyotard's anti-hermeneutic. His catalogue of defeated ideals presents just such a picture:

> 'Auschwitz' refutes speculative doctrine . . . 'Berlin 1953, Budapest 1956, Czechoslovakia 1968, Poland 1980' (I could mention others) refute the doctrine of historical materialism: the workers rose up against the Party. . . . 'May 1968' refutes the doctrine of parliamentary liberalism. . . . the 'crises of 1911 and 1929' refute the doctrine of economic liberalism. And the 'crisis of 1974–1979' refutes the post-Keynesian revision of that doctrine. The passages promised by the great doctrinal syntheses end in bloody impasses. Whence the sorrow of the spectators in this end of the twentieth century.[4]

Lyotard does not present this list of failures as a proof of the inadequacy of certain political doctrines, but as evidence that no historical event, or series of events, can be adduced in support of a belief in 'progress', or to deny its possibility. To make such claims, Lyotard would argue, is to attempt to translate between 'phrase regimens', which, as already noted, he believes impossible: ethico-political judgements and historical judgements belong to different phrase regimens.[5] Again, Lyotard falls prey to his own argument. How can it be feasible to adduce historical evidence, as Lyotard manifestly does, to deny the possibility of its effectiveness as evidence? If this simply illustrates the contingency and radical incomprehensibility of historical events then a kind of 'metanarrative' of the sublime is called upon to interpret history, and to legitimate its discreteness from speculative reason. Contingency precludes even the certainty of itself.

The figure of the circle appears perilous, endangering the future, or endangered by it. This needs to be addressed if Paul's interpretative possibilities, including his category of 'hope', are to be realized. I have already outlined an understanding of the relation between his writing and Ricoeur's formulation of the hermeneutic circle. What room is there left for hope once the circle is closed? What sense can be made of a circle that is not 'vicious'? Is not the idea of an 'open circle' oxymoronic? The simple logic of circularity is deceptive when applied to understanding and interpretation, whose laws are not geometric. Dennis Schmidt offers a re-reading of the hermeneutic circle by placing it in a philosophical tradition which has made varied and contradictory uses of the figure.[6] From sign of completeness, unconditionality, and oneness, the circle has been translated to signify radical temporality and contingency. It has stood for thought's perfection and its self-deception. The concentric circles of Hegel's philosophy have given way (maybe) to Heidegger's heterocentric structure of *Dasein*. Schmidt reads Heidegger's notion of the future as 'not yet' alongside Ernst Bloch's formulation of the principle of hope, with its relation to historical dialectics, to speak of the future as 'not yet given with the given'. So the circle, as image of the return of the same, or homecoming, is conditioned by an understanding of the present as impotent to close the circle of the future: the recognition that 'home is a place where we have not yet been'.[7] Because of its temporality, understanding is never closed by the present as though the present were the point at which the circle returns to its origin. There is always a dislocation, a slippage, a disjunction, which breaks out toward the new, and this conditions the way in which the hermeneutic circle is perceived: not interpretation's closure, but its entanglement. So, Schmidt observes, 'today we use the image of the circle not to indicate that matters are simple, clear, or closed, but that they are complex and entangled . . . beyond what is immediately evident. . . .'[8]

On this account, the hermeneutic circle is an expression of the future's 'radical openness, as well as . . . its more or less hidden determination by the past'.[9] Furthermore, hope appears not only as an openness, but also as the possibility of that openness, because it transgresses the present, denying its power to totalize the real. As Schmidt says, Bloch's principle of hope insists that 'the real is never exhausted by the present'. The very idea of possibility is predicated upon hope. Philosophers as diverse as William James (1842–1910), Martin Heidegger and Ernst Bloch have valued the category of possibility higher than that of present reality, and hope is recognized by Bloch as 'not only a basic feature of human consciousness, but, concretely corrected and grasped, a basic determination within objective reality as a whole.'[10] There is a distinction here, between subjective hope (hoping), and objective hope (that hoped for), which assumes, as Wayne Hudson says, 'that subjective hope has an objective correlate (which remains to be identified and then produced)'.[11] The debt to Edmund Husserl's notion of intentionality is evident in this, and the phenomenological project, in fact, extends into Bloch's work along the line of the hermeneutics of hope which he developed in *The Principle of Hope* (1959). The latter interprets advertisements, daydreams, religious beliefs, and various forms of cultural production, as evidence of a future-directedness that is not confined to human consciousness.

Because of the future orientation of the human world, philosophy, for Bloch, must break with the Platonic doctrine of *anamnesis*, and with all the subsequent backward-looking models of epistemology (including Hegel's). The world is not a completed entity, but a yet-to-be-determined process, so any philosophy that is to be adequate in describing it must forsake the static objectifications inherited from the metaphysics of totality, and be open to what will arise in the future. Such philosophy Bloch calls 'Open System': 'Open system attempts to grasp the not yet known, not yet become, still arising elements in the world, and is oriented towards the future and the new.'[12] This has an antecedent in what Bertrand Russell calls Aristotle's 'religion of progress and evolution', but cannot work wholly within categories which derive from the notion of 'final causes', and the quest towards 'God's static perfection'.[13] Bloch's neologisms ('Front', 'Novum', 'Real Possibility', etc.) attest to this need to trespass the borders of an inherited conceptuality. A considerable debt is owed to Kant here, which is evident in the relationship between Bloch's category of the 'not-yet' and Kant's postulates of practical reason. Both notions represent unreached realities which orient the dialectical movement of history.

As an interpreter (or re-interpreter) of Marxist theory/praxis, Bloch draws on its utopian strain. His insistence on the open, unfinished, problematic character of the world, offers the possibility of radical hope towards a maximalist realization of Marx's social vision. Hope, then, cannot be confined to human consciousness. It must have its roots in the objective possibilities of the world. Bloch's approach to this is to think the subject–object relation, not as a dualism, but as a process. He derived from Hegel the idea that this process overcomes the problems associated with a mind-independent objective reality, and a subjective reality devoid of objective status. Subject could become substance 'through dialectical subject–object mediations in history'[14]: 'That which is within is, and remains the key to that which is without; yet the key is not the substance, and the substance of the key lies as well in the object house (as yet hardly on its way to completion) that is the world.'[15]

Subject and object, then, are 'not yet' identified, but their identity is a goal of human action. The ontological and epistemological openness of the world gives human will and action a status which allows hope to arise. This hope is directed towards utopian realization by Marxism, which replaces Kant's 'God' postulate with a human ideal. 'Learned hope' (*docta spes*), is distinguished from the universal tendency to look forward, by means of its detour through dialectical materialism. It is a hope that is not deceived by the negative signs that the world manifests, nor deflected by other-worldly (religious) consolation, but is seen, in a dialectical-materialist manner, as setting goals for theory/praxis by its utopian function. Utopianism remains effective, for Bloch, because he denies the premisses upon which objections to it are based. He does not accept that it is not grounded in material reality, nor that it is an effect of a subjectivism which ignores the indefeasible character of that reality. If there is no fixed and finalized form to reality, as Bloch contends, then not only is utopia productive, it is also expressive of the character of reality as unfinished. It is a necessary effect of a mutable ontology, in a world which is processual, and in which new elements constantly arise as products of human intervention and labour.

Hope, as openness to the future, can be seen as a hermeneutic principle in Bloch's readings of a range of cultural productions. What does this mean for Pauline interpretation? How can philosophical hope for a utopian society open up the hermeneutic field, and question both the kind of closure that would insulate texts against resistant readings, and the sealing up of 'phrase regimens' into discrete, untranslatable discourses? It is already possible to pit Bloch's 'learned hope', with its grounding in material reality, against Lyotard's denial of the interrelation between history and speculative reason; to refuse to be deceived by the negative signs. Jürgen Moltmann's theology of hope provides a means of relating theological hope to the politico-philosophical hope of Bloch, and so prepares the ground for an examination of Pauline hope as the required break in the hermeneutic circle.


## MOLTMANN'S BLOCH

### Renewing Hope

Towards the end of the nineteenth century, Johannes Weiss and Albert Schweitzer re-interpreted the content of Jesus' teaching to emphasize its eschatological bearings over against the liberalism descending from Strauss, Feuerbach, Renan and Comte. The Jesus of liberal theology is a moralist whose teaching is detachable from the supernatural elements in the Gospels' accounts of his life. The latter came to be seen as unhistorical accretions, arising between the time of Jesus' death and the writing of the Gospels.[16] A religion of humanity was distilled from the Christian tradition, taking on its moral teaching but rejecting both its historicity and its theological dogma. This is a system familiar to English readers, chiefly through the work of George Eliot, who translated Strauss's *Das Leben Jesu* in 1846, and whose novels are shot through with deontic formulations based on the morals of a humanist value system, for which Christianity is little more than a metaphor.[17] Matthew Arnold's view was much the same: all that remained of 'The Sea of Faith', he famously lamented, was 'Its melancholy, long, withdrawing roar, / Retreating, to the breath / Of the night-wind . . .'[18]

John Macquarrie observes that although Weiss and Schweitzer set the direction for a theology determined by eschatology and Jesus' teaching of the coming Kingdom of God, they did not remodel it in line with this insight. He sees the early Karl Barth, Rudolf Bultmann, Wolfhart Pannenberg and Jürgen Moltmann as theologians who have made serious attempts to reconstruct theology in this mode.[19] For Moltmann, all that remains of the eschatological orientation of primitive Christianity is the view of history as 'saving history', and eschatology as a concern with 'final events'. There are two versions of this eschatology: a transcendental version which equates the eschaton with the 'present of eternity', and an existential version concerned with decisions which possess personal finality.[20] These eschatologies, he says, obscure 'the real language of eschatology', and derive from the Greek '*logos* of the epiphany of the eternal present'. They confine eschatology to the margins of theology, making it an appendage of Christian dogmatics. Taking his cue from Martin Buber's re-interpretation of the theology of the Old Testament, Moltmann re-thinks New Testament theology as expectation, hope:

From first to last, and not merely in the epilogue, Christianity is eschatology, is hope, forward looking and forward moving, and therefore also revolutionizing and transforming the present. The eschatological is not one element of Christianity, but it is the medium of Christian faith as such, the key in which everything in it is set . . .[21]

Buber (1878–1965) contrasted the God of the desert wanderings of Israel, the God of promise for the future, with the gods of the 'epiphanic' religions. The difference in the resultant religions is that between 'presence' and 'promise', a difference which opens the way for hope. Moltmann outlines the characteristics of promise as 'a declaration which announces the coming of a reality that does not yet exist'.[22] Because the promise speaks of a future, it instils a sense of history which is not cyclic, but which breaks free of the myth of the 'eternal return of the same'.[23] The futurity of the promise means that it contradicts present reality and creates a tension, an interval of hope and freedom to obey or disobey. Israel's history shows that hope, undefeated by either disappointment or fulfilment. There is always a surplus when promises remain in excess of their fulfilment as the ' "not yet" of expectation surpasses every fulfilment that is already taking place now. Hence every reality in which a fulfilment is already taking place now, becomes the confirmation, exposition and liberation of a greater hope.'[24]

The interval between promise and fulfilment raises the question of interim obedience. Moltmann sees the law (*Torah*) as the ethical side of the covenant, and obedience as the product of hope, with the consequence that the commandments cannot be seen as rigid norms, but are an adumbration of the future. The theology of the God of the promise is taken into the New Testament by focusing on the resurrection rather than simply asserting, with Weiss and Schweitzer, the primacy of the coming kingdom of God in Jesus' teaching. 'Christianity', Moltmann insists, 'stands or falls with the reality of the raising of Jesus from the dead by God. In the New Testament there is no faith that does not start *a priori* with the resurrection of Jesus.'[25]

The resurrection re-orients the sense of a realized eschatology in the Gospels' interpretation of the Old Testament messianic prophecies as fulfilled in Jesus, by directing the teaching about the kingdom towards hope for universal resurrection. The possibility of an eschatological fulfilment in the coming of the Holy Spirit (Pentecost), Moltmann asserts, is overcome by the still-current, unredeemed state of the world. Thus Paul speaks of the Spirit not as fulfilment but as the 'earnest' of the coming kingdom (2 Corinthians 1:22; 5:5), and of the expectant 'travail' of the whole creation (Romans 8:22). The resurrection can only be understood, then, in terms of hope for the future. It demands, in that case, a re-definition of history, not only because history, since the Enlightenment, has excluded the possibility of such an event, but also because it points towards a possible future.

## The Resurrection of History

Moltmann argues that the view of history which excludes the resurrection is found expressed in the work of Ernst Troeltsch, and his insistence on the existence of a 'correlation . . . between all historical processes'.[26] Only on the grounds of similarity can historical events be recognized as such. The vicissitudes of history are only understandable as instances of a 'common core of similarity'. This is the case that Hume made against the occurrence of miracles – a case which I consider to be rendered problematic by C. S. Lewis. According to Hume, there is 'uniform experience' against the miraculous, but, Lewis argues, 'we know the experience against them to be uniform only if we know that all the reports of them are false. And we can know all the reports to be false only if we know already that miracles have never occurred'.[27] The apparent sophistry of Lewis's argument, which might seem like a technical objection to an empirical gesture, should not detract from an appreciation of his basic objection to Hume's claim. There is *not* 'uniform experience' against the miraculous, not even in our own cynical times, and it can only be claimed that such is the case by rejecting all reports of miraculous occurrences on the grounds that what they attest is impossible.

Troeltsch's argument, like Hume's, is circular: miracles are precluded as unhistorical in order to support an argument for history as that which precludes the miraculous. For Hume, Nature is uniform, making it possible to gauge the probability of an occurrence. But how probable is such uniformity? It cannot be known from experience since 'uniformity has to be assumed before experience proves anything'.[28] Judgements about the probability of the miraculous, then, must begin with a conclusion. With regard to the resurrection, history cannot exclude it without pre-judgment of its probability, based on an assumption of uniformity. To claim that historicity is based on a principle of similarity, is to abandon history to metaphysics, to relate all its events to a *logos* of identity, to conceive of history 'as the movement of a resumption of history, as a detour between two presences'.[29] How probable are any excessive events or processes (the Holocaust, Apartheid, 'freak' accidents, the so-called 'big bang' etc.), when judged by their similarity or dissimilarity with other events or processes accorded historical status? Theodor Adorno raises a similar question in relation to social critique:

> Criticism of tendencies in modern society is automatically countered, before it is fully uttered, by the argument that things have always been like this. . . . But even if things have always been so . . . the eternity of horror nevertheless manifests itself in the fact that each of its new forms outdoes the old.[30]

I do not want to suggest that Adorno's work can be called upon as a witness to the likelihood of the miraculous, but that the rejection of miracles on the basis of 'correspondence' or 'similarity' has far-reaching and wide-ranging ramifications. The principle of similarity can be evoked to stave off resistance to received ideas, norms and practices. It can occur as an interpretative tradition, a circularity which closes off the possibility of new meanings. It can have, in fact, precisely the effect which Norris ascribes to the hermeneutic circle. I imagine that some unstated principle of selection is applied by those who wish to preclude miracles without ruling out the possibility of historical change.

For Moltmann, the historicity of history consists in the character of the event as past encounter with possibility. 'Unborn future lies in the past', he says, and 'fulfilled past can be expected from the future'. He sees positivistic historicism as reducing history to 'realities that can be dated and localized, without noticing the realm of future possibilities that surrounds these realities so long as they are "historic" realities'.[31] The view of history which Moltmann is rejecting is that which derives from backward-looking models of epistemology and ontology in the wake of the Platonic doctrine of *anamnesis*. In this respect Bloch's principle of hope requires a re-orientation of history that accords well with Moltmann's requirement that history be re-defined in terms of the resurrection rather than *vice versa*. Whereas history is described as a movement from cause to effect by positivist historiographers, Bloch conceives it as a transition between possibility and reality, mediated not by causal necessity, but by tendency, which he calls 'the energetic of matter in action'.

'Tendency', then, is not passive, but is the 'energetic' 'driving forward' of 'matter in action'. This is only 'weakly' so in the extra-human world, and must be activated by human agency. The dialectical progress of this movement in history is towards the manifestation of a content – not, for Bloch, Hegel's 'Absolute Spirit', but utopian realization of the subject of history. The latency of the potentiality in matter, which tendency moves to realize, is related, by Moltmann, to the Christ-event, while the hope of the resurrection, revealed by God's raising Jesus from the dead, is seen as uncovering 'a historic process of mediation between subject and object'.[32] The still-unredeemed world is open for the future of Jesus Christ. The Kingdom of God is not awaited passively. It is to be activated by Christian mission. So promise is also a demand for action:

> The *pro-missio* of the kingdom is the ground of the *missio* of love to the world. It is the ground of the outgoing of the spirit in bodily obedience, because and in order that the 'inward' may become the 'outward', reality become rational and reason real – as Hegel put it . . .[33]

## 'Crucified Hope'

If the world is accurately represented by open system, if it is an unfinished process, then there is no guaranteed progress towards utopian realization. For Bloch, the process is decided 'by the bravery of hope on the front line of the present'.[34] That hope is only maintained by human will. Wayne Hudson points to an antinomy in Bloch's work here, in that the open, experimental character of the world makes hope possible, and yet Bloch also wants to authenticate the possibility of success.

Moltmann interposes a certainty available only to faith. It is the point at which a theology of hope has to dissociate itself from Bloch's project. Moltmann's certainty lies in the conviction that 'with the experiment "man" and the experiment "world" God had joined a hope'.[35] He sees Bloch's contribution in the fact that he does not reduce human openness to the future to a kind of inwardness, but aligns 'man's openness to the world' with an ontology of the world's openness to man. The openness of humanity, apparent in hope, corresponds to the openness of the world, apparent in its possibilities. But subjective hope can only be transformed into learned hope by a change of conception of reality. It must stand against non-purposive positivism and non-commital idealism, and must prevail against the mythical and philosophical 'eternal return of the same'.[36] The point of hope is, therefore, the emergence of the new. Biblical apocalyptic has to be demythologized to replace the unmediated transcendent end with an 'immanent transcending without transcendence'. There is a dialectical mediation of subjective and objective hope for the 'humanization of nature' and the 'naturalization of man'.[37] But Moltmann points out that, in the process of making the 'transcendence of the creator . . . immanent in the creating matter', in order to activate the possibility of hope, nature is re-mythologized in a way that reverses the de-mystifying of nature by Judaism and Christianity.

A similar problem is associated with the place of the negative in the dialectic of possibility and hope. The power of the dialectic is assumed to negate the negative, but, Moltmann claims, the negation drawn into this process is ontologized as 'not-yet-being', and is not identical with 'nothingness itself'. It is here that Christian hope is activated as faith in the God 'who quickeneth the dead, and calleth those things that be not as though they were' (Romans 4:17). So, unlike Bloch's principle, Christian hope is not open to the possibility of disappointment, but comes by way of actual disappointment: through crucifixion to resurrection. It is learned hope 'in that it knows concretely the overwhelming power of the negative and of the judgement over all being and its possibilities, and yet is still hope. As "crucified hope" it can be resurrection hope.'[38]

At the close of the previous chapter, this structure of hope emerged from the consideration of Romans 4. The hope-in-belief that was there opposed to and divided from empirical hope, can be identified now with learned, resurrection hope. It is not deceived by the negative, nor deflected by the illusory, but arises in the 'as though' of Romans 4:17, confronting and passing through negativity. The interpretative possibilities of this hope are drawn from the power of faith to call the sign to account. The power of the negative can then be confronted and re-interpreted in the light of hope, because the appearance of the world is not allowed to totalize the future. That is to say, present reality can be read in terms of the possibility of a different kind of knowledge which it does not yet admit: 'I shall know even as I am known' (1 Corinthians 13:12).

The hermeneutic circle (understood now as a figure of entanglement), that was observed in the work of faith, language and understanding, is allowed, by dint of its orientation in hope, to be a reading for the future, which calls into question the constraints of the present. This orientation also limits the power of tradition to determine understanding. The foregrounding of hope questions the circularity of hermeneutics, but is itself a product of that process as the direction set by the 'pre' of pre-understanding, pre-supposition. This entanglement is not evident in Schmidt's description of the future as 'not yet'. 'We need to remember', he says, 'that the present juncture in history . . . is the locus of liabilities as well as vantage points'. The 'need to remember . . . the present' encodes a version of *anamnesis*: presence is already a return of the same. The present tense of Schmidt's writing belies the avowed limits of presence, so fraught with liabilities. Those same liabilities must also relativize his claim that 'it is quite difficult to hold onto the simple truth that the present ultimately has no special privileges'.[39] The present *is* privileged in that it is the place from which we interpret. This privilege is never attenuated, but is limited in its scope by the temporality of the interpretative act, by its 'more or less hidden determination by the past', and by the direction it receives from hope.[40] This renders assertions about the 'radical openness' of the future problematic, because the future is not totalized by present assumptions – even the assumption of its openness. Hope is that orientation which moves from *pro-missio* to *missio*, for the sake of the future, which is radically unknowable in its content, yet is shaped by the history beginning with resurrection as it is grasped by hope-in-belief: learned hope.

It is freedom that is liberated by hope. A freedom for 'stubborn resistance to consensus values . . . a genuine challenge to prevailing institutional norms'. Moltmann writes:

> The gospel of the kingdom and of the justice of God in Christ can enter into a co-operative endeavour with social-revolutionary work for 'those who labour and are heavily-laden' and political work for 'those who are humiliated and offended', precisely because it goes beyond this in promising justification of the sinner and the resurrection of the dead.[41]

Ricoeur takes up this 'freedom in the light of hope' from Moltmann, and examines it in philosophical terms.

## RICOEUR'S MOLTMANN

### The Hope of Freedom

In his sonnet, 'That Nature is a Heraclitean Fire and of the Comfort of the Resurrection', Gerard Manley Hopkins wrote of the transforming power of resurrection hope:

> ... world's wildfire, leave but ash:
>     In a flash, at a trumpet crash,
> I am all at once what Christ is, since he was what I am, and
> This Jack, joke, poor potsherd, patch, matchwood, immortal
>     diamond,
>         Is immortal diamond.[42]

The brevity of life, and the constant flux of the world, are depicted as 'nature's bonfire', in an image borrowed from the early philosopher Heraclitus. With an apocalyptic 'trumpet crash' the residual 'ash' of natural decay is transformed into 'immortal diamond'. The immeasurably prolonged stress which transforms common carbon into rare and valuable diamonds, is contracted into an instant. Hopkins traces a Heraclitean process, from water (in the images of rainfall in the first quatrain), through earth (in the second quatrain) to fire (from line 9). This dynamic metaphysics offers no real hope, but only endless repetitions fuelled by endless strife. Bloch cites the same tradition in his rejection of cyclic philosophies, opposing his *Novum* to 'the Heraclitean and Stoic doctrine of world conflagration, according to which the Zeus-fire takes the world back into itself and similarly, in periodic cycles, releases it again'.[43] The 'comfort of the Resurrection' breaks into the cycle, not without stress, but with a force that outweighs nature's dynamic, an excess that is evoked, within the metaphorical economy of the poem, by instant transformation: 'In a flash' diamond emerges from the mud. Diamond suggests fire made permanent, and the play of colours associated with its refractory property evokes the possibility of flux within a stable form. The excessive stress of the Resurrection is a disruption of form represented by the technical strategy of the poem in its transgression of the restrictions which govern sonnet composition. Without the semblance of the sonnet form there would be no sense of exceeded constraints. It is just this kind of freedom, in its exceeding of law, that Ricoeur elaborates in his approach to Moltmann.

Ricoeur takes up Moltmann's theology of hope, defining freedom in the light of hope as 'the meaning of my existence in the light of the Resurrection'. The Resurrection is not an end of hope in the fulfilment of promise:

> The Resurrection, interpreted within a theology of promise, is not an event which closes, by fulfilling the promise, but an event which opens, because it adds to the promise by confirming it.

The Resurrection is the sign that the promise is henceforth for all: the meaning of the Resurrection is in its future, the death of death, the resurrection of all from the dead.[44]

Approaching a question of religious freedom, he discerns three levels on which it can be understood: the psychological level, on which faith is treated as an act of choice; the ethico-political level, which asks about the right to profess a specific religion; and the freedom that 'pertains to the religious phenomenon as such'. The last of these three levels is examined, not to the exclusion of the others, but as 'the completion of the discourse of freedom'.[45] This examination initially involves recapitulating Moltmann's re-interpretation of the Resurrection to unmask its hope content, hidden by the Greek christologies of manifestation and divine presence.

The psychological approach to religious freedom is seen in terms of choice. Existentialism ('from Kierkegaard to Bultmann') is aligned with the philosophies of the eternal present, coming down from Parmenides (5th century BC), in that the temporal and communitarian aspects of freedom are ignored in the attention to personal instantaneous decision. This ethics of the present is traced in Stoicism and Spinoza (1632–77), with their rejection of hope and fear. Hope is also opposed to Nietzsche (1844–1900) and Freud (1856–1939) in their homage to necessity. It is the power of imagination, the 'creative imagination of the possible'. Freedom's ethical dimension is seen as a question of law. Moltmann's insistence that the law is the the ethical dimension of the promise, means that freedom's relation to the covenant is mediated by law. The translation of the obedience to the law into resurrection hope is marked with reference to Paul, so that 'with Saint Paul this obedience is no longer transcribed in terms of law; obedience to the Law is no longer the sign of the efficacy of the promise; rather, the Resurrection is the sign'.[46]

A 'new ethics' emerges here, in Moltmann's observation that the renewed promise of the Resurrection involves an obligation, a mission 'which engages the present, proceeds from the promise, opens the future'. Again, the existential decision is left behind in a mission towards social and political freedom: the promise of the kingdom that comes by an active engagement of the human will.

The psychological and ethico-political dimensions of freedom are 'expressions', for Ricoeur, of the '*kerygmatic center* of freedom', which is the proclamation of the Resurrection. Freedom in the light of the hope of the Resurrection is given two categories: 'in spite of' and 'how much more'.[47] The first category is identified by recognizing that '[t]he peculiar *aporia* for every thought about hope appears with death', as Moltmann says.[48] Freedom in the light of hope, then, is freedom 'in spite of' death. The kerygma of the Gospels is read as: 'the living Lord of the Church is the same as Jesus on the cross'. The question of the identity of the crucified and the living arises in the 'hiatus between the Cross and the apparitions of the Resurrected. The empty tomb is the expression of this hiatus'.[49] Hope must carry this discontinuity – the hiding of the kingdom under its contrary, the Cross. Hope, then, becomes paradoxical. It takes on the form of that not-yet-knowledge of 1 Corinthians 13:12.

Ricoeur formulates the second category of freedom, that of 'how much more', as the inverse of the 'in spite of', speaking of an *economy of superabundance* in Paul's rhetoric (especially Romans 5:12–20, which he quotes). Paul speaks of the more than sufficient, over-efficacy of divine grace in Jesus, to outweigh the power of death. Freedom is to be 'at home' in this economy. Once more, the distance from existentialist versions of freedom is marked: '[f]reedom in the light of hope of resurrection has a personal expression, certainly, but, even more, a communitarian, historical, and political expression in the dimension of the expectation of universal resurrection'.[50] The mediation between a personal hope and a social hope is the excess of transforming power that Hopkins noted in the instant appearance of 'immortal diamond': 'In a flash, at a trumpet crash'.

The second half of the essay Ricoeur devotes to relating the kerygmatic hope to philosophical discourse. Whereas Moltmann takes up Bloch's utopian orientation and speaks of the kingdom of God in terms of social action aimed at its realization, Ricoeur seeks an 'interpretation which incessantly separates hope from utopia'. In fact, that separation is not fully established by Ricoeur's ensuing argument. The primary philosophical analogue of kerygmatic hope is Kantian postulation. Thus Hudson: 'Open system inherits Kant's postulates of practical reason, his stress on the primacy of hope, his postulate of an unreached Real and In General'.[51] Ricoeur seems to use 'utopia' in a way that opposes it to material reality when he insists that '[t]he passion for the possible must graft itself onto real tendencies, the mission onto a sensed history'.[52] Bloch, as already observed, saw utopia as precisely this kind of hope. The world as process has utopia in place as a limit situation, a postulate of practical reason which demands and directs human action. Ricoeurian hope turns out to be remarkably akin to Bloch's principle, despite their different interpretations of the utopian. Hope is characterized as that which opens systems: 'The theme of hope has precisely a *fissuring* power with regard to closed systems and a power of *reorganizing* meaning'.[53] The primacy of hope in Kant, therefore, leads to the important assertion that his philosophy is 'a philosophy of limits and not a philosophy of system'.[54]

Because religion is, for Kant, a question of hope, Ricoeur scrutinizes the sequence that moves from pure reason, through practical reason, to the philosophy of religion. The dialectic of pure reason gives rise to the critique of transcendental illusion, and the 'domain of hope', he insists, 'is quite precisely coextensive with the region of transcendental illusion'. The Kantian critique, however, does not displace hope, but 'is essential to an understanding of hope'. It does not rule out the possibility of any legitimate thought of the unconditioned, but implies that the transcendental illusion proceeds from 'the filling-in of the thought of the unconditioned according to the mode of the empirical object'. It is only the legitimate thought of the unconditioned that gives rise to the transcendental illusion. So, reason limits the claim of the empirical to provide knowledge of the unconditioned, the thought of which arises as a kind of prosopopeia or catachresis.

Practical reason gives the will a goal: the highest good. The critique of the transcendental illusion (that truth is always conditional upon the truth of its underlying premise, so to know the world unconditionally requires the establishing of an ultimate premise known unconditionally) forbids speculation about the highest good, and positions it as 'the completion of the will', so, 'it does not permit any knowledge, but only a demand'. This direction of the will leads to the postulates of practical reason (God, freedom and immortality, for Kant) which 'designate an order of things to come to which we know we belong'. Ricoeur sees freedom as pivotal to this notion of postulation. This is not the freedom entailed by duty ('ought implies can'), but a freedom that has objective reality. The postulation is that 'we exist according to this supreme vow'. The other two postulates (God and immortality) indicate that this freedom is a 'freedom in the light of hope'. Immortality is an effect of the will toward the highest good: the possibility of its realization. It is therefore the hope of the postulate of freedom and is thus 'the philosophical equivalent of the hope for resurrection'.[55] The postulation of the existence of God is seen as the origin of the synthesis of morality and happiness, a connection which is beyond our power. It is a future connection which allows Kant to bring religion to the question 'What can I hope for?'

## Freedom and Evil

The problem of evil inevitably accompanies that of freedom. Are we free to choose between good and evil? Turning to Kant's 'Essay on Radical Evil', Ricoeur sees the postulate of freedom confronting the conclusion that freedom for the highest good is also the propensity for choosing badly. This is the problem of hope without faith which Moltmann confronts in Bloch. The openness of the future is ambiguous. Again, this is the political crisis of interpretation in the 'postmodern' era. Politically repressive forces will appropriate meanings as readily as liberal, progressive ones. The problem is acute for the interpretation of history, as Christopher Norris has pointed out.[56] It is the need of the moment to re-think the category of hope with this in mind. It is not just a question at the level of ethics. It is determined by the very issues of meaning and interpretation which have emerged through this discussion. Interpretative freeplay confronts the same dilemma of choice, and the ethics of reading is predicated upon the epistemological problems addressed by Kant. Ricoeur writes:

> The 'postulate' of freedom must henceforth cross through, not only the night of knowing, with its crisis of the transcendental illusion, but also the night of power, with its crisis of radical evil. *Real* freedom can spring up only as hope beyond this speculative and practical Good Friday. Nowhere are we closer to the Christian kerygma: hope is hope of resurrection, resurrection from the dead.[57]

The philosophical approximation of hope of resurrection here seems to be precisely the kind of 'post-Hegelian Kantianism' that Ricoeur advocates. The 'death of God', the content of the 'speculative Good Friday', appears to be 'a universalizing of the historic Good Friday of the god-forsakenness of Jesus'.[58] This Hegelian view of the death of God, as a moment in a dialectical process, is open to the criticism levelled by Feuerbach: 'the God who reconstructs himself on the basis of his own negation is no true God, but on the contrary a self-contradictory, atheistic God'.[59] Hegel's universalizing move masks the historical particularity of the Good Friday event, and the uniqueness of the Gospel testimony to the Resurrection. Ricoeur may be right, as far as philosophical discourse is concerned, that '[n]owhere are we closer to the Christian kerygma', but, to the extent that he is so, he is also over-optimistic about the very task of 'approximation'. In a note at the end of the essay, he goes some way toward reconciling the historical Jesus with the philosophical principle. Pointing out that 'Kant is in no way interested in the historicity of Christ', but views him as an archetype, he goes on to observe that this 'archetype is not at all an idea that I can give myself arbitrarily'.

Hope, then, comes to rest in a historical person rather than an arbitrary symbol, an event rather than an ideal, 'an archetype and not a simple example of duty'. Christ is not a principle, but one who confronted the 'night of knowing'. Re-iterating Moltmann's insistence that 'Christianity stands or falls with the reality of the raising of Jesus from the dead by God', now takes on a greater significance. It is no longer just to see the Resurrection as a sign of hope rather than fulfilment, but to make hope an historically determined category rather than a function of idealism.

Ricoeur's essay, whilst it does not distinguish between the possibility for the future of an historic event, and the a-historical universalizing of that event as a myth of the dialectic of Absolute Spirit, does effect a limited approximation. It puts philosophical discourse 'into a relation of proximity with kerygmatic and theological discourse', by virtue of an analogy between hope and postulation. It is possible to sustain this effect, without falling prey to Feuerbach's critique, if the 'speculative Good Friday' is seen in terms of the Christian kerygma: 'the living Lord of the Church is the same as Jesus on the cross'. In other words, the speculative Good Friday is read as taking place within the same history as the Resurrection. A 'speculative Easter Sunday' is not the assertion that 'God reconstructs himself on the basis of his own negation', but the re-reading of history to include the Resurrection, as Moltmann suggests. The limitation of Ricoeur's approximation is that hope is not altogether comparable to the process of Kantian postulation; rather, the very process of postulation is an effect of hope.


## KANT AND HAMANN

### Hope and Reason

In more recent work, Ricoeur has returned to the issues of practical reason, freedom, and political hope, to argue the discontinuity between the practical order and the theoretical.[60] Kant is read as hypostasizing one aspect of practical experience, moral obligation, at the expense of 'desire'. His universalization of the moral imperative implies 'that the practical order is amenable to a system of knowledge . . . comparable to the knowledge and the science required in the theoretical order', opening the door, Ricoeur thinks, to the assumption that a 'science of praxis' is possible. Not that this development is Kant's responsibility, but that 'by constructing the concept of the practical a priori after the model of that of the theoretical a priori, Kant shifted the investigation of practical reason into a region of knowledge that does not belong to it'.[61]

Such an objection could lead to the kind of anti-cognitivist approach prevalent in postmodern theories of freedom, such as Lyotard's appeal to the sublime as a kind of anti-philosophical trope which undoes any claim to link the practical order with the theoretical.[62] Ricoeur circumvents this danger by pressing for a *critical* theory which derives practical reason from the realm of intersubjectivity, via a critique of ideology. That critique goes by way of the Hegelian concept of the will, which, instead of opposing reason-determined will to free choice at the intersection of duty and desire, proposes 'a dialectical constitution of willing'. The idealization of the State that follows from this 'in which the will of each individual recognizes itself in the will of all' is not taken up. Hegel failed to note the possibility whereby the State, far from becoming increasingly 'an institutional mediation of freedom', constrains and represses. But this is not the most telling objection, since individual freedom *must* be mediated institutionally if there is to be social freedom. Ricoeur contends that it is the radical ontological distinction of subjective mind and objective mind (*Geist*) in Hegel that is most dangerous. 'One may wonder', he muses, 'whether this hypostasis of mind, elevated in this way above individual consciousness and even above intersubjectivity, is not responsible for another hypostasis, that of the State itself'.[63] Practical reason must derive, then, from intersubjectivity if it is to avoid an undialectical relation between individual and institution, between freedom and law.

If ideology, at one level, has the function of social integration, a critical approach to it, according to Ricoeur, can transform practical reason 'from knowledge into critique'. If, however, practical reason subtends the theory of knowledge (as Onora O'Neill has argued), such a transformation is meaningless: practical reason is already critique.[64] Ricoeur identifies three functions of ideology. The first function corresponds to its most familiar guise, false consciousness.

This is found to have a depth dimension in its role of filling the credibility gap between a claim to authority and a belief in its legitimacy. The layer of legitimation is, in turn, found to conceal a further layer: 'the symbolic systems constitutive of action itself'. Utopia is related to ideology as subversion is to integration. The delusive appearance of utopian thought is also an opening of 'the field of the possible . . . beyond that of the actual'. In contrast with ideology (understood as a function of social integration), utopia appears as the function of social subversion, so that '[u]ltimately what is at stake in utopia is the apparent givenness of every system of authority'.[65]

As might be expected, Ricoeur is not content to oppose utopia to ideology. He shows that they 'dialectically imply each other' since the fact that ideology mediates social ties means that it also opens a gap for the 'eccentric' appearance of utopia; and utopia, in its eccentricity, tending towards disintegration, allows ideology its integrative function. This inter-penetration, however, also allows the critique of ideology from a utopian source.

Although Thomas More's original utopia is geographic, Bloch's seems to be temporal (*Uchronia* is Ricoeur's term). It is a question of possibility, and so of the future. A chronology is thus implied in this practical reason (as a critique of ideology from a utopian source) which closely resembles Johann Georg Hamann's (1730–88) 'rejection of the Enlightenment distinction between eternal and temporal truths':[66]

> What would the most exact and careful knowledge of the present be without a divine renewal of the past, without an inkling of the future. . . . What a labyrinth the present would be for the spirit of observation, without the spirit of prophecy and its clues from the past and the future.[67]

Here, there is no closure of the past nor of the future, but a reciprocal openness and exchange which defines the present. The tendency to view the past as complete and as sealed off from the present and the future renders both the present and the future dark. It is Ricoeur's contention that the past must be 'reopened' and its extinguished possibilities 'rekindled'. He writes: 'in opposition to the old saying that the future is open and contingent in all respects while the past is definitively closed and hence necessary, we must make our expectations more determinant and our experience more indeterminant'. Those determinant expectations must be 'finite and relatively modest' so that they can engender '*responsible* commitments'. This is to resist purely *utopian* expectations in favour of strategies for action, but action that is cognizant of the postulates of practical reason, so that 'every expectation must be a hope for all of humanity'.[68] Kant's notion of the *sensus communis* includes this 'maxim . . . of enlarged thought' in the requirement 'to think from the standpoint of everyone else', not as an insistence upon the possibility of a divinatory act of interpretation, but as an agreement to avoid working from maxims which cannot be agreed upon by others, allowing the Categorical Imperative to become a hermeneutic principle.[69]

In the process of postulation, then, the influence of the future works back towards the past to recover its hope-contents, illuminating the present with potential. Hamann's chronology is similar, but, for him, the influence of the future is not an effect of practical reason. He proposes a dialectic of observation and prophecy, of the present and the absent in which 'the spirit of observation and the spirit of prophecy are expressions of a single positive power . . . and in fact presuppose one another, are related to and mutually affect one another'.[70] This is an approximation of 1 Corinthians 13:9: 'For we know in part and we prophesy in part', which Hamann quotes at this point. 'Observation', the appearance of the world, far from determining the future is conditioned by it in hope: 'The future determines the present', says Hamann, 'and the present determines the past, as the purpose determines the constitution and the means to be used'.[71]

### Faith *versus* Reason

Despite the similarity between these chronologies, Hamann's philosophy developed out of his antipathy towards Enlightenment values, especially as exemplified by Kant, whilst Ricoeur expressly draws on Kant and the Enlightenment tradition. Hamann was far from being an irrationalist, but saw reason as limited by faith. The interplay of faith and reason that he outlines may serve to re-orient the account of hope that emerged from from Ricoeur's re-examination of 'Religion within the Limits of Reason Alone' in 'Freedom in the Light of Hope'.

Although decisively influential in the rise of the German *Sturm und Drang*, particularly in his effect on Herder, Hamann remains little read in the English-speaking world. Apart from J. C. O'Flaherty's study (1952), R. G. Smith's book (already mentioned), a chapter in

F. Beiser's *The Fate of Reason* (1987), and Isaiah Berlin's recently published volume, *The Magus of the North* (1993), reference to him is
largely restricted to brief allusions and footnotes in connection with
Herder.[72] Hamann was a native Königsburg, and a contemporary of
Kant. They knew each other and, despite profound differences of
belief, Hamann described Kant as a 'helpful and unselfish man,
basically good and noble in his disposition, talented and worthy',
in a letter to Herder in 1785.[73]

In 1758 Hamann had had a dramatic conversion experience, whilst
on a visit to London. It convinced him that 'God was always com-
municating with him, if he would only listen'.[74] The world, as well as
the Bible, was God's word, and, he maintained, 'all nature's treas-
ures are nothing but an allegory, a mythological picture of heavenly
systems – just as all events of world history are silhouettes of more
mysterious actions and disclosed miracles'.[75]

With such a hermeneutical view of the world and the word it is
not surprising that Hamann's philosophical concerns took a dis-
tinctly linguistic turn which makes him seem decidedly modern at
times. It was this concern with language that dominated his criticism of Kant and furthered his case for the incapacity of reason to
legislate in matters of faith. He saw Kant as performing a second
phase of purification of philosophy. Before Kant:

> The first purification of philosophy consisted in the partly misun-
> derstood and partly unsuccessful attempt to render the reason
> independent of all tradition and belief in tradition. The second
> purification is even more transcendental, and results in nothing
> less than independence of experience and its everyday induction.[76]

Profoundly influenced by the English empiricists, especially David
Hume (to whose work he introduced Kant), Hamann anathematized
what he perceived as Kant's hypostasis of reason. Reason, he argued,
exists only in language which is 'nothing more than the customs
and conventions of a culture'. To purify reason language itself must
be purified. Enlightenment reason, like its rationalist forebear, is
founded upon two connected premisses: 'Receptivity of language
and spontaneity of ideas! From this twofold source of ambiguity
pure reason draws all the elements of its disputation, its scepticism
and its criticism.'[77] Neither of these premisses can be granted since
'the visible and audible signs of language belong to experience'.[78]

If, however, O'Neill is right to refer to Kantian reason as 'a practical and collective task', constructed on the plain of experience, and not an algorithmic hypostasis, much of the force of Hamann's critique is deflected. This is not to devalue it, but to apply it as a language-oriented re-inforcement of this version of Kantian ethics.

In a move that may remind us of Derrida's word-play, Hamann makes his point about language by recourse to the word 'metaphysics':

> This hereditary defect and leprosy of ambiguity clings to the very name of metaphysics, and is not removed, far less transfigured, through being traced to its birthplace in the casual synthesis of a Greek prefix. But even though it is granted that in the transcendental topic the empirical distinction of *behind* and *beyond* mattered still less than the *hysteron proteron* in an *a priori a posteriori*, yet the birth-mark of the name widens out from the brow to the very heart of all knowledge . . .[79]

Metaphysics, the 'behind' or 'beyond' of physics, is marked by its name as determined by the study of the physical. An empirical science thus precedes it and places it, gives birth to it. The name itself determines this order and remains as a 'birth-mark', signalling the provenance of the discourse that announces its own purity and autonomy. The fact that the name is a result of a 'casual synthesis', far from mitigating its effect actually adds to the empirical, real world condition of its claims. If there is a profound dualism between the rational and the sensible, then reason and language are also separated. Reason cannot be universal and a-temporal and yet have language as its vehicle or instrument. Beiser sums up the threat to Enlightenment thinking posed by Hamann's linguistic turn when he points out that the authority of reason is thus endangered since 'its principles will no longer be universal and impartial, binding for every intelligent being. Rather, they will simply express the values, traditions, and language of a culture'.[80]

Hamann's project was not an attempt to found a philosophy of the irrational, but to make room for faith alongside reason. Language relativizes reason, but faith holds language in place, calling it to account. In 1759, Hamann wrote to Kant disparaging the latter's attempt to win him back for Enlightenment thought. In this letter he placed the role of reason in his thought quite precisely: 'Reason is not given to you in order that you may become wise, but that you may know your folly and ignorance'. He went on to quote Hume's objection to Christianity as unreasonable: 'Mere reason is insufficient to convince us of its veracity'.[81] Whereas Hume's response is to reject faith in favour of reason, Hamann sees the very limit of reason marking the point of faith's departure. This is crucial for the relationship between faith and reason, and finds its way into Søren Kierkegaard's (1813–55) work as a founding moment in *Fear and Trembling* (1843): 'faith begins precisely where thought stops'.[82] Faith outbids reason by making sense of the absurd. Reason can be surpassed, for Hamann and for Kierkegaard, but faith cannot: 'Faith is the highest passion in a person. There perhaps are many in every generation who do not come to faith, but no one goes further'.[83]

There is a problem here which the diversionary, ironic and pseudonymic strategies of Hamannian and Kierkegaardian style do not subvert or dissolve. In order to go beyond reason and find meaning in its other, it is necessary to reassert reason within the absurd, to carry an argument through and beyond the reason/faith border. The very condition of meaning is faith, but to mean is to stay within reason. Derrida makes the point against Foucault's attempt to write a history of madness. The trial of reason involved 'may be impossible, for by the simple fact of their articulation the proceedings and the verdict unceasingly reiterate the crime. ... Order is then denounced within order'.[84] Further, to propose a strict dualism which allows a border between reason and faith is to ignore the very point at which Hamann wants to diverge from Kant: just as reason cannot be purified of experience because of its investment in language, neither can faith. If this is inverted, and the argument for the role of faith in language (put forward in the first two chapters) is accepted, then faith is a condition of both language and reason. Faith does not begin where thought ends but re-emerges there from its hiddenness in language, and is revealed by the finitude of reason that it reveals.

The Lisbon earthquake of 1755 threw the question of reason into sharp relief. Leibniz's optimism provided the focus for eighteenth-century debate about whether or not this is the best of all possible worlds.[85] The catastrophe in Lisbon raised the question not only of theoretical optimism but of divine providence, without which the world would appear meaningless and life hopeless. The human condition would be absurd. What troubled eighteenth-century minds were the implications for reason if there were no rational grounds for a belief in providence. 'If we cannot accept that our lives are meaningless, and if reason tells us that this is the case, then why should we remain loyal to reason?' Beiser asks.[86] Kant and Hamann were divided over this issue too. The former remained confident in his reason and, to a certain degree, confirmed a Leibnizian optimism. This is not to suggest that Kant retained an uncritically sanguine outlook, but that his exchange with Hamann around this time gave 'the young Kant reason to reconsider his optimistic rationalism'.[87] Human finitude, Kant had argued, prevents us from seeing events like the Lisbon earthquake in their divine perspective. Hamann's response was to accuse Kant of transcending reason in order to defend it, appealing to the unprovable assertion that this is the best of all possible worlds, and to God, about whom reason can make no assertions. In a letter of December 1759 he wrote: 'If you want to prove that the world is good, then do not appeal to the world as a whole, for we human beings cannot know it, and do not refer to God, for only a blind man with staring eyes can see him'.[88]

Hamann was not a thoroughgoing pessimist, but he saw hope as residing in faith and not in reason. This was another direct consequence of his conversion experience and the concomitant impression of the world that makes of both nature and history 'a sealed book, a cloaked witness, a riddle which cannot be solved unless we plough with some other ox than our reason'.[89] History has meaning, but only when it is understood in hope, eschatologically. History is not thus denied, but its totalization in the present is refused, and the semiotics of history is transgressed towards a hermeneutic. R. G. Smith writes of Hamann's sense of history as a picture or allegory that it 'is not the destruction of the events which compose mundane history, but rather the introduction into them of a meaning greater than themselves – greater, that is, than any single event or separate chain of events . . .'.[90] This brings the discussion back to the question of the future and the chronology already discussed: 'the future determines the present and the present determines the past'. Hope, as it arises from faith, then, opens up the present and decentres it, preventing it from totalizing the real, but also circumvents assertions about the 'radical openness' of the future, which are judgements from a present. It is meaningless to make judgements about the future whilst acknowledging the interpretative liabilities of the present. All we can know of it is hope.

## READING PAUL (3)

### Subject and Object: The Future Now

Returning, briefly, to the theme of justification, a theological dilemma, associated with interpretations of Paul, provides a clue to the role of hope in this discussion of his hermeneutic possibilities. Anthony Thiselton, utilizing Wittgenstein, examines the question of whether justification is present or future in Paul. The Wittgensteinian principle employed is 'the phenomeneon of "seeing . . . as . . .", of seeing x as y'. The famous duck-rabbit image is reproduced to illustrate the point: '*What* is seen remains the same; *how* it is seen depends upon the significance of function of the phenomenon within a given system, frame of reference or setting in life'.[91] In terms of the theological debate, Thiselton argues that both the present and the future claims about justification are true, so that 'we have been justified' (in Romans 5:1) does not contradict 'the righteousness for which we hope' (in Galatians 5:5).[92] What differs is the frame of reference: '[h]istory and eschatology each provide a frame of reference in which a different verdict on the believer is valid and appropriate'. The future, eschatological justification can be anticipated in the present by faith: 'from the historical viewpoint justification is still future, but by appropriation of the eschatological verdict it is possible to live by faith in the present experience of being justified'.[93]

Faith here is not external to justification but is criterial to it. To have this faith is part of what justification is and entails. This, again, marks the influence of the future upon the present, with faith as mediation. The relation between justification and meaning has already been explored (in the previous chapter). Here, a futurity appears which reveals the expectation of meaning appropriated by faith: that other kind of knowledge that is hoped for and towards which hermeneutics presses on.

Similar considerations occur in Sanders' assessment of Paul's soteriology:

[T]he verb 'save' in Paul is generally future or present, but only once past (aorist) tense. Even here, however, Paul writes that 'we were saved in *hope*' (Romans 8:24). . . . Especially striking is the use of the present passive participles 'being saved' and 'being destroyed' . . . consummation is still in the future. We may finally note that the resurrection is future.[94]

The complexity of Pauline hope is manifest in this theological formulation. It corresponds neither to presence nor absence but causes a reciprocal exchange between them which is unrecognizable in the hypostatic models deriving from Plotinian metaphysics. It is equally unrecognizable in the hypostasis of the future characterized as 'radically open'. This, again, invalidates the claims that Paul's writing is the site of an emergent Graeco-Christian tradition which can be divided from and opposed to a Judaic one, or that it represents Christianity's complete investment in a metaphysics of presence derived solely from Platonism. In fact, as Gabriel Josipovici argues, there is something specific in Paul's soteriology, a tension between the epochal event of conversion on the Damascus road and the ongoing inner conflict, that seems to derive neither from Hebrew nor Greek metaphysics:

> This struggle within the self between warring factions is something with which literature has made us so familiar that it is hard to realize that it is not the only way to think about the self . . . Dostoevsky . . . made the explicit point in his *Notes from Underground* that it was a concept unknown to Plato or to the philosophical tradition descended from him, and implied that only a Christian vision of man could make sense of it.[95]

This struggle is expressed in Romans 7:19–23:

> For the good that I would I do not: but the evil which I would not, that I do. Now if I do that I would not, it is no more I that do it, but sin that dwelleth in me. I find then a law, that, when I would do good, evil is present with me. For I delight in the law of God after the inward man. But I see another law in my members, warring against the law of my mind, and bringing me into captivity to the law of sin which is in my members.

Josipovici sees this as an internalizing of religious imperatives that demands the recounting of personal experience (as Paul does in Acts 22 and 26, and again in Galatians 1), if it is not to render faith untenably subjective. Such testimony is the precursor to Augustine's *Confessions* and, through Bunyan's *Grace Abounding to the Chief of Sinners*, to modern autobiography. This is an over-simplification of Pauline interpretation based on a failure to attend to at least two important factors: Paul's rhetorical strategy in constructing his Letter to the Galatians, and his use of allegoresis. The latter is examined in more detail in Chapter 5. The point about Paul's rhetoric is made by David Aune: 'The narrative of Galatians 1:13–2:21 has a defensive tone and is intended to establish Paul's credibility, for in deliberative rhetoric the *ethos* or moral character and conduct of the speaker, if unknown or in doubt must be established.'[96]

Paul's experience is adduced in support of his case, to testify to his character as reliable witness. Admittedly, this is not necessarily incompatible with recounting experience as a concretion of internal processes, but it does suggest the possibility of an alternative interpretation. This alternative emerges as Josipovici takes his case a step further, claiming that, for Paul, 'all externals are meaningless, part of the Old Law, the domain of the Devil', and adding that 'if history itself is allegorized and internalized, if everything that happened takes on a purely spiritual meaning, then it becomes vitally important to give spiritual meanings some sort of objective status or the whole is in danger of simply disappearing'.[97]

A lot depends on those 'ifs', especially the 'if' applied to 'purely spiritual meaning' in Paul. There is no 'purely spiritual meaning' in Paul, but, as I hope to show, a dialectic of spirit and letter in which these two poles of language are seen to be constituted by their reciprocal relationship. Already the direction of Pauline hope-in-belief militates against a 'purely spiritual meaning' and its correlative subjectivism. Recalling Bloch's subject-object relation (and the identity of the two as a goal of human action), brings this more clearly into view. Romans 8:19–22 reads:

> The creation waits in eager expectation for the sons of God to be revealed. For the creation was subjected to frustration, not by its own choice, but by the will of the one who subjected it, in hope that the creation itself will be liberated from its bondage to decay and brought into the glorious freedom of the children of God. We know that the whole creation has been groaning as in the pains of childbirth right up to the present time (NIV).

Here, the creation has a subjectivity for which 'the sons of God' are object. Clearly, from the context (especially verses 15–17 of the same chapter) 'the sons of God' refers to 'those who are in Christ Jesus' (v. 1). This inversion of the subject-object relation is deepened by the prosopopeia of 'choice', 'freedom' and 'groaning', and a world pregnant with its own future.

Whereas for Bloch the unfinished character of the world leaves room for human action to work towards a realization of objective hope, for Paul the eschatological finiteness of the world is the condition for objective hope. The difference between these varieties of hope is marked by the point Moltmann makes against Bloch, that there is no guarantee against disappointment in Open System. For Paul, hope is not vulnerable to disappointment but arises out of it: 'tribulation worketh patience; And patience, experience; and experience, hope: And hope maketh not ashamed' (Romans 5:3b–5a). Tribulation, suffering causes hope to emerge by contrast with the present contents of the world, but its appearance is mediated by experience and patience. Tribulation is not causally linked with hope. Hope arises as an interpretation of suffering, based upon a temporality that allows the future to determine the present. Such a determination depends upon the justifying faith which Paul has been elucidating in Romans 4, and which was examined in the previous chapter. Hope's disruptive power breaks into the present when the negative appears, irrupting in defiance of tribulation, and demanding a future.

Because Pauline subjectivity is not absolute, but reciprocally defined by the 'creation', the internal struggle which Josipovici witnesses cannot be seen as a simple interiorizing of religious experience. It is also a phenomenology of 'freedom in the light of hope'. The context does not allow a binary opposition between internal and external, which would make the external 'meaningless', to govern the interpretation. The 'law', the epitome of externality, is not written off as the 'domain of the Devil' at all. On the contrary, 'the law is holy, and the commandment is holy, and just, and good' (Romans 7:12). Not only so, but this holy, just and good law is also 'spiritual' (v. 14). It is in place to define goodness and its opposite: 'I had not known sin, but by the law' (v. 7); akin, in fact, to the postulates of practical reason. This is a hopeful re-placing of the law, resisting the backward-oriented interpretation which allows a tradition to totalize meaning. That tradition is neither allowed to be completely determinant nor simply abandoned. It is subjected to 'the kind of stubborn resistance to consensus values . . . that would constitute a genuine challenge to prevailing institutional norms'.[98]

## The Hermeneutical Significance of Conversion

Paul's repeated recounting of his conversion experience is not, then, an attempt to 'give spiritual meanings some sort of objective status'.

In Acts 22 and 26, he uses it as an evangelistic message designed to show the transforming power of an encounter with Christ. He is careful, on both occasions, to emphasize the complete reversal of his position: from persecutor of believers to persecuted believer. But the conversion has another, hermeneutic significance which can be glimpsed in its recounting in Galatians 1:13 & 14:

> For ye have heard of my conversation in time past in the Jews' religion, how that beyond measure I persecuted the Church of God, and wasted it: And profited in the Jews' religion above many my equals in mine own nation, being more exceedingly zealous of the traditions of my fathers.

A controlling interpretation is seen to have determined belief and action to the point where 'zeal for the traditions' gave rise to an oppressive force. Paul at no time claims a causal link between the tradition and his action in its propagation, rather, he acknowledges in the signifiers of excess ('beyond measure' and 'exceedingly') that a certain interpretation of that tradition instituted his campaign of persecution. What caused a re-reading of that tradition was the Damascus road conversion when, he says, 'it pleased God . . . to reveal his Son to me' (vv. 15 & 16).

There is a striking parallel between Paul's dramatic *volte-face* and Hamann's London experience, not just in the drama of a sudden and sublime occurrence, but also in the hermeneutic ramifications of both events. Hamann's conversion convinced him that experience was hermeneutical, since the world was God's word. He could have found this in Paul: 'For the invisible things of him from the creation of the world are clearly seen, being understood by the things that are made, even his eternal power and Godhead; so that they are without excuse' (Romans 1:20).

Paul's experience became, for him, a founding moment in a new hermeneutic, an event that broke in upon 'the traditions of (his) fathers', and subjected them to scrutiny in a new light. Under this new apprehension the law became the interpretant of human action rather than its determinant. For Hamann, reason was in the place of law as he resisted the new institutional norms of Enlightenment thought. The parallel is made clear in a passage already quoted (in part):

> Reason is not given to you in order that you may become wise, but that you may know your folly and your ignorance, as the

> Mosaic law was not given to the Jews to make them righteous, but to make their sins more sinful to them.[99]

Hamann's conversion repeats Paul's and carries its resistant hermeneutic into the conflict of interpretations at the point when that conflict becomes critical: Kant's epistemological turn. For both Paul and Hamann, it is the experience of conversion that re-orients hermeneutics (as also for Augustine), and sets up a resistance to received ideas by virtue of an eschatological sense which unsettles the totality of presence and its determination by the past in backward-looking models of interpretation. Paul's recountings of his conversion experience attest to the irruption of hope into the present so that his personal history is also prophetic. As R. G. Smith writes of Hamann: 'the end of history is present in man's personal life, and this end is God's complete action in his Word. . . . that is, the completeness of his action, is what makes it possible for all historical events to be recognized as signs'.[100]

This future guarantee of signification is a hermeneutic of hope appropriated by faith. The light on the road to Damascus is thus proleptic, eschatological, a sign of hope and an axial point in the history of interpretation and the interpretation of history.

# 5

# The Letter of the Spirit

... for the letter killeth, but the spirit giveth life.

(2 Corinthians 3:6b)

## OPPOSITIONS

Sin has been defined often – among others by Malebranche and by Kant – as the inversion of the natural relationship between the soul and the body through passion. Saussure [here] points at the inversion of the natural relationship between speech and writing. It is not a simple analogy: writing, the letter, the sensible inscription, has always been considered by western tradition as the body and matter external to the spirit, to breath, to speech, and to the logos. And the problem of soul and body is no doubt derived from the problem of writing from which it seems – conversely – to borrow its metaphors.[1]

Derrida, in *Of Grammatology*, provides impressive evidence for the place of these correlative oppositions in the western metaphysical tradition from Socrates to Saussure. Writing, the body, sensibilia are external, subordinated to speech, spirit and the intelligible, which are internal. The critical force of Derrida's work consists in de-stabilizing these oppositions, not to assert their inverse, but to question the epistemic foundations of western thought by showing these founding oppositions to be unsustainable. He might have quoted Origen's deliberation on the 'spiritual senses':

He [Christ] is called the true sight, therefore, that the soul's eyes may have something to lighten them. He is the Word, so that ears may have something to hear. Again, he is the Bread of Life so that the soul's palate may have something to taste.[2]

The list continues, so that Christ is also the 'spikenard' for the soul's sense of smell, and the 'Word made flesh' for the soul's hand to touch. Just as Saussure could only resort to metaphors derived from writing in order to define *la langue*, so Origen resorts to the realm of the sensible in order to speak of the highest (most inward) experience of the soul. His term for discerning God's will by means of those senses, *enoptike*, seems, as Andrew Louth suggests, to mean 'insight' – a term which yokes the inward intelligible realm with the realm of the senses.[3] It is the tradition of interpretation coming down from Origen which places Christian hermeneutics as vulnerable to deconstruction, because the Platonic model with which he works depends upon the stability of the oppositions which Derrida subjects to scrutiny. Paul falls prey to the same treatment to the extent that an unbroken line is maintained, which situates his interpretation of the Hebrew Bible as the originary text in a tradition which includes Origen and the inheritors of his allegorical method. A concern of this chapter, therefore, will be to show a dislocation in that tradition by subjecting a central interpretative gesture in Origen's *De Principiis* to deconstruction, and then questioning deconstruction itself with Paul's text.

Underlying this move is an appreciation of the irony involved in adopting a deconstructive approach to Origen's text in order to locate a point of slippage in the interpretative tradition to which he belongs, whilst at the same time advancing objections to the deconstructive project. But it is just this irony which effects the rupture. It is an aporia within deconstruction that it should depend upon the positing of a Graeco-Christian metaphysics (as opposed to a Judaistic grammatolatry), which, the deconstructor would claim, informs western interpretation from Paul onwards, and is constructed out of persistent oppositional thinking. The oppositional stress, which it can be used to highlight in Origen, also questions the veracity of its presupposition with regard to Paul, especially his distinction between the letter and the spirit.

Hope is still the dominant theme here. In this chapter it appears in the very resistance to a continuing tradition which is represented by an approach to Origen. At the level of theoretical development, hope is what prevents the letter/spirit distinction from being identified fully with the stratification of meaning found in Origen and throughout the Middle Ages.

In the final section of the previous chapter it was noted that Pauline hope disrupted one Platonic opposition – that between presence and absence. The correlation between that opposition and the others noted here is particularly marked in the privileging of speech over writing because of the former's claimed self-presence. The intelligible/sensible dichotomy is another version of the same concern – the intelligible lines up with presence in its immediacy, whereas the sensible is mediated by the perceptual faculties, and so, in a sense, absent. If Pauline hope disavows the rigidity of the presence/absence dichotomy then the system of oppositions that cluster around it must also be affected, and what Derrida identifies as the 'metaphysics of presence' must be under strain in Paul's thought. Hope's disruptive power was also noted by Kant in his *Critique of Pure Reason*, in its transgression of the boundary between the practical and the theoretical orders. It involves beliefs which enable those who hold them to conceptualize willing and acting. In other words it enables postulation and prompts action.[4] This insight is particularly important when the focus on Paul's work shifts to the role of love in his hermeneutic in Chapter 6.

Transgressive hope, then, labours against both the reductive stratification of meaning and the closing off of theory from practice. In Paul's formulation it mediates between faith and love. Given its central role, the structure of hope must work through the whole of Paul's hermeneutic, fracturing the image of its Platonic heritage, and questioning the easy assumption that it can be defined as a straightforward privileging of the spirit over the letter, speech over writing, presence over absence, intelligible over sensible, without any serious consideration of what the letter/spirit distinction entails, and how it fits into a broader view of Pauline interpretation.

## BODY, SHADOW, SPIRIT AND LETTER

### From Letter to Spirit

In *The Slayers of Moses*, Susan Handelman represents Paul's interpretative method in the very oppositional terms under discussion: 'For Paul', she asserts, 'the spiritual meaning utterly nullifies the literal meaning, and allegory becomes the technique through which he uses the law to destroy the law'.[5] Keeping faith with a received opposition, the 'spiritual' and the 'literal' are held apart as though naming two completely discrete levels of meaning, one of which can be accentuated at the expense of the other. It is possible to read Paul's hermeneutic as questioning the rigidity of this stratification which it also sets up: showing signs of slippage between the spirit

and the letter. If this is the case then it is no more possible to privilege letter over spirit than to see the spirit as nullifying the letter.
The distinction implies an irreducible reciprocation.

Handelman's concern with Pauline interpretation is part of an
investigation of 'the emergence of rabbinic interpretation in modern literary theory', through the work of Freud, Lacan, Derrida and
Bloom. Derrida is characterized as 'erecting' a 'new religion of writing' which is opposed to Christianity in its presumed complicity
with Greek metaphysics, and is predicated upon a perceived relation
between contemporary and rabbinic models of interpretation. The
disjunction of what is made to look like Graeco-Christian thought
and Jewish thought she locates in Paul's antinomianism and the
interpretative strategies which he employs to disenfranchise the letter
of the law:

> One of Christianity's central interpretive axioms was the distinc-
> tion between 'spirit' and 'letter'. The severity of this differentia-
> tion justified the Church's overthrow of the authority of Rabbinic
> law, the divine text of the Jews, as mere 'letter'. For the Church the
> true 'spirit' was the New Testament through Jesus. In this attitude
> the Church followed, in the main, a Hellenistic way of thinking,
> and a Greek metaphysic as well as metaphoric.[6]

The 'metaphoric' refers to Christian insistence upon incarnation as
the central divine act: 'The Word became flesh and dwelt among
us'. This, the argument goes, is a literalization of metaphor under
the guise of spiritualizing interpretation. A certain tension might be
noticed here: spiritual interpretation is only the literal in disguise,
but the literal itself is only masked metaphor. If Ricoeur is right to
see metaphor as a linguistic trope which demands a hermeneutics
of discourse, then Handelman's description of Christian interpretation uncovers a strong connection between the movement from sign
to text and that from letter to spirit. The 'spiritual' meaning cannot
'nullify' the 'literal' without loss to itself. This crossing between the
spirit and the letter is not a localized accident of Handelman's text
– it is the structure of Pauline interpretation. I hope to show that this
is the case in the process of undertaking the re-thinking of contemporary hermeneutics necessitated by such a claim. These implications
are far-reaching indeed, particularly for deconstruction inasmuch
as it depends upon an opposition between Graeco-Christian thought

and Judaic thought, with the latter seen as offering the possibility of a non-Christian alternative to western metaphysics.

## Allegory

The letter/spirit distinction is closely associated with allegory. The initial quotation from Handelman illustrates this proximity. The destruction of the law by the law is said to be brought about by allegory as a technique capable of being used to 'nullify' the letter by calling forth the spirit. But what is allegory? How can it supplant the letter? The assumption that it is necessarily a negation of the literal is founded upon the interpretative distinction between allegory and typology. James Barr defines the difference, as traditionally perceived, thus: 'typology is based on historical correspondences and thus related to the Bible's own historical emphasis, while, judged by that same emphasis, allegory is non-historical and anti-historical'.[7]

Handelman, in seeking to distinguish between an historical emphasis in Hebrew thought that maintains literal interpretation, and an allegorizing emphasis in Graeco-Christian thought that tends toward the negation of history, follows the tradition that defines typology and allegory as Barr suggests. His counter-claim is that the presumed anti-historicity of allegory depends upon the choice of examples used to define it, and that the example of Philo has been decisive in this process. The influence of Philo upon Christian interpretative practice is, predictably, strongly emphasized by Handelman, but she claims that whilst Philo retained a degree of historical literality, his Christian interpreters did not. She quotes Rosemary Reuther as arguing that Paul's antinomianism was based on an allegorizing of the law which freed the Christian from outward observance, replacing a dialectical relationship between spirit and letter in Philo with a dualistic one.[8] Barr makes the point that allegory, as used in Christian exegesis, is not always and of necessity anti-historical: 'the way in which allegory works upon a text in relation to history depends upon the allegorical method in itself but also upon the question of what kind of text it is in the first place'.[9]

He goes on to cite the example of Augustine's famous gloss on the parable of the Good Samaritan in which each element of the story is given an interpretant, rendering the parable allegorical of the work of incarnation. This, Barr suggests, is allegory moving from a-historical fiction towards an understanding of what were, for the allegorist, historical events. According to Barr, this typifies

Christian allegory-making better than the example of Philo. Since Philo was not a Christian, this seems highly plausible.

Implicit in Barr's discussion, but left undeveloped by him, is a distinction within the term 'allegory' itself, between what is written as allegory (without historical reference), and allegorical interpretation of a text from literal to figurative or from figurative to literal. These terms will need to be investigated, but it is necessary, for the sake of clarity, to pursue first the role of allegory (in its most general sense) in the early post-Biblical era.

The connection between Paul's letter/spirit polemic and allegorical interpretation has been used to force the gap between a Graeco-Christian hermeneutic under the aegis of Platonic metaphysics, and the rabbinic tradition of interpretation which provides '[a]n alternative tradition to that of Europe's metaphysics', providing 'support for the project of deconstructing that metaphysics and its "logo-centric" interpretation of texts', as Boyarin puts it. Such a differentiation has a long history. Before the violent yoking of Greek and Christian thought, the conflict between Greek and Jew was familiar. Paul was aware of it, and was expressly unwilling to implicate his work in it. In 1 Corinthians 1:22 & 23 he is explicit on this point: 'For the Jews require a sign, and the Greeks seek after wisdom: But we preach Christ crucified, unto the Jews a stumblingblock, and unto the Greeks foolishness'.

His use of allegory as a rhetorical device has been understood as a means by which Paul made such preaching 'wisdom' for the Greeks much more than a 'sign' for the Jews, as if the appeal of allegory was to one more than the other. Historically, this is dubious. Allegory predates Greek civilization, having its roots in pre-Biblical Babylonian and Egyptian interpretation. 'There we find', according to Gerhard Von Rad, 'the mythological conception of an all-embracing correspondence between the heavenly on the one hand, and the earthly on the other'.[10] Also, Christian allegory, particularly in Paul's usage, can be seen as having developed from Judaic practice as much as from Hellenistic. R. P. C. Hanson gives an account of the use of allegory in rabbinic exegesis, characterizing it as being deliberately discouraged at least as early as the third century because it spiritualized history and played into the hands of the Christians.[11] He also claims that Philo (whose strategic importance to Handelman's argument has already been noted) was influenced by Palestinian allegoristic interpreters.

The other side of this argument is equally instructive. Christian exegesis did not develop solely according to an allegorical imperative which demanded that all Scripture be subjected to a spiritual reading which excised its literality. Beryl Smalley tells a story of continual consultation that has Christian exegetes looking to their Jewish counterparts for interpretative guidance, Origen, Jerome and Andrew of Saint Victor being the most notable. Andrew claimed to have been instructed on the literal sense of the Pentateuch by French Rabbis.[12]

Origen, whilst he developed an allegorical hermeneutic which has been decisive for Christian interpretation and its inheritors, did not simply see the literal sense as 'nullified' by spiritual interpretation. In Book IV of his *De Principiis* he delineated a theory of interpretation which drew heavily on his reading of Paul. He allowed scripture three senses, based upon a similitude with a tripartite humanity: 'For as man consists of body, and soul, and spirit, so in the same way does scripture.' The simplest reader 'may be edified by the "flesh", as it were, of the scripture, for so we name the obvious sense'. The next stage of reading competence grasps the 'soul' of the text, while the 'perfect man' understands the spiritual meaning.[13] This begins the further analysis of the letter and the spirit which became the 'fourfold sense' which was current during mediaeval times, and the seven senses that Angelom of Luxeuil claimed to discover in some scriptures.[14] 'Superfetation of το 'εν', as T. S. Eliot puts it.[15]

Handelman engages with Origen as 'an inheritor of Pauline antinomianism and the Christian teaching that the Old Testament merely prefigures or foreshadows the New.' But Origen does not write off literality altogether. He relegates it to the realm of the simplest understanding, and affirms that 'it is possible for those ambitious of a deeper meaning to retain the profundities of the wisdom of God, without setting aside the commandment in its literal meaning'.[16] The vicissitudes of the dynamics of literal and figurative senses, suggested by Origen's disavowal of their mutual exclusion, is traced by Hans Frei. He shows a development from the untroubled co-existence of literal and spiritual readings of Scripture, in which the literal was equated with the historical, through a polemical break between them after the inversion of the direction of Bible-interpretation in the eighteenth century. This inversion meant that whereas reality had once been incorporated into the narrative configuration of a unified history, given in the Bible, the meanings of the Biblical narratives came to be interpreted in the light of a history external to it. This reversal in the direction of the literal interpretation led to its divergence from figural modes of reading since these modes no longer seemed to be credible extensions of the new literal meanings.[17] Thus, what has come to be perceived as an absolute break has a historical mediation. There is no reason, then, why the dialectical understanding which Handelman sees in Philo should not also be discoverable in Paul.

So far, it seems to be the case that although allegory works, in interpretation, to enforce a separation between the letter and the spirit, it is not a device that renders this distinction absolute. Nor can it be used to mark a hermeneutic break between Graeco-Christian thought on the one hand, and Judaic thought on the other. These observations are further confirmed by Erich Auerbach's critique of what he calls 'figural interpretation', a term which includes both allegory, in its interpretative mode, and typology:

> Figural interpretation establishes a connection between two events or persons in such a way that the first signifies not only itself but also the second, while the second involves or fulfils the first. The two poles of a figure are separated in time, but both, being real events or persons, are within temporality. They are both contained in the flowing stream which is historical life, and only the comprehension, the *intellectus spiritualis*, of their interdependence is a spiritual act.[18]

Here, the logic of figural interpretation stresses temporality and historicity. The spiritual interpretation is an act of historical connection, a conjoining of the temporally disparate which does not delete the letter but re-writes it according to a particular world view. The events or persons linked by such a hermeneutic have no empirical connection: temporal extension offers no necessary link. Such linkage requires that 'both occurrences are vertically linked to Divine Providence, which alone is able to devise such a plan of history and supply the key to its understanding'.[19] Auerbach makes an explicit contrast between such a conception of history, 'magnificent in its homogeneity', and the 'mentality of classical antiquity'. The world-view which makes this kind of historical hermeneutic possible is Judeo-Christian: 'This is allegory in a special sense which is born directly out of the Judeo-Christian understanding of history as the work of God. It contrasts sharply with classical allegory'.[20]

Handelman sees Auerbach as providing support for a view of

allegorical interpretation as unhistorical. She quotes from *Mimesis* (1946): 'antagonism between sensory appearance and meaning ... permeates the early, and indeed the whole, Christian view of reality'.[21] Auerbach, at this point, is discussing Paul's method of interpreting Scripture for a non-Jewish world, which meant finding meaning in Jewish history which could be made relevant beyond its cultural context. Handelman interprets this as 'the central tendency of Christian thought from its beginnings to displace meaning away from text and word'. This is ironic in the context, as the very world-view in which the historical text registers meaning is that which Christianity inherited from Jewish cosmology: the 'vertical' dimension of Auerbach's account of the temporality of figural interpretation. In fact, the 'antagonism' which Handelman reads as a 'displacement' is the necessity of interpretation and the imperative of what Harold Bloom, the hero of Handelman's story, would call 'belatedness'.

## A 'Tension' Theory of Allegory

So far, I have accepted a notion of the literal which equates it, more or less, with historical reference, and have argued that figural interpretation does not nullify that historical reference but inscribes it within a particular world-view. If this inscription is a creation of meaning, then the question of the relation between history and the texts in which it is recorded is raised. It is beyond the scope of this work to develop an approach to historiology, but the issue can be pursued by pressing the notion of literal meaning as it has been used to disenfranchise the realm of spiritual meaning. In order to achieve this, the questions of history and its textuality have to be ignored. If those questions are re-vivified within the discourse against spiritual meaning, the tension between the letter and the spirit is restored, resisting resolution towards either pole. Preferring the letter to the spirit returns language either to Adamic onomathesia or to an impenetrable opacity which can serve no real purpose. To allow the spiritual meaning the power to nullify the literal is to detach meaning from language in a way that makes the latter obsolete. Where could such meaning reside? To what would the spirit give meaning? If, however, meaning is the product of difference, then the literal-historical and the spiritual must each have its other.

Dispensing with the spiritual meaning (in its figural guise) became possible by means of the splitting of the literal, as observed by Frei. Later in this chapter I will come back to the fecundity of the literal in its seemingly limitless potential to divide and subdivide. For now, it must suffice to observe that wherever and whenever the literal splits apart, the power of the spirit is manifest in the disruption.

Tracing the movement of the letter/spirit relation requires a return to the work of allegory and its role in Paul's approach to interpretation. In Galatians 4:21–31 he makes explicit reference to allegory (the only such reference in his writings), in interpreting the story of Sarah, Abraham and Hagar in Genesis 21. He refers to the citation of this passage as *allegoroumena*. This has been translated variously as: 'Which things *are* an Allegory' (KJV, 1611); 'Which things *contain* an allegory' (RV, 1881); 'These things *may be taken* figuratively' (NIV, 1973) (my emphasis). The historiographic character of the Genesis text can be seen to be acknowledged with increasing confidence, as a shift is evidenced from an understanding of Paul's hermeneutic as calling for the text to be treated as an allegory, through calling for a recognition of the possibility of treating it as an allegory, to a position where its status is historical but it is being interpreted allegorically in this context. The Greek *allegoroumena* keeps these possibilities in place, and allows a tension theory of allegory to emerge which holds off the will to substitute one level of meaning for another, resisting the reading of allegory as a nullifying of the letter by the spirit.

'Allegory', traditionally, names a narrative mode which is thought to offer the possibility of calling forth a different narrative which it encodes or cryptically represents. The strategy of interpretation by which a text is seen as suggesting a secondary discourse, outside of itself, has been called 'allegoresis'. C. K. Barrett, commenting on the use of allegory in Galatians, sees little need for the distinction: 'there is little difference in effect between "These things are written in allegorical form", and "These things are (here and now) being allegorically interpreted"'.[22] The 'little difference' is, at times, that between fiction and historiography, and whilst the disruption of the levels of meaning laid by the distinction is at work within the undecidability of *allegoroumena*, the latter is undecidable only because of that distinction. Paul neither evokes nor denies the literal-historical, but his text holds the tension and interprets the originary text, within this tension, by means of its interplay with a text from Isaiah (54:1) – a move which seems to owe as much to midrashic precedents as to Philonic allegoresis. Allegory, in Paul's usage, then, is far from being a simple device for replacing the letter with the spirit.

The structure of *allegoroumena* is also that of the letter/spirit distinction (the former being a device of the hermeneutic that enables the latter). Outlining this structure demands a closer look at the moments in Paul's text from which his hermeneutic has been elaborated.

## Origen

It has already been noted that Origen saw Scripture as having three senses: analogues of body, soul and spirit. Smalley has shown that this was decisive for Christian interpretative practice (at least until the Reformation and Luther's demand for a return to the 'literal' sense), overshadowing the Antiochene school, whose exegetes did not approve of Origen's allegorical method. In formulating his interpretation, the author of *De Principiis* drew heavily on his reading of Paul, seeing in the letter and the spirit homogeneous levels of meaning, rigidly fixed. Such homogeneity, however, is disrupted at source by the very hermeneutic which begets it. The following quotation from Book IV of *De Principiis* juxtaposes terms from Paul's letters, illustrating an assumption of discreteness between levels of meaning, and, at the same time, calling that discreteness into question: 'the interpretation is "spiritual", when one is able to show of what heavenly things the Jews "according to the flesh" served as an example and shadow, and of what future blessings the law contains a shadow'.[23]

The interpretative opposition at first appears to be that between the spiritual and the corporeal, but this is thrown off balance by the use of 'shadow' placed as a cognate of 'flesh', so that 'the Jews "according to the *flesh*" served as an example and a *shadow*' (my emphasis). Immateriality and substantiality intertwine here in a way that is reminiscent of de Man's reading of Coleridge in 'The Rhetoric of Temporality'.[24] Coleridge's attempt to state the case for symbol over allegory in *The Statesman's Manual* is read as actually subverting the opposition by discovering them to be of 'common origin beyond the world of matter'.[25] What Coleridge sought to assert of symbol (its 'material richness' as against the 'phantom proxy' of allegory) he compromises by averring its 'translucence of the eternal through and in the temporal'. Conversely, allegory is seen to come into the fullness claimed for symbol by means of its potential for combining 'the parts to form a consistent whole': the synechdochal structure of the symbol (as part of the totality which it represents) gains nothing for it.[26]

In Origen, the same failure to hold apart the poles of an opposition between substantiality and insubstantiality suggests a reading of Paul which is insufficiently aware of the dialectical tension in its use of allegorical interpretation, and seeks to establish a dualism which has since been used to define Paul's interpretative stance. Origen draws on the *'allegoroumena'* passage in Galatians in an attempt to appropriate Paul's authority for his own brand of allegorizing, claiming that the apostolic writer considers 'that those do not understand it (i.e. the law) who do not reflect that allegories are contained under what is written'.[27] There is a 'translucence' to the text for Origen, that Paul's interpretation uncovers. Reading this against the undecidability of *allegoroumena*, and in terms of the effect of de Man's sense of allegory as designating 'primarily a distance in relation to its own origin', twists Paul's hermeneutic free of the Origenist tradition, allowing it to be re-read.

Such a re-reading can be broached from the point already noted in Origen and its analogue in Handelman: where the spiritual and the literal intertwine, and corporeality mingles with its shadow. The passage from Origen (quoted above) brings together 2 Corinthians 3:6b and Colossians 2:16 & 17:

[T]he letter killeth, but the spirit giveth life.

Let no man therefore judge you in meat, or in drink, or in respect of an holyday, or of the new moon, or of the sabbath days: Which are a shadow of things to come; but the body is of Christ.[28]

Handelman draws together the same verses, quoting Colossians 2:16 & 17 after having asserted that '[f]or Paul, the spiritual meaning utterly nullifies the literal'. Origen, and his interpretative descendants, have sought to calibrate these twin oppositions so that 'spirit' and 'body' collaborate to nullify 'letter' and 'shadow'. This provides the background to Handelman's contention that Christian spiritualizing interpretation is a dissimulation, a mask for the literalizing of metaphor. 'Spirit' becomes a cognate of 'flesh': unmask the literal and you find the spiritual masquerading as the 'literal'. The polyvalency of the Greek *skia* further solicits the instability of the surface of Paul's hermeneutic. Translated as 'shadow', it has among its definitions: 'shade of one dead, phantom'.[29] Its incorporeality should chime with that of 'spirit' in its opposition to 'letter'. Instead, it is found as a cognate of 'letter', opposing 'spirit'. Thus the literal meaning dwells with the spiritual in symbiosis, dying to itself in a continual process of deference and reassertion which energizes meaning. The necessity of scripture, of *écriture*, this collaboration, collocation and mutuality continually re-surfaces throughout the history of interpretation.

Returning Paul to this more complex pattern of interpretation is also to attend to the historical imperatives which gave rise to his writings. The conflict of interpretations between Jew and Greek meant that Paul, a Jewish apostle to the Greeks, had to be heard within both cultural discourses. I have already quoted his response to this demand in 1 Corinthians 1:22–23; adding verse 24 shows the trajectory of this response:

> For the Jews require a sign, and the Greeks seek after wisdom: But we preach Christ crucified, unto the Jews a stumblingblock, and unto the Greeks foolishness; But unto them which are called, both Jews and Greeks, Christ the power of God, and the wisdom of God.

Paul's interpretative strategies call 'both Jews and Greeks' by disrupting the categories and levels of meaning which his text inherits from two cultures, two epochs, two languages.

## THE LITERAL SPIRIT

### Developments of the Spiritual Sense

The double hermeneutic which informs Paul's spiritual letters as he writes the letter of the spirit becomes the history of interpretation. In the Middle Ages the tension at work in Paul's use of allegory is manifest in the fact that 'biblical exegetes clearly used it in the sense of figural interpretation in which the historical actuality of the figure establishes the validity of that for which it stands'.[30] Without the letter there was no spirit. When the Reformation asserted the pre-eminence of the literal sense the tension re-asserted itself within literality:

> Whereas all agreed that the literal sense of Scripture (as opposed
> to the spiritual sense) was the basis of Christian doctrine, the lit-
> eral sense itself could be interpreted either literally or figurat-
> ively. Both the Catholic doctrine of transubstantiation, and the
> Zwinglian denial of the real presence, are founded on different
> interpretations of the same texts . . .[31]

This dividing of literality against itself led to the questions of the
text which gave rise to modern critical concern with authorship, date,
integrity, genre, occasion and purpose of composition and redac-
tion. These were all felt to be ingredients of the literal sense. If such
details could be ascertained then the spiritual meaning could rest
on a firmer foundation. The same point can be made about Robert
Lowth's revolutionary claim that much of the Bible is poetry (1741).
The latter's focus on 'the text as a document from a particular concrete historical situation' was not an attempt to undermine the old
typological and mystical interpretations, but 'to put such readings
on a sounder scholarly basis'.[32]

Versions of literality began to supply the spiritual sense with different kinds of material, and the focus shifted from 'typological and
mystical readings' to metaphor and symbol. For the Romantic interpreter, the letter is not a veil over the spirit, but its 'conductor', in
Coleridge's term.[33] The Reformation had set in motion the process
of 'internalization' in interpretation. Luther's stress on personal
faith, the spread of new translations of the Bible, and the inevitable
multiplying of divergent accounts of its teaching, with the rise of
printing, had effectively questioned the interpretative authority of
the Church, and cast the individual in the role of personal exegete.
In Romantic interpretation it is not just the Church's hegemony that
is overthrown; the authority of the Book is also open to doubt and
speculation. For Coleridge, the Bible's authority is based not upon
religious reverence, but on our individual experience of its affective
power.[34]

The Victorian response to the Bible was to opt for a kind of proto-
demythologizing, attempting to make of Christianity a moral praxis,
extrapolated from a Bible increasingly traduced by the burgeoning
scientific age. Authority shifted again; this time in favour of scientific discourse. Matthew Arnold insisted that religion, as such, was
not discredited by science, but its 'proofs' in miracle and prophecy
were. Get rid of the *Aberglaube*, he says, and reassert the deontic
values.

At this point it is probably worth noting that the moral sense of Scripture, the sense beloved of the Victorians, was, for the mediaeval exegete, one stratum of the spiritual meaning. Cassian's influential formulation included only one literal sense (the historical), and three spiritual senses.[35] Patristic writers were not able to maintain such distinctions with any degree of rigidity or consensus. Smalley writes: 'St. Gregory said that history was the foundation of allegory, yet he sometimes denied the historical sense; St. Augustine admitted that in rare cases one might deny a literal meaning in favour of the allegorical'.

Smalley goes on to show a continued project of keeping the senses of Scripture apart. John the Scot re-divided them into mystery or allegory, on the one hand, and symbol, on the other. This dichotomy transgressed the letter/spirit distinction by making symbol include metaphor, parable, doctrinal discourse and history, whilst allegory maintained the interplay of history and its 'meaning'. Paschasius reasserted a primary literal-historical sense as the basis for inter-pretation to discover a spiritual sense.[36] Letter and spirit inhere in each other, rendering the whole project of demythologizing, whether in its Victorian humanist or Bultmannian form, untenable. What, after all, are moral value and *kerygma* if not re-inventions of the spiritual sense? How can such senses be held apart from the other senses which texts bear?

As the Higher Criticism reduced the Word of God to a document whose history and authorship required investigation, and the process of secularization elevated literary texts, the problems of hermeneutics began to be explored in the newly-developing field of literary criti-cism. The early twentieth century versions of criticism reacted against the historicism of the nineteenth century and the subjective stress of the Romantic era. The so-called New Criticism (1940s–50s) sought a new kind of objectivity which would sever the text from the bio-graphy of its author. Titles like *The Well Wrought Urn* (1947), and *The Verbal Icon* (1954), bear eloquent witness to the objective pre-tensions of the style.[37] Effects such as paradox, ambiguity and irony replaced concern with authorial meaning, and were adduced in sup-port of claims about the uniqueness and autonomy of the poetic text. The New Criticism saw, particularly in poetry, what another age had seen in the Bible – a language that transcended itself, that could not be totalized by interpretation. The important New Critical notion of 'tension' became a kind of cryptic sublime which poetry expressed but which the critic could not approximate in prose. The best efforts of criticism remained subservient to literature. A new kind of Scripture emerged, which separated the letter from the spirit more rigorously than any previous interpretative mode.

When structuralism took over, the distinction remained intact, giving rise to oppositions like expression/content, story/discourse, speech/writing, surface structure/deep structure. Derrida's deconstruction of Saussure's semiology (the latter forming the founding work of the structuralist enterprise) shows its investment in precisely the set of oppositions to which that between the letter and the spirit was imagined to belong. I have attempted to show that the effect of Paul's hermeneutic, far from being ultimately defeated by deconstruction, is actually demanded by it, and begins to appear in a new light, not as consonant with deconstruction, but questioning its power to undo interpretation.

This brief, partial and caricatured history of spiritual interpretation highlights not only the resilience of Paul's hermeneutical insights, but also the crucial role of deconstruction in re-opening the debate. Deconstruction enables the de-stabilizing of oppositions which unsettles the tradition of interpretation culminating in the hypostatic models of New Critical and structuralist thought. Despite the willingness of some interpreters to name deconstruction as the death or excoriation of spiritual interpretation, it simply demands that the letter/spirit dichotomy be re-read. To the extent that deconstruction denies the possibility of a spiritual pole in interpretation, it falls prey to its own work, as Derrida says it always must; for the distinction is nothing less than the possibility of meaning.[38]

The patristic writers could not hold their proliferating levels of meaning apart because those levels always occupy the same textual space. The spirit and the letter cannot be separated. Yet they are not identical. Despite this paradox, they do not cancel each other out because, as Sollace Mitchell says, 'no sense can be made of writing except as the mark of an intentional activity'.[39] Once the move from writing to intentional activity has been made, the very distanciation which puts meaning into doubt is also a limit to its proliferation. What Frank Kermode says of narratives is potentially true of all texts: they 'have to mean more, or other, than they manifestly say'.[40] This is also to say that more than one level of meaning inhabits the same textual space. Perhaps this is only a continued splitting of the literal into strata, without the benefit of any nomenclature, but what imperative drives the process if not that of the spiritual meaning? Heterogeneity, the anti-totalizing drive of postmodern theory, is a contender. But heterogeneity would then be in the place of the spiritual meaning, the transcendental signified, the encrypted message concealed by the surface of the text, and all the different versions of literality would simply serve to provide it with material, just as, for the patristic writers, the literal senses served the spiritual.

## Deference

The problem of interpretation is not, then, one of keeping letter and spirit apart, but one of legitimating choice between levels of meaning, or what Ricoeur calls 'isotopies'.[41] But choice is never problem free. To choose between interpretations is a reduction of possibilities which cannot altogether evade the charges of obscurantism and ideological naïveté. What informs, constrains, motivates or enables a particular choice? What interests are served by it? What system of values gives currency to the content of the interpretation? I have already argued that following the index of faith discernable within language, through its work of hope, indicates a direction for interpretation which is not merely ideological, because faith is criterial to language whereas ideology is its product. Access to faith, however, within rationality, is restricted to language, but since the rational does not contain faith, but is ruptured, exceeded and limited by it, faith also ruptures, exceeds and limits language.

Those discourses which attempt to shrug off either faith or reason, or both, in search of a realm of post-religious, post-Enlightenment freeplay, are efforts to mean without meaning, to speak and to write without language. They also employ an interpretation of interpretation, choose it and forget the act of choosing, the act of interpretation involved in the choice. The point is Derrida's in 'Structure, Sign and Play in the Discourse of the Human Sciences'. He says that there are two interpretations of interpretation:

> The one seeks to decipher, dreams of deciphering a truth or an origin which escapes play and the order of the sign, and which lives the necessity of interpretation as an exile. The other, which is no longer turned toward the origin, affirms play and tries to pass beyond man and humanism . . .[42]

So, interpretation divides into two camps with different, divergent interests. To simply assert two incompatible modes of interpretation, however, would be to repeat the kind of oppositional gesture that Derrida has so effectively put into question. There is an opposition here, but no question of choosing, Derrida claims:

> For my part, although these two interpretations must acknowledge and accentuate their difference and define their irreducibility, I do not believe that today there is any question of *choosing* – in the first place because here we are in a region (let us say, provisionally, a region of historicity) where the category of choice seems particularly trivial; and in the second, because we must first try to conceive of the common ground, and the *différance* of this irreducible difference.[43]

Here, choice is not at the level of potential meanings; it is at the level of hermeneutic theory, but the same problems are in place. Does choice not seem trivial precisely because it reduces heterogeneity by means of obscurantism and ideological naïveté? Why should informed, critical and deliberate choice be seen as trivial? To choose, in this case, is not to return to to binarism, but to resist it, because the formulation of the alternatives masks the tension of spiritual interpretation and the historical interweaving of the letter and the spirit. Freeplay is a false alternative because any interpretation of interpretation must keep faith with language, must progress beyond the order of the sign towards a hermeneutics. For my part, I do not believe that there is any question of *not* choosing without reasserting a simple opposition, reducing interpretation to a bi-polarity of totalization and/or anarchism.

Already, within the formulation of *différance*, there is a limit to freeplay. The undecidability of Derrida's term, between 'differing' and 'deferring' is itself a mask and an exclusion of the third term. To 'defer' is not only to 'put off' or 'postpone', but also to yield to the wishes, judgement or authority of another. *Différance* is also deference. This is not merely an accident of English etymology. It is the logic of meaning as the product of difference. In order for language to work as a system of differences, every term must also 'defer' to the others within that system, allowing them to decide its value and determine the perimeters of its deployment. Deference opens a wound within deferral, weakening its power to postpone meaning. It is profoundly hopeful – the desire for, and the belief in meaning in the midst of deconstruction's threat to it. As a mode of difference and a challenge to deferral, deference re-casts *différance* so that 'putting off' is divestment as much as postponement. The deferral of meaning arises in tandem with a divestment by which the sign dies to itself in order to free language from a closed order, opening the way for hermeneutics.

The delineation of deference as a hermeneutic principle returns the discussion to Paul. As I attempted to show in Chapter 2, Jesus is more than just a figure of religious devotion for Paul. He is also the axial point for his interpretation. The *kenosis* (self-emptying) of Philippians 2 is the primal act of divestment:

Have this mind in you, which was also in Christ Jesus: who, being in the form of God, counted it not a prize to be on an equality with God, but emptied himself, taking the form of a servant, being made in the likeness of men; and being found in fashion as a man, he humbled himself, becoming obedient even unto death, yea, the death of the cross. (Philippians 2:5–8, RV)

Kenotic humiliation and obedience become exemplary for the sake of community – the sharing of meaning and the unity of understanding: 'each counting other better than himself; not looking each of you to his own things, but each of you also to the things of others' (Philippians 2:3b–4, RV). Harold Bloom takes Paul's *kenosis* as a version of strategic misprision, a power play which enables a later poet (ephebe) to 'empty out' the precursor along with his/her own self-emptying, in an attempt to assert a discontinuity between them.[44] Handelman compares this to the alleged attempt by New Testament writers to empty out the Old Testament by means of Christ's kenotic act: the incarnation of the Word.[45] In fact, Paul's emphasis in Philippians 2 is on establishing a communitarian outlook among the believers: 'that ye be of the same mind, having the same love, being of one accord, of one mind' (v. 2, RV). His approach to the Old Testament represents the will to establish a community of interpretation, to find meaning there in the light of Christ's broadening of its relevance: 'Is he the God of the Jews only? is he not also of the Gentiles?', Paul asked the Roman church (Romans 3:29).

In its exemplary role *kenosis* institutes the interpretative imperative of deference which is criterial to this broadening of the scope of Paul's message, and, ultimately, to any social theory of language. This emphasis recalls the transgression of the theory/practice opposition by hope, observed at the beginning of the chapter. The theory of language and interpretation requires the practice of deference, and the realm of their conjunction is precisely that of hope.

## EXCEEDING JUSTIFICATION

### Defining 'Hope'

Hope must involve desire. Stewart Sutherland, steering a course between the accounts of hope offered by H. H. Price, Jonathan Harrison and J. P. Day, makes the point that it is not sufficient to characterize hope as a belief that something is possible. Bad eventualities are possible but are not objects of hope.[46] The disruptive quality of hope, in its relation to the categories of temporality, can be identified in desire. As Geoffrey Harpham shows, desire is always deferred or displaced with regard to its goal:

> The satisfaction of desire is the death of desire, a desire instantly satisfied is desire erased and therefore not desire at all. We can only call by the name of desire an impulse whose goal is frustrated, deferred, or displaced. In other words, any desire that is known to us must contain within itself a restriction on its own freedom that operates as a stabilizing force.[47]

The structure of desire, or what Derrida refers to as its 'coherence in contradiction', contains the structure of Pauline hope: 'hope that is seen is not hope' (Romans 8:24). Is hope, then, identical with desire? Clearly not, since hope involves a disposition of belief lacking in desire. Desiring that something be so does not require that the desiring subject believes that it might become so. This, Sutherland recognizes as a point of agreement between the three British philosophers with whom he is concerned. Before relating this to the letter/spirit polemic, it will be worth looking at Sutherland's essay on hope in a little more detail.

The problem with hope, defined as a coalescence of possibility and desire, even where the possibility shades into belief, is that it does not distinguish between Micawberish optimism and the kind of hope that can take its place in Paul's economy, alongside faith and love. In order to refine the definition Sutherland appeals to the work of Gabriel Marcel. The crucial question for Marcel is one of 'the intentional object of hope': he is unwilling to reduce hopes 'of' and 'for' to hopes 'that'. Sutherland writes: 'The underlying premise is that if we analyse statements of hope into statements of hope that, then that involves providing an adequate description or at least characterization of the object of hope'.[48]

Preoccupation with details of hope's object only reinforces the Freudian view of hope as illusion. By the same token, religious hope falls prey to the Marxian verdict on religion – that it is a reality-denying narcosis which deflects human action. Sutherland, whilst suggesting that Marcel overstated the case, also points out that his work alerts us to the subtlety of hope's relationship to its content: it cannot be reduced to what Bentham called 'the felicific calculus'.

In outlining his own version of hope as 'a moral vision of what might be', Sutherland makes four significant points. Firstly, he says, hope deals in 'pictures rather than empirical predictions and descriptions'. Its depictions of the future are symbolic, so futurity is a matter of interpretation: hope is hermeneutical. Secondly, the visionary character of hope includes a degree of uncertainty, so that its object is 'neither inevitable nor impossible'. The third point is a corollary of this uncertainty: 'hope focused by vision is hope that is discussable'. Hope is not fixed by clear and distinct ideas of the future, but, as hermeneutical, is subject to a conflict of interpretations. A critical vocabulary is required that can be brought to bear upon such social visions. 'It would even be possible', Sutherland writes, 'to talk of an education into, or indeed out of hope'. The relationship between real-world conditions and visionary hope may degenerate. This is Sutherland's fourth point. The very discrepancy between world and vision, however, gives hope its critical force as a 'basis for the critical evaluation of our world, rather than a flight from it'. Its purchase upon the world will depend upon the inclusion of the 'empirical realities of human life' as an ingredient of hope. Contrasting the visions of hope offered by religious and secular thought, heaven versus utopia, Sutherland concludes that the two differ in that 'the secular vision must ultimately believe that such a goal is achievable/possible through the efforts of men and women', whilst the 'religious view is not bound to such a belief, and in many forms rejects it'.

This conflict was observed in Moltmann's assessment of Bloch, but it is a difficulty which Sutherland cannot resolve. He wants, on the one hand, to include the element of belief in hope, but it vanishes from the argument whilst he constructs his vision, in order to make room for 'the degree of uncertainty which is essentially part of hope'. Without this uncertainty, he seems to think, hope will ossify into deadly particularities, and return to illusions incapable of any critical role. In effect, the whole edifice is erected on this uncertainty principle, and that uncertainty stems from the hermeneutical character of hope as symbolic vision. It is ironic to base what is claimed to be a justification of 'hope's place in the Pauline trinity of faith, hope and charity' on a hermeneutic negativity when Pauline hope suggests a great deal of confidence: 'our hope of you is stedfast, knowing . . .' (2 Corinthians 1:7a).

A clue to the depth of this difficulty can be found in a line already quoted: 'It would even be possible to talk of an education into, or even out of hope'. This bears a superficial resemblance to Bloch's notion of 'educated hope'. The profound difference, however, is that Bloch sees hope at work prior to the process of 'education', so that one is not educated 'into' hope, but pre-existent hope is itself in need of education.[49] The very nature of hope is at stake in this distinction. If it is a belated picture-making, as Sutherland seems to suggest, then it is also an effect of desire which motivates it. The structure of hope with which he begins (belief and desire in coalescence) cannot hold. Hope, then, cannot be identical with moral vision. Rather, it is what subtends and produces that vision. Without this further distinction, the symbolic visions in need of interpretation are a species of dream-work, the figures of a repressed desire, and hope has the character of a neurosis condemned to misinterpret its own text.

Rejecting Sutherland's account does not necessarily involve the denial of a negative element at work within hope, or make of it a principle of undifferentiated assertion. It is simply to make way for a different account, one which acknowledges the tension marked by his claim of uncertainty. Harpham's notion of 'resistance' is useful here. He speaks of 'the ubiquity of resistance as a structuring principle intrinsic to desire'.[50] Desire is not resisted from without; no sense can be made of it unless there is an inherent tension. 'What ethics, literary criticism, and even psychoanalysis call desire', is not 'an independent energy that exists prior to repression', but is 'a speculative construct inferred from repression', so repression is actually 'a condition of desire itself . . .'.[51]

The resistance within desire marks the asceticism 'common to all culture', the self-denial and discipline which allows the distinction between culture and its opposite.[52] *Kenosis* can be recognized now as 'a structuring principle intrinsic to . . .' hope, carrying the force of resistance beyond desire. The negative moment within desire, and therefore within hope, is never an uncertainty with regard to hope's object, but an intrinsic part of the hope that is not reducible to vision, is not seen: for 'hope that is seen is not hope'.

## Obscurity: The Crisis of Faith

In order to elucidate this structure, and relate it again to the interpretation of the letter and the spirit, I turn to an essay by Lynn Poland
on Augustine.[53] Poland's concern is to explain Augustine's puz-
zlement over the pleasure of allegorical interpretation, and to relate
allegoresis to the experience of conversion. The principle of similarity she identifies at work in both allegoresis and conversion is the
negative moment which precedes each – the obscurity of the text
to be interpreted, and the distance from God of the subject of conversion. If Harpham is right, then even the desire for God is shot
through with resistance. This certainly seems to have been the case
for the desert fathers, who committed themselves to the search for
a closer union with God through self-denial. As a transgression of
the self, conversion itself suggests the resistance which Harpham
uncovers. This, in turn relates conversion to language as 'the transgression of the self by the "word of another"'. Again, Harpham
asserts '[l]anguage *is* conversion'.[54] Poland reveals Augustine's taste
for interpretation, seeming to revel in the process more than in the
discoveries of exegesis. His constant questioning of the affective
power of allegorical interpretation in the *Confessions*, suggests that
'the delight and power he experiences in interpretation exceeds
theological justification'. The obscurity of some Scriptural passages
serves to excite the curiosity of the reader. As Poland says, quoting
Augustine:

> [T]he *res* 'are presented in a more winning manner, that being as
> it were withdrawn, they may be desired more ardently, and being
> desired may be with more pleasure found'. Allegory's power to
> enflame and seduce thus threatens to become gratuitous, without
> theological necessity, a rhetorical game of hide and seek for the
> purpose of producing pleasure.[55]

The excess and resistance of allegoresis relate it to the work of hope
as what Ricoeur calls the 'economy of superabundance', implied in
Paul's use of the rhetorical 'kal ve-chomer' or 'how much more'
argument, common in Rabbinic discourse.[56]
 For Poland, the gratuitousness in Augustine's sense of allegory is
also the locus of its 'religious function', in that 'allegorical exegesis
repeats in miniature the crisis through which loss and death become
gain and eternal life'. Just as Freud's grandson repeats the process

of loss and gain in the 'fort . . . da . . .' game, the interpreter repeats
the loss and gain of conversion by overcoming the obscurity of the
text in 'a test that must be continually repassed'. Poland writes:
'Textual obscurity creates a crisis for faith, and provides the occasion
to reconfirm the faith on which the possibility of allegorical interpretation depends'.[57] A complex interrelation of faith, hope, language
and interpretation places allegoresis as a paradigm of hermeneutics
in general because 'language is conversion', and allegoresis repeats
the process of conversion, constantly returning to the principle of
faith as justification.

Augustine's allegoresis exceeds theological justification in order
to produce an exceeding justification of allegoresis, of interpretation, of language. This excess is already emergent in hope's rupturing
of temporality, and the straining of the oppositions noted at the
beginning of this chapter. Where the letter and the spirit seem to
repeat and renew the oppositional thinking of Platonic metaphysics,
the tension within *allegoroumena* unsettles it, exposing it to the force
of excessive hope. The closure that the Pauline distinction seems to
bring to the text's meaning, ending the hope of new interpretation,
is converted into the *jouissance* evident in Augustine's 'rhetorical
game of hide and seek'. Harpham again:

> 'How can it harm me', Augustine implores God, or his reader, 'if
> I understand the writer's meaning in a different sense from that
> in which another understands it?' How can it harm me? This pre-
> face to transgression announces an erosion of control for the inter-
> preter aware of the infinitude of truth.[58]

Hope, then, exceeds faith as justification, pressing on (with) texts to
make them yield further meanings. The resistance within hope casts
interpretation in the role of temptation, and gives rise to an ethics
of reading. For Augustine, such an ethics was reducible to the principle of charity or love: 'We must meditate on what we read till an
interpretation be found that tends to establish the reign of charity'.[59] Again, the direction of hope is towards the other. Interpretation finds its goal in the realm of social interaction, and the third
term of Paul's trinity (charity or love) is implied by following through
the hermeneutic implications of the first two (faith and hope).

The process of conversion at the root of Paul's, Augustine's and
Hamann's hermeneutics, is the moment of encounter with the radically other – the point at which subjectivity begins to fracture, and
interpretation is forced to take a longer route through a contextual-

ized, socialized version of understanding, recognizing the interdependence which language encodes, its intersubjectivity: the cryptogram of love.

Isaiah too tells of such a moment of conversion when, confronted with a vision of God, the prophet finds himself questioned by an absolute otherness which threatens his selfhood. In the ecstasy he cries out: 'Woe is me! for I am undone; because I am a man of unclean lips, and I dwell in the midst of a people of unclean lips: for mine eyes have seen the King, the Lord of hosts' (Isaiah 6:5). *'I am undone'*: it is subjectivity that is questioned. What results is the socialization of the prophet's vision. He recognizes that he 'dwells in the midst of a people', and that he is identified with them by 'unclean lips' – the social recognition is linguistic. The commission which follows is a command to 'Go, and tell this people ...' (v. 9).

READING PAUL (4)

## Blinded by the Light

Tiresias is the seer, but blind. Oedipus sees with his eyes, but his understanding is blind. When he loses his sight, he receives vision.[60]

The account of Saul's conversion in Acts 9 involves a similar play of blindness, sight and vision. On the road to Damascus to arrest the Christians there, Saul encounters 'a light from heaven' (v. 3). This arresting light not only prevents his progress, but also leaves him blind: 'and Saul arose from the earth; and when his eyes were opened, he saw no man: but they led him by the hand, and brought him into Damascus' (v. 8). After three days in Damascus, without food or drink, Saul is visited by a man named Ananias to whom God has appeared in a vision. Ananias' vision includes an account of Saul's own, simultaneous vision, in which he (Saul) sees Ananias come and lay hands on him, miraculously restoring his sight. The working out of both men's visions does indeed produce the healing of Saul's eyes: 'and immediately there fell from his eyes as it had been scales: and he received sight forthwith' (v. 18).

The 'light from heaven' was a light that blinded. Within that blindness vision opened. What is this vision? It is a vision of the restoration of lost sight: vision itself. There is a crossing over, here, between the noumenal and the phenomenal which parallels the work of hope. The noumenal 'light from heaven' induces a phenomenal occurrence – Saul's blindness. That phenomenal occurrence is the occlusion of phenomenality, the eclipse of appearance. In place of phenomenal sight, noumenal vision opens, but only to adumbrate a return to sight, an apocalypse or unveiling of the physical eye. The blindness which Saul experiences reveals the blindness of his understanding, highlighted by the question addressed to the voice accompanying the heavenly light: 'Who art thou, Lord?' (v. 5). The progress from blindness, through vision, to sight, issues in an enlightened under- standing – the result of conversion: 'and straightway he preached Christ in the synagogues, that he is the Son of God' (v. 20). The answer received to the inquiry on the road ('I am Jesus whom thou persecutest', v. 5), becomes a new language of proclamation, a new interpretation of the Scriptures and of the life of Jesus.

The essay by Paul Ricoeur ('Consciousness and the Unconscious'), quoted at the head of this section, has a relevance beyond the com- parison between Oedipus and Tiresias, on the one hand, and Saul and Ananias on the other. In it, Ricoeur attempts to uncover the character of consciousness as a task rather than a given, in the light of Freud's ego psychology, Husserl's phenomenology and Hegel's phenomenology of spirit. This begins by identifying a problem for Husserlian phenomenology: the foundational consciousness is re- vealed as de-centred by the unconscious in psychoanalysis, and as false consciousness by Marxism. Consciousness, then, 'does involve a type of certainty, but this certainty does not constitute true self- knowledge'. Although reflection 'points back to the unreflected', the unreflected 'is no longer able to constitute a true knowledge of the unconscious'. Consciousness becomes a task in that the 'self- adequation which we could call self-consciousness in the strong sense of the word comes not at the beginning but at the end. It is a limit-idea – a limit-idea which Hegel called absolute knowledge.'[61]

A full-scale examination of subjectivity in the work of Paul would be a major undertaking. What is of interest here is the hermeneutical strategy of Ricoeur's synthesis of Freud and Hegel, its interplay of light, darkness, blindness, sight and vision, and how this relates to Pauline hope and the hermeneutics of the letter and the spirit.

Ricoeur formulates the problem of consciousness as a task by turn- ing to its crisis in the passage from childhood to adulthood, revers- ing the analyst's effort to elucidate the analysand's subjection to his or her childhood. He does this by turning to Hegel's 'succession of spiritual figures', for suggestions of forms 'which would be irreducible to Freud's key signifiers – the Father, the Phallus, Death, the Mother . . .'. He finds three regions of meaning: possession, power and value – economic, political and cultural objectivities, which undermine the 'psychology of consciousness'.

The difference between Hegel's and Freud's respective critiques of consciousness ('For both, consciousness is what cannot totalize itself') has to do with the two directions already observed: analysis and synthesis – consciousness as effect (Freud) and as limit-idea (Hegel). These are two dialectically opposed hermeneutics. Ricoeur illustrates this by re-reading Sophocles' *Oedipus Rex* in the opposite direction to Freud's account. Whereas Freud shows Oedipus constrained by a pre-ordained fate to murder his father and marry his mother, Ricoeur shows him progressing towards the knowledge that he has done so, towards self-knowledge. Tiresias, the blind seer, is the only one who knows the truth about Oedipus, '[t]hus Tiresias and not Oedipus is the center from which the truth proceeds'. So, Ricoeur says: 'there are indeed two types of hermeneutics. One is oriented toward the resurgence of archaic symbols and the other toward the emergence of new symbols and ascending figures . . .'[62]

These two hermeneutics cannot remain in opposition because there is a human responsibility to grow out of childhood, to posit an eschatology that breaks out of repetition and constitutes a 'contrasting history'. 'The unconscious', Ricoeur adds, 'is the origin or genesis, while consciousness is the end of time or apocalypse'. So consciousness does not simply languish in the darkness of its prehistory. Hope is intrinsic to it inasmuch as it represents an identity of these two hermeneutics:

> [A]n identity which leads us to say that a phenomenology of spirit and an archaeology of the unconscious speak not of two halves of man but each one of the whole of man . . . finite consciousness is perhaps no more than the way, open to a limited and mortal destiny, of living the identity between spirit . . . and the unconscious . . . .[63]

## Growing Up

The passage from childhood to adulthood, the responsibility to grow up, is important to Paul's interpretative method, as are the themes of eschatology and revelation. The thematic of childhood and adulthood, or immaturity and maturity, is interwoven with the thematic of love and wisdom. It is important, in the treatment of self-involving categories like 'maturity' and 'wisdom', to establish their constitution in the realm of intersubjectivity. For Paul the categories of 'wisdom' and 'maturity' can only be understood in terms of community. He calls the Corinthians 'babes in Christ' because there is 'envying, and strife, and divisions' among them (1 Corinthians 3:1–3). In 1 Corinthians 2:6, the message of wisdom is for the mature (*teleos*). This is held out to the members of the Corinthian church as something, as yet, beyond them, precisely because they are 'babes'.

The opening verses of 1 Corinthians 3 set up an opposition between the spirit and the body as a correlate of the difference between the mature and the immature. But the discreteness of its terms cannot be maintained:

> And I, brethren, could not speak to you as unto spiritual, but as unto carnal, even as unto babes in Christ. I have fed you with milk, and not with meat: for hitherto ye were not able to bear it, neither yet now are ye able. For ye are yet carnal . . . (3:1–3a).

Carnality is that condition which cannot be fed with 'meat' (the extrapolation of flesh). Meat is for the mature, for the 'spiritual'. This chiasmus, which places the cognate of the body ('meat') alongside the spirit, and in opposition to a carnality that is unable to come to terms with its own cognate, parallels closely the interweaving of body, shadow, spirit and letter. The theme of maturity, like that of the spiritual interpretation, effects a reciprocation between the terms of apparent oppositions. Here, the thematic of love is what disrupts the stability of the poles. Love is what is lacking in the Corinthian outbreak of 'envying, and strife, and divisions'. Interpretative factionalism has created division: 'one saith, I am of Paul; and another, I am of Apollos' (v. 4). The divisive interpretation that has caused the Corinthian Christians to oppose Paul to Apollos is immature and carnal, unworthy of the message of wisdom: maturity is inseparable from community.

1 Corinthians 13 takes the theme of maturity into its discourse on love, as Paul relates it to the emergence of perfect (*teleion*) knowledge: 'When I was a child, I spake as a child, I understood as a child, I thought as a child; but when I became a man, I put away childish things' (13:11). The orientation of Paul's hermeneutic is

futural. It is directed toward the eschatological emergence of the perfect, toward that new order of knowledge which will remove the tinted glass ('For now we see through a glass, darkly', 13:12). It is clear that the light which blinded him on the way to Damascus opened his new vision. The falling away of scales from his eyes was prophetic of the apocalyptic clearing of his vision. Conversion is not the sudden, miraculous advent of maturity, but the promise of it. Conversion sets in motion the work of interpretation that is oriented 'toward the emergence of new symbols and ascending figures', but not without the revelation of blindness. It looks towards the overcoming of its childish thought and understanding, and prophesies its own hermeneutic potential.

At this stage it is possible to envisage how Ricoeur's double hermeneutic may be thought. A familiar metaphor of conversion (or a familiar alternative to the trope of conversion) is that of re-birth. John's Gospel recounts the exchange between Jesus and Nicodemus, in which Jesus says: 'Except a man be born again, he cannot see the kingdom of God' (John 3:3). Whilst Paul does not use this language of re-birth, he approximates it with the repeated references to new creation: 'we also should walk in newness of life' (Romans 6:4); 'if any man be in Christ, he is a new creature' (2 Corinthians 5:17); 'in Christ Jesus . . . a new creature' (Galatians 6:15). The hermeneutic that is oriented towards preceding forms, and that which is oriented towards completed consciousness, become identifiable as the testimony to a proleptic experience of conversion which posits both a new innocence and a new maturity, simultaneously. Just as cognates of 'flesh' are not kept apart from those of 'maturity' and 'spirit', and the phenomenal and noumenal are entwined in the experience of conversion, so the hermeneutic of hope disrupts the categories of temporality, exercising a revision of antecedent forms in its drive towards the uncovering or apocalypse of the *telos*, towards maturity or perfection.

Ricoeur warns against 'an easy eclecticism in which consciousness and the unconscious would be vaguely complementary'.[64] The dialectic must not be 'caricatured' by this kind of compromise. The only way to avoid such a compromise is to understand that the two types of hermeneutic are the same. At this point he refers to the two hermeneutics as 'that of the Day' (consciousness) and 'that of the Night' (the unconscious). I believe that hope has the power to elucidate that dialectic because it draws the regions of temporality into itself, asserting the 'Day' in the 'Night', and, by virtue of the resistance intrinsic to its structure, the 'Night' in the 'Day'. Light, the possibility of the phenomenal, is also the symbol of the noumenal, and the condition for temporality. As Derrida points out in 'White Mythology', the light of the sun is the ultimate (and originary) metaphor of both the intelligible and the sensible, and, therefore, unsettles such oppositions.[65] When Ricoeur refers to 'the light of hope' his two hermeneutics are already entwined. Hope is a kind of Enlightenment which 'maketh not ashamed' (Romans 5:5). It is not a revelation of guilt or the uncovering of a malignant pre-history, but neither is it a world-denying thesis of ultimate bliss. It emerges, Paul says, not as the denial of tribulation but as its product, mediated by patience and experience (Romans 5:3–4).

**'The Glory that Excelleth'**

Paul's text brings the themes of light, shadow and interpretation together in 2 Corinthians 3 – the most important passage on the letter/spirit distinction in his work. In that passage he addresses the only problem of interpretation: authority. His, it seems, has been questioned by the Christians at Corinth:

> Do we begin again to commend ourselves? or need we, as some others, epistles of commendation to you, or letters of commendation from you? Ye are our epistle written in our hearts, known and read of all men . . . (2 Corinthians 3:1–2)

Not content to legitimate his authority by appeal to his autobiography (as he does in Galatians), he turns his antagonists into his text. The questioning of Paul's authority is thus a kind of false consciousness in need of interpretation. They have not read themselves correctly. The correct interpretation means recognizing that they must read the text of their own constitution as a community: 'Ye are our epistle'. Paul's authority derives from the very existence of the Corinthian Church. They are only a community at all inasmuch as they have previously accepted Paul's interpretation of Scripture and of Jesus: 'Forasmuch as ye are manifestly declared to be the epistle of Christ ministered by us, written not with ink, but with the Spirit of the living God; not in tables of stone, but in fleshy tables of the heart' (3:3).

The letter of the Spirit is no less material than that written in ink. It is written 'in fleshy tables of the heart'. Once again the spiritual crosses through the physical, and is not undialectically opposed to it. The speech that is self-present and belongs exclusively to the realm of the spirit is nowhere in evidence. There are only kinds of writing and versions of interpretation. The Corinthian interpretation, a free play of ideas in the absence of Paul's authority, is checked by the demand that they re-read themselves, and do so spiritually. The control is clearly theologically determined: 'Not that we are sufficient of ourselves to think any thing as of ourselves; but our sufficiency is of God; Who also hath made us able ministers of the new testament' (3:5–6a). That theological appeal, however, is not just claimed as Paul's revealed right to interpret. In fact it is formulated as a limit to that right. Paul does not allow himself to fall prey to the self-delusion which has beset the Corinthians. The confrontation with God's otherness, the ecstasy of conversion, has provided him with a model for reading. The letter can be mis-read, interpreted wrongly in immaturity, and work against love. Multiplying interpretations split the readership into factions, so that 'one saith, I am of Paul; and another, I am of Apollos' (1 Corinthians 3:4). The spirit is the principle of love, working towards consensus, giving life to language as a social phenomenon.

Paul allows the spirit to take precedence over the letter, not as the founding opposition which holds apart spiritual and material, noumenal and phenomenal, speech and writing etc., but as the hope of language which must work towards maturity. The spiritual meaning is not the nullification of the literal meaning by means of allegory, nor by any other means. 'Literal meaning' is an oxymoron, because literality is the death of meaning: 'The letter killeth, but the spirit giveth life' (3:6). The literal has never been able to remain intact. Again and again it has been split apart by the power of the spirit. Logically and historically the letter divides and re-divides, and with it people divide, one against another. The letter is the mark of intentionality, the symbol of rule-governed activity, and is everywhere in need of interpretation. This is a spiritual imperative.

The two kinds of writing of which Paul speaks in 2 Corinthians 3, are that 'in tables of stone', and that 'in fleshy tables of the heart' (v. 3). The former invokes the Sinaitic revelation and the tablets of stone inscribed by the finger of God, while the latter invokes Jeremiah's prophecy of a writing in the heart: 'I will put my law in their inward parts, and write it in their hearts' (Jeremiah 31:33). Relative glory attends these inscriptions, with the 'economy of superabundance', associated with hope, suggested by the implied 'how much more' of verses 7 and 8:

> But if the ministration of death, written and engraven in stones, was glorious, so that the children of Israel could not stedfastly behold the face of Moses for the glory of his countenance; which glory was to be done away; How shall not the ministration of the spirit be rather glorious?

The inanimate writing (in stone) comes with the sign of the noumenal – the light that irradiates the face of Moses. Moses reflects the glory of his revelation. He is not blinded by the light but blinds others. Unlike Paul's experience, no vision opens within this blindness, rather, the light is veiled. The withholding of this light becomes a metaphor for the withholding of the spirit. Moses' veiling of his face suggests to Paul a concealment of meaning, in that God has not appeared to all Israel, but only to Moses. His absence leaves the letter dead. The veil, which protects the Israelites from the blinding light, itself blinds them, covering their understanding and preventing them from seeing the light.

In Paul's conversion, the blinding light is also the beginning of vision, the dawn of understanding. He writes of the glory of this new understanding as a 'hope':

> Seeing then that we have such a hope, we use great plainess of speech: And not as Moses, which put a veil over his face, that the children of Israel could not stedfastly look to the end of that which is abolished. But their minds were blinded: for until this day remaineth the same veil untaken away in the reading of the old testament; which veil is done away in Christ (3:12–14).

The influence of his conversion experience seems strong in Paul's writing here. The removal of the veil in Christ, is very reminiscent of the change from 'who art thou, Lord?' (Acts 9:5), to the preaching of Christ, 'that he is the Son of God' (Acts 9:20), with 'veils' and 'scales' occupying similar roles. The 'hope' of a new understanding gives rise to boldness. It is a proleptic, prophetic hope that interprets itself as the inheritor of a tradition, a prophetic tradition in which Jeremiah also stands. Jeremiah prophesied a writing on the heart, but a veil is interposed: 'even unto this day, when Moses is read, the veil is upon their heart' (v. 15). The veil that hid the full glory of the written word at Sinai now prevents its translation into Jeremiah's heart-inscription, leaving the letter dead, denying it access to the spirit for want of conversion. For Paul, then, interpretation requires that scales and veils be removed, and only an encounter with the radical otherness of God can begin this enlightenment. Enlightenment does not complete the picture. It is simply the birth of hope.

Returning, briefly, to the problem of reflection with which Ricoeur begins his essay, 'Consciousness and the Unconscious', it is possible to re-read it in the light of Paul's elucidation of letter and spirit. Reflection has a new meaning once it has passed through the kind of questioning which Paul raises before the Corinthian Christians. He sees reflection as transformation because consciousness, in the act of interpreting, turns from itself towards the other, and in reflecting the other, the self is re-focused, re-created, transfigured: 'But we all, with open face beholding as in a glass the glory of the Lord, are changed into the same image from glory to glory, even as by the Spirit of the Lord' (v. 18).

Understanding may still be 'through a glass, darkly', but the opacity grounds a reflection. The field of the unreflected is the otherness of God that cannot be subsumed under self-consciousness. Self-reflection becomes speculation on the 'same image', as the glory 'which was to be done away' is transformed into 'the glory that excelleth' – the other light which arrests, blinds, envisions and opens hope for meaning and maturity.

# 6
# Love and Do as You Like

Though I speak with the tongues of men and of angels, and have not charity, I am become as sounding brass, or a tinkling cymbal (1 Corinthians 13:1).

## THE IDEOLOGY OF FREEPLAY

The importance of re-discovering Paul's hermeneutic is not far to seek. The interpretative 'freedom' of contemporary models of the reading process is potentially inimical to the very liberty which it, superficially, seems to establish. If there is no control upon meaning discoverable as an extrapolation of language itself, then any kind of power interest can be brought to bear to make texts do the work of tyranny and oppression.

One of the tenets of modern textualism tends to render the biographical details of the author irrelevant to the meaning of the text. This has been celebrated as not only the 'death of the author', but also as the 'birth of the reader'.[1] This is no more the discovery of libertarian thinkers like Barthes than of conservative critics like T. S. Eliot. The latter's deeply disturbing essay, 'Tradition and the Individual Talent', with its almost neurotic repetition of cognates of 'death', expresses a similar conviction.[2] The whole New Critical ethos that followed Eliot's lead laboured under this apprehension. As a reaction against the New Criticism, poststructuralist thought has done little to allow the more unpleasant aspects of the author's personal history to be subjected to scrutiny, effectively ignoring the way in which texts affect and are affected by lives.

Even without such a consideration, the influence of a principle like Heidegger's notion of 'authenticity' can be questioned on the basis of its oppressive potential. Marjorie Grene, for example, criticizes the individualism of the 'authentic' individual, devoid of any sense of social responsibility, having no care for the welfare of others, seeking only its own selfhood: 'to view the existence of others only as a means to my freedom is worse than not good enough – it is positively evil'.[3] In this light, Heidegger's influence upon hermeneutics is not just to be regretted, but actively opposed. This must involve, *pace* Ricoeur, some model of reading which does not merely issue in a revised self-understanding, but which is communal, socialized, and directed towards the other. It would be fruitless to deny the influence (albeit indirect) of Heideggerian hermeneutics on this study. As Derrida says: 'We must begin *wherever we are* . . . : in a text where we already believe ourselves to be'.[4] Breaking the cyclical movement of the hermeneutic circle, by means of a transgressive hope, I have attempted to work both within and against the vicissitudes of the contemporary scene.

This chapter undertakes an elucidation of the principle of charity. Derived, initially from Paul *via* Augustine, the principle is traced in Bakhtin's dialogism and Levinas' turn to the other, before being returned to a renewed understanding of Pauline charity in relation to language and interpretation. Language is seen as a social phenomenon which is not possessed nor enclosed by any individual, nor ultimately totalizable by any élite. Paul's writing espouses love as the overriding theme of language, and the only goal of hermeneutics: 'Follow after charity', he advised the Corinthian Christians (1 Corinthians 14:1a).

The theoretical and the practical, already entwining in the category of hope, are inseparable in the economy of love, as the acknowledgment of, and deference to, the other, implied in every linguistic act. To speak or to write is to enter the realm of intersubjectivity. Love, in this sense, like faith and hope, is always already in place, and self-understanding is subordinated to interaction. Hermeneutics begins to look more like a 'sociological poetics', in Bakhtin's term, than a private enterprise governed by the post-authorial (but now seemingly authoritative) ideology of free play. In this I follow Hamann in some of the implications of his hermeneutical insights. As Beiser says of him: '[h]is mystical vision means that we have no privileged access to ourselves'.[5] The only route for consciousness is through the hermeneutics of language, through a realm of social interaction. Hamann's linguistic turn also issues in his insistence upon the unity of art and life, of theory and practice. This reveals the complicity between the poststructuralist divorce of text and context, on the one hand, and the metaphysics of rationalism, in its analysis and categorization of facets of experience which 'springs from a craving for tidy scientific classification', but which 'distorts the facts, congeals the continuous flow of the living sense of nature and of God into dead fragments, and kills the sources of the true sense of reality.'[6]

In this way Isaiah Berlin characterizes Hamann's response to Rationalism and the Enlightenment. The re-unification of art and life, in some measure, chimes with deconstruction's overturning of oppositional thinking, especially in its questioning of the opposition which enables scientific discourse: participation *versus* distanciation. The distanciation of writing is also a participation in some discourse, whose rules it either obeys, or in contrast to which it can be defined. The poststructuralism which has buried the author with such pagan ceremony is left with the embarrassment of its desire to overthrow Enlightenment values, returning it to participation in the very exercise of distanciation demanded by the rise of science: author and text, life and art, language and reality are kept apart.

If the distanciation of writing is also the death of the author, then meaning is an effect of participation. The instability of the opposition dispels the illusion that the text is a free form. It does not overcome textuality, but is the attenuation of its autonomy; which is to say that meaning is produced socially as cultural agreement. The notion of culture is itself premised upon this assent, upon this ascesis or self-denial, which subverts the appeal to private meanings, as Harpham's *The Ascetic Imperative* shows: 'Asceticism, we could say, *raises the issue* of culture by structuring an opposition between culture and its opposite'.[7] The deconstruction of this opposition, far from undermining Harpham's claim, reinforces it. What that deconstruction shows is that 'nature', as an opposite of 'culture', and as 'prior' to it, is preceded by a culturally agreed concept of 'nature'. Derrida writes: '*Before all determinations of a natural law there is, effectively constraining the discourse, a law of the concept of nature*'.[8] Asceticism, the practice of self-sequestration, removes the subject from 'culture', creating an opposite by which culture is defined:

> To contemplate the ascetical basis of culture . . . is to recognize that an integral part of the cultural experience is a disquiet, an ambivalent yearning for the precultural, postcultural, anti-cultural, or extracultural.[9]

Culture and its opposites imply, and even produce one another. Their meaning is differential, but because of the *nature of culture*, also *deferential*, arising in the sociality of language, and giving rise to it. The principle of deference, as outlined in the previous chapter, is entailed both by the play of difference, and by the *kenosis* of cultural agreement, of culture constituted by the 'ambivalent yearning' for its other.

'Love and do as you like', said Augustine, and this is a hermeneutic principle as well as a matter of practical ethics.[10] 'Do as you like', without the conditioning of love, could well serve as the maxim of contemporary literary theory. Re-introducing love is not a return to Augustine's Christianized version of Platonic metaphysics. Augustine represents a juncture of interpretation, a moment at which a hermeneutic appeared (or re-appeared), only to vanish with the rejection of Platonism and its alleged successor, Christianity. The work of love, which disappeared under the discourses of reason, science, and imperialism, needs to be re-vivified in the age in which reason has come under threat from the anti-rationalist tendency in postmodernism; in which science has broken up into increasingly narrow and more specialized fields (none of which expressly recognizes its linguistic construction); and in which imperialism is discredited and collapsing. Love is at odds with neither reason nor science, but they have been allowed to totalize the field of interpretation from the Enlightenment until the current era of poststructuralism, obscuring the demands of love as it carries the discovery of faith through into praxis; following the orientation of hope (and understood as its mission, task, or goal).

Augustine's charity principle, in that it postulates an interpretation 'that tends to establish the reign of charity', can also be compared to Kant's Categorical Imperative. If, as O'Neill says, Kantian reason is predicated upon the necessity of refraining from proceeding according to strategies that others cannot adopt, then Augustine's injunction is simply to interpret reasonably. According to Paul, 'charity', like O'Neill's account of Kant's construction of reason, 'seeketh not its own' (1 Corinthians 13:5).

'Love and do as you like' suggests both an ethical demand and the recognition that interpretation can resist received ideas and mores. The only principle that can be called upon to govern the field is one which language yields to itself. The constraint already belongs to the co-implication of language and culture, and their mutual investment in the sharing of meanings, the possibility of agreement in the economy of difference/deferral/deference. Meaning is not a given of language and culture, but its promise, mission, task and hope; what Paul, in writing to the Thessalonians, called 'a labour of love' (1 Thessalonians 1:3).

## THE WEIGHT OF LOVE: AUGUSTINE'S CHARITY PRINCIPLE

### A Careful Liberty

According to Etienne Gilson, charity is not only the key factor in Augustine's theology, philosophy and theory of interpretation, but is also an ordering principle of his work. This is offered in explanation of a tendency, observed in Augustinian thinkers such as Pascal and Malebranche, towards non-linear modes of thought. Exposition of the work of Augustine and his later disciples demands a different kind of treatment, one which acknowledges that it is love and not knowledge that constrains them. 'Now in order to arouse love', Gilson claims, 'we do not prove, we show'. Augustine does not want to merely inform his readers. He wants to change them. In order to produce this effect (or at least to create a text that might become instrumental in beginning to produce that effect), digression, adumbration, conjecture and lacunae are employed to make room for the reader. This rhetoric aims to 'set them on the path of inquiry, show them the attitude they should adopt...'[11]

The careful liberty to 'love and do as you like' is manifest in this partial authority which seeks to control the reader's response whilst making way for the autonomy of the text and the possible recalcitrance of the reader. The text has a hidden order, to which the reader may become subject if the rhetoric is on target: 'In Augustine's works the digression that always seems to break the order of the discourse is really the order itself'.[12] It might be said that discourse manifests its own order, which is hidden by the expectation of linearity. (The linearity of writing itself is a kind of digression since the text is always in a dialectical relationship with the reader, and every act of reading is, to adapt a phrase from Auerbach, 'fraught with background'). Love demands the disruption of this order, initiating a double movement that both opens the text up to interpretation, and also restricts that interpretation with an ethical demand. The charitable text is also the erotic text, the text that *'desires me'*, as Barthes puts it, but it does so in the hope that I will be a good lover, observing the rhetorical procedures.[13]

### Epistemological Reminiscence

Underlying the apparently 'lacunose and deficient' (Gilson) text, is a theory of language which isolates the individual in a way that is at odds with the best insights of charity as a way of reading. In *The Teacher*, Augustine is in dialogue with his son, Adeodatus (who, he insists in the *Confessions*, was responsible for all the words ascribed to him[14]). Their subject is speech, the main contention being that nothing can be taught by means of signs that is not already known:

> We learn nothing by means of these signs we call words. On the contrary . . . we learn the force of the word, that is the meaning which lies in the sound of the word, when we come to know the object signified by the word. Then only do we perceive that the word was a sign conveying that meaning.[15]

The thing must be known in itself in order for a sign to be related to it. Augustine is not arguing that the pre-existent soul recognizes things by *anamnesis* of its prior contemplation of the Platonic Forms. The eponymous 'Teacher' is Christ, so that when someone hears me speak, they are 'taught not by my words but by the things themselves which inwardly God has made manifest'.[16]

This epistemological reminiscence is closely related to Augustine's theory of sensory perception. He understands perception as the soul's use of the body as its instrument. A problem arises for him in that, in his hierarchical universe, soul is higher than body, and the inferior cannot be allowed to act on the superior. He has, therefore, to produce a theory of perception which will give the initiative to the soul rather than the body in the act of perceiving. Whatever the body experiences, it cannot affect the soul. Augustine inverts the neo-Platonic notion that the fallen soul is trapped in a body against its will and best interests, and insists that the soul loves the body which it animates. A desire to protect the body from harm, to warn it of any danger to its health or comfort, gives rise to perceptual sensations. Sensations pass from the soul to the body, enabling the latter to respond to any changes in its environment. Perception, then, is not the passivity of the body, but the activity of the soul. Similarly, language does not bear knowledge to us, but becomes meaningful because of an already-borne knowledge. The distance separating Augustine from contemporary theory is evident here. Language, and not the soul, the modern account would say, structures our perceptions; what we know is not what we perceive for ourselves, but what comes to us along with language: metaphysics, ideology, culture.

What is the consequence, in the light of what Augustine argues in *The Teacher*, of his later insistence that 'things are learnt by means of signs'?[17] Is there simply an inconsistency in his thought or did he revise his earlier position? Pursuing these questions leads to an understanding of his attitude to language and communication which makes it necessary to re-work the principle of charity through the work of some more recent thinkers.

Andrew Louth makes a synthesis of such diversities by appeal to the work of love. He argues that language is 'fractured and of itself frustrates communication, producing an illusory community of meaning, to some extent, fortunately, given the nature of fallen man.' But, he continues, 'it can also be a means of redemption'.[18] The fault line which fractures language has already appeared: it runs from *The Teacher* to *On Christian Doctrine*. Signification depends upon a prior grasping of reality, but 'things are learnt by means of signs'. The 'illusory community of meaning' is a community because 'signs affect the mind according to the arrangements of the community in which each man lives'.[19] It is illusory since 'every heart is closed to every other heart'.[20] Hence the loss and gain of language, which, although the result of the Fall, goes some way towards mitigating its effect. Mind can only connect with mind by way of the public realm of signs. The intelligible must cross through the sensible, the interior through the exterior. So, although language might have redemptive potential, it also exposes the intelligible to misinterpretation in its indirectness, 'and the Platonist in Augustine deeply distrusts it'.[21]

## (Meta-)Physical Love

Isolation of mind from mind, and the interiority of truth, lead Augustine to the brink of pessimism with regard to communication. The impetus to qualify this negative assessment is theological, and stems from his consideration of the incarnation of the Word, in *The Trinity*. The incarnation cannot be allowed to be ineffective, so a different, more positive assessment of communication is required. Accordingly, Augustine posits the idea of 'the word within', prior to language, and of which language is the 'body'. Just as the Word, in the incarnation, did not cease to remain in God, so the word remains within when spoken. Crossing through the sensible realm, the evocation of the intelligible word gives rise to 'something similar' in the soul of the addressee.[22] Compromised by a law of representation, the evoked intelligible word is 'something similar', a similitude within truth. The immediate, internal presence of truth is just another sign. Even on Augustine's own terms, the communication of mind with mind needs some justifying principle if it is to remain true to the vicissitudes of fractured language and frustrated communication where the intelligible confronts the sensible.

Louth sees love as the needed remedy. The love that motivated the incarnation underlies 'the utterance of the human word that seeks genuine communication'. Love has been undone by the Fall, and the gap is not altogether bridged by language. Yet language is the best expedient, and is at its most effective when motivated by love: the genuine desire to communicate. Louth refers to this work of love as 'the deeper level of intention'. Meaning has become reducible, again, to intention, and the whole problematic of hermeneutics comes into view, not only in the history of justification, but also because the apprehension of intention can only be expressed, even by Augustine, as 'something similar' to its originary word.

The problem with the principle of charity, as it appears here, is that it bears the weight of an assimilated metaphysics which insists on the oppositions in play in Augustine's treatment of language. Love, that 'deeper level of intention', is a product of divine illumination, and is purely intelligible. In the ordered universe, with its hierarchical levels, love is the motive power. The order of things, imposed by a God who is love, is not just to be accepted, but should be willed by the rational human subject. Augustine thinks of love, the will and the soul as intimately connected. The soul operates upon voluntary decisions, and the principle of the will's orientation is love.[23] In the *Confessions*, he compares the motion of the soul, driven by the will, to physical bodies and their gravitation:

> The body by its own weight gravitates towards its own place. Weight goes not downward only, but to its own place. Fire tends upwards, a stone downwards. They are propelled by their own weights, they seek their own places. . . . Out of order they are restless; restored to order, they are at rest. My weight is my love; by it I am borne withersoever I am borne.[24]

Love is the movement towards order and rest. This compulsion drives the will to desire the universal order. Love, for Augustine, is a purely internal principle, which is consonant with its intelligible status in his system. Such a principle is in need of re-interpretation, not only because of its investment in Platonic categories, but also because, as Augustine himself acknowledges, language is a social phenomenon.

To order interpretation according to the dictates of an inaccessible domain of selfhood returns it to purely private judgements, devoid of any social constraints. Indeed, Augustine is aware that interpretation is multiple: 'One God', he says, 'hath tempered the Holy Scriptures to the senses of many ...'; '... that may be manifoldly understood in the mind which is in one manner signified by bodily expression'.[25] As long as love is an internal constraint, making its own demands on the text, the alterity of the other, to which language should awaken the speaking, reading, hearing or writing subject, remains unaccounted for. Interpretation, in this economy, can respect only a hidden norm, and will not admit of criticism. Its arcane agenda may also be the product of 'similarities', which are signs masquerading as wonders: hypostases of culture in the garb of freely-formed personal opinions.

In order to combat the power of self-love, a revised principle of charity must have regard to the work of deference. It must not be just directed towards the other, but remain open to the otherness which limits and defines it. As Paul says: 'Look not every man on his own things, but every man also on the things of others' (Philippians 2:4). Love's interiority does not appear to pose any problem for Augustine. If it acts like a natural force, a directive impulse, then it cannot fail to find 'its own place'. That this place will be reached without regard for any contrary will is immaterial since the twin loves, of God and my neighbour, will mean that 'its own place' is utopian. But the physical metaphor exacts its own price on the effectiveness of this notion, in that it defines the intelligible and internal in terms of the sensible and external. The passage, quoted above, is at its heart an empirical gesture: 'Fire tends upwards, a stone downwards.' Further, the perception is relative to the scientific discourse of its time. Newtonian physics proposes an external force acting on the object to 'pull' it downwards – gravity. Thus Hamann's observation about the 'birthmark' of metaphysics is relevant here. The metaphysical construct 'love' is an extrapolation of a physics.

A revised principle of charity, then, must not rely upon the weight of love, but must propose a 'gravity' – the pull of the other, as an external force which gives 'weight' its scale of values, its means of assessment. A contemporary (and more technical) principle of charity is, in fact, proposed by Donald Davidson, in his essay 'On the

Very Idea of a Conceptual Scheme'. A conceptual scheme is a way of organizing experience by which 'individuals, cultures or periods' make sense of the world. Conceptual relativism is a set of doctrines, in various disciplines, which holds that such schemes are incommensurable, or mutually untranslatable, so that 'what counts as real in one system may not in another'.[26] Davidson cites the examples of Whorf's linguistic relativism, and the scientific relativism of Kuhn and Feyerabend. Their claims are ultimately unintelligible, he argues, since, in order for reality to be divided up or organized differently in different schemes, there must be an underlying reality upon which those schemes are imposed. If such a reality exists, then the claims of conceptual relativism lose their ontological force.

Davidson's argument is subject to the objection that questions of ontology are bracketed in the epistemological discussion. Conceptual relativism, is, after all, an epistemological argument, and the loss of 'ontological force' may be no loss at all if the epistemological force remains intact. Even if there is a value-free reality underlying the multiple interpretative strategies of different languages, cultures and epochs, how can it be known apart from our perceptual framework? Davidson's other objection to conceptual relativism has more critical leverage, but only serves to deepen the sense of impasse. He points out that if one conceptual scheme is not translatable into another, there is no position outside of those schemes from which their failure to calibrate can be observed, so there is no possibility of verifying the relativist position. Of course, this does not establish an alternative position either, but leaves the issue in abeyance.

Davidson's principle of charity is his attempt to offer an alternative to conceptual relativism which avoids its debilitating effect on communication. He rejects 'the very idea of a conceptual scheme' in favour of the assumption that strategies of making sense do not differ radically from one culture, period or individual to another:

> Charity is forced upon us; whether we like it or not, if we want to understand others, we must count them right in most matters. If we can produce a theory that reconciles charity and the formal conditions for a theory, we have done all that could be done to ensure communication. Nothing more is possible, and nothing more is needed.[27]

This is a long way from Augustine, yet it draws out the thread of charity as an interpretative imperative, and incorporates deference to others ('we must count them right in most matters'). But there is still a considerable amount of ground to be made up if the theoretical implications of deferential charity are to be worked through. Davidson's assertion leaves an ethical gap in interpretation, marked by the phrase: 'if we want to understand others'. Is there an ethical imperative which can make up the loss of power through the 'if', and that can overcome the paradox of a 'charity' which is 'forced upon us'? The problem noted with regard to Augustine is still unresolved. That is to say, charity is still an internal principle which makes demands within the interpreting subject. In Davidson, these demands are partly objectified by the failure of conceptual relativism to establish its claims, but the 'if' remains a threat. I can still turn my back on the other, and deny my social responsibility. What is required, then, is to show the social character of language; to show, in effect, that it is beyond the reach of what I want to be the case, and that to forsake the principle of charity is to mistake my investment in language for ownership of a resource.


## SOCIOLINGUISTICS

Contemporary literary theory bears witness to the linguistic construction of society and, to a lesser extent, the social constitution of language. In *Of Grammatology*, Derrida discusses the interrelation of the two in the work of Rousseau, quoting the following passage:

> I leave to anyone who will undertake it, the discussion of the difficult problem, which was most necessary, the existence of society to the invention of language, or the invention of language to the establishment of society.[28]

How could these co-implicated phenomena ever be separated in their origin? How, Derrida asks, could language spring out of the prehistoric 'dispersion'? That dispersion can never be dispensed with, he says, since it 'determines the *natural condition* of language'. He then goes on to expand this insight into the familiar deconstruction of the nature/culture opposition. There is a sense in which this is tendentious and ideological, despite the claim that deconstruction works within the dynamics of the text under scrutiny. What it fails to bring to light is the extent to which language and society are mutually dependent. The implication is there, but Derrida pursues his case against 'phonocentrism', and ultimately 'logocentrism', at the expense of the social, ethical question.

In fact, at this stage in his argument, he cannot engage with language as a social phenomenon because his earlier focus on the sign has set the deconstructive project up as a critique of semiotics – an analytic gesture which tends away from context and relation, away from the realm of shared meanings, towards a relentless unmasking of the signifier behind every signified. He elaborates an inverse semiotics, a semioclasm. One of the consequences of this emphasis is that theorists have subsequently sought to draw attention to failures of meaning in texts, that supposedly 'open a space for new readings', whilst apparently ignoring their own jeopardized status.

Sociological language theories have become almost as diverse as psychological and textological theories. Sociolinguistics is an established discipline with a widening field of research. Names as well known as Basil Bernstein and William Labov can be adduced as evidence. But the contemporary situation in linguistics and the literary theory which draws upon its insights, still advances versions of semiotics, whether in the form of semioclastic de-stabilizing of meaning, or semiolatrous elaboration of structure.

Although sociology and linguistics have developed independently of one another, they have approached one another in sociolinguistics. Their long-standing, mutual disregard, according to Pier Giglioli, owes something to Saussure's distinction between *langue* and *parole*. 'For', Giglioli's explanation runs, 'if *langue* is defined as a set of grammatical rules, existing in the mind of everyone, it becomes unnecessary to bother with the study of actual speech in social interaction'.[29] Quite so, but the claimed *rapprochement* between sociology and linguistics has not produced a re-working of the theoretical base. It comes about as the recognition that language encodes sociological factors, whether in differences between restricted and elaborated codes (Bernstein), or the logic of non-standard language forms (Labov). The *langue/parole* distinction remains intact, but *parole* becomes the focus of attention as an approach to sociological questions, rather than as an approach to *langue*. Even if the distinction were to remain, the social aspect of language should require it to be modified since, if *langue* is a 'psychic imprint', as Saussure calls it, the study of *parole* will always lead back to psychological, rather than sociological, models of language.

Giglioli hints at the problem when he says that 'attempts to establish direct relationships between grammatical rules and social structures have generally failed'. This is bound to be the case as long as 'grammatical rules' are treated as a purely psychological problem. On the other hand, correlations have been discovered, he claims, between 'systematic variations of speech behaviour' and the 'underlying constraints of a system of social relations'.[30] If this is so, then the study of language held in thrall by the semiotic moment is condemned to present a distorted image of its material, because the sign, in its Saussurean manifestation, belongs to an a-social, a-historical realm. In this tradition, social context is an appendage, an optional sub-discipline within linguistics. The very name of 'sociolinguistics' attests to this lineage and commitment.

## BAKHTIN

### Language and the Class Struggle

Before sociolinguists had begun to speak of register variation, Mikhail Bakhtin (1895–1975) formulated a rough typology of sociolect:

> There is interwoven with . . . generic stratification of language a professional stratification of language, in the broad sense of the term 'professional', the language of the lawyer, the doctor, the businessman, the politician, the public education teacher and so forth, and these sometimes coincide with, and sometimes depart from, the stratification into generes.[31]

Here, the social marking of speech and writing patterns is partly the product of technical specification, but also creates (or at least helps to create and does much to sustain) power differentials in a stratified society. Bakhtin's account of the interaction between sociolects places language in a synechdochal role: the agonistic of heteroglossia is seen in part/whole relation with the class struggle. Each language variety will come into being in an ideological en-clave, and its specificities of intonation, grammatical construction, semantic and stylistic combinations will be endemic. 'Language is created', Bakhtin insists, 'within the bounds of a definite value horizon. Therefore, it is not possible for two significantly different social groups to have the very same language'.[32]

He is concerned with social realities, and not with abstracted systems and structures. He seeks an understanding of the way in which language is used in defining and determining relationships, and what is at stake in the process. If the situation that obtains linguistically is the index of social reality, then the interactions between heteroglossic strata become the indices of social change. At the heart of Bakhtin's thought, therefore, is the notion of dialogism: a theory of language as the product of many diverse, competing and heterogeneous voices.

Underlying this claim for the historical process of meaning, is a theory of the 'multiaccentuality' of the sign. Signs become signs, for Bakhtin, only by means of interaction between consciousnesses. Consciousness itself can only come about in semiosis, and so is itself a social construct. Since signs are forged in dialogue, they are necessarily conditioned by social organization. Any change in social formations will register in the sign, and only by tracing this process can the relationship between signification and existence be understood. As with the typology of sociolects, class differences are not coterminous with sign communities, so that, although no two social groups have 'the very same language', the isoglossic boundaries are neither rigid nor wholly distinct. 'As a result', Bakhtin says, 'differently oriented accents intersect in every ideological sign. Sign becomes an arena of the class struggle'.[33] This struggle is the sign's 'multiaccentuality'.

Clearly Bakhtin is not a sociolinguist since he recognizes no distinction between the theory of language and the study of society. He objects to the objectification of language found in Saussure and his inheritors, upon which later sociolinguistic theories are based. In fact, he works out his philosophy of language between what he sees as two extremes: individualistic subjectivism and abstract objectivism. The former position is associated with Romanticism, and describes language as an active creation governed by the individual psyche. This tradition is seen as stemming from Hamann and Herder, finding its most important representative in Wilhelm von Humboldt, and coming via Karl Vossler and Benedetto Croce. Its antithesis, Cartesian in origin, developed through Leibniz's notion of a universal grammar, and found its most characteristic form in Saussurean structural linguistics. In the case of the latter, language is represented as a closed system of norms, the laws of which are removed from the ideological realm, and are inert and immutable.

Bakhtin is opposed to these positions with equal vehemence because, on the one hand, although '[w]e are most inclined to imagine ideological creation as some inner process of understanding', we do so without noticing the extent to which it 'unfolds externally, for the eye, the ear, the hand. It is not within us, but between us'.[34] On the other hand, the system that is constructed by the Cartesian tradition 'is merely an abstraction . . . the product of deliberation . . . of a kind by no means carried out by the consciousness of the native speaker . . .'[35]

What is lacking from both of these extremes is an appreciation of the irreducibly social nature of 'the concrete reality of language'. Bakhtin's central term for the instance of language in its social setting is 'utterance'. The spoken or written utterance always has a context. It is never neutral, but is always 'expressed from a point of view, which for Bakhtin is a process rather than a location'.[36] It, therefore, encodes differences in value and places them in a dialogic relation with those of preceding and subsequent utterances. By virtue of this situational specificity, the conventionality of the linguistic sign is historically determined. The very notion of the arbitrariness of the sign, found in Saussure, gives rise to this insight, for it entails mutability. The historical situation that prevails, the socioeconomic, ideological and sociolinguistic environments, will produce the historical utterance:

> Social evaluation therefore mediates between language as an abstract system of possibilities and the concrete reality of language. Social evaluation determines the living historical phenomenon of the utterance, both from the standpoint of linguistic forms and the standpoint of meaning.[37]

Meaning will thus be determined by the speaker and his/her orientation to the hearer. There is a dialogic context determining the nature of the sign in its concrete historical usage. There is also a dialogical relationship between the speaker and his/her own discourse, that will orient even interior discourse toward 'a possible audience, toward a possible answer . . .'[38] Every aspect of language is socially determined, and the historical utterance is the product of social situations. There is, then, a struggle for meanings, in which language becomes an arena of social conflict, with the ruling class striving to assert 'correct' uniaccentuality in every ideological sign, and the plurivocity of everyday use keeping meanings open and mobile. The process is an ongoing one, which has no end or *telos*, but which generates society in what Bakhtin calls 'the unfinalizable depths of man'.[39] Many voices compete in and for the ideological sign, subverting the monologism of claims to authority, but enabling language to function as a social reality, as *the* social reality. The sign is no longer the characteristic mode of language, but is subordinate to the utterance, since language 'may not be divorced from the concrete forms of social intercourse'.[40] The very definition of the sign is subject to the same conflictual forces as any other definition: it 'is defined by the *social purview* of the given time period and the given social group'.[41]

## Dialogism

Bakhtin's work is dialogical not only in content, but also in form, methodology and publication history. He never simply offers an outline statement of abstract theory. In *The Formal Method in Literary Scholarship*, he enters into dialogue with the Russian Formalists, and all his ideas take shape against the tenets of Formalist doctrine. Nor is his treatment of that doctrine anything approaching simple dismissal. At the end of the work he remarks (possibly for reasons of political expediency) on his indebtedness to Formalism as a foil against which to sharpen Marxist scholarship. A similar attitude prevails in his treatment of the philosophy of language, where, as already mentioned, he defines the social theory against the background of subjective and objective theories. Also, in the works on Dostoevsky and Rabelais surveys of previous criticism are included. In the case of *Rabelais and His World*, Bakhtin shows how different epochs have produced readings of Rabelais according to the ideological preoccupations then extant, or as Tony Bennett puts it: 'The effect of Rabelais' work is not viewed as an invariant one produced and guaranteed by the text itself, but as a matter for concrete historical specification'.[42]

By its own logic, Bakhtinian dialogism takes its place in a discourse of history as a response to what has gone before, and in the expectation of some kind of answer. It recognizes its own condition as a concrete historical utterance in an ongoing, open-ended dialogue. But it also recognizes its own heteroglossic condition in the question of authorship surrounding the attribution of texts to Medvedev, Voloshinov and Kanaev: 'It is not within us, but between us'. The notion of ideological creation as socially determined is given a peculiar potency by this sense of authorship as interpersonal. It gives rise to a real historical dilemma with regard to the 'correct' ascription of texts to names. But this also serves to highlight the ideology of individualism which dictates that such ascription should be a dilemma for our age and our culture. For Bakhtin the individual is dialectically related to society in much the same way as the literary text is to the literary environment. Whilst the individual voice is not to be denied its heteronomy, 'the individual consciousness can only become a consciousness by being realized in the forms of the ideological environment proper to it: in language, in conventionalized gesture, in artistic image, in myth, and so on.'[43] This prevents the study of language from slipping into either solipsism or scientism. Consciousness is produced in language which is produced between one consciousness and another: an interaction both produced by and productive of the environment, whether literary, ideological or socioeconomic.

George Myerson has pointed out an important theoretical problem with Bakhtin's notion of dialogism. In *The Argumentative Imagination* (1992) he claims that the distinction between the dialogical and the monological is treated 'as if that difference were not a matter of interpretation'.[44] What Bakhtin fails to recognize is the hermeneutical power of the 'dialogical imagination': the interpretation involved in even the most monological utterance. This is a two-fold power, in that, distinguishing between the monological and the dialogical is an act of interpretation, and also, the most monological utterance is re-interpretable in terms of its internal otherness, its dependence, its intertexts, its rhetorical blindspots. This is so because dialogism is a version of the recognition that language is never unitary. 'Dialogue' is not an extra-linguistic option in interpretation; it is an intra-linguistic criterion of interpretation. Monologism is always a dissimulation, an ideologically determined ascesis.

Similarly, Harold Fisch convicts Bakhtin of forgetting the dialogism within the discourse of authority in his treatment of the Bible. What Bakhtin, in his *Aesthetics of Verbal Creation*, refers to as 'naïf confessional', and regards as a concern for the extra-mundane, Fisch shows to be highly socialized. Taking on Bakhtin's privileging of the novel, Fisch shows the investment of that form in biblical models. *Joseph Andrews*, for example, is not straightforward parody of the Joseph narratives at the end of Genesis, but 'genuine . . . accommodation and imitation'.[45] The same is true of the biblical allusions in *Silas Marner*. The social world of the novel is shot through with biblical motifs and structures.

Introspective confession in the psalms was normative for Bakhtin's understanding of the whole of the Bible, which he saw as 'sanctified, closed rather than open, not admitting the possibility of an ongoing discourse in which the reader can participate'. Accepting the psalms as paradigm case, Fisch argues that not only have the psalms been internalized and renewed in various social settings over centuries, but they are also as much social forms as personal poems. They often have public themes and worship settings, so that 'the two voices, the private and the public, interact and alternate'. Phrases that seem personal and intimate are found repeated in other psalms, so that 'far from being a private mode of lyricism, the celebration of a unique moment of introspection, such a poem draws attention to its communal character. It invites our participation.'[46] However monologically a text is interpreted, its investment in shared forms can be re-discovered and dialogue renewed. Even a text as 'sanctified' and as 'closed' as Bakhtin perceived the Bible to be, is not immune to its own participation in language.

## Kenosis

For Bakhtin, Dostoevsky had created 'a completely new type of artistic thinking . . . something like a new artistic model of the world'. The characters in his stories are not 'voiceless slaves' inhabiting a homogeneous world in which the author is a transcendent, God-like, controlling consciousness, but 'free people', 'unmerged voices and consciousnesses'. They produce 'a genuine polyphony of fully valid voices', and are never reduced to a 'multitude of characters and fates in a single objective world, illuminated by a single authorial consciousness'. They have 'equal rights', and their individual worlds are not forcibly merged 'in the unity of the event'.[47]

This kind of polyphony of heterogeneous voices speaking from disparate worlds, each with its own agenda and its own rights and demands, recreates real-world heteroglossia, which does not just illustrate Bakhtin's theory, but is actually formative of it. Clark and Holquist write: 'Dostoevsky was decisive in shaping Bakhtin's thought'. His authorial position is, in a sense, God-like, but not closely akin to the God of the Old Testament. 'Dostoevsky is rather a Christ to his characters. . . . In the best kenotic tradition, Dostoevsky gives up the privilege of a distinct and higher being to descend into his text, to be among his creatures.'[48]

Kenosis, the self-emptying of Christ in the incarnation, is of fundamental importance to Russian Orthodox Christology, and plays a significant role in Bakhtin's thinking.[49] Clark and Holquist mistakenly oppose this to 'a Pauline contempt for the here and now, a revulsion for the body', apparently not noticing that the kenotic tradition stems from Paul (especially Philippians 2). It is precisely this kenotic power at work in language which re-functions the concept of love, translating it from an internal principle into one which transgresses the borders of the internal and the external. To come to consciousness I must share meaning, must find myself as part of the interactive linguistic environment. The self-conscious subject may imagine its self-identity, but in order to assert that identity it must differentiate itself from others. This differentiation is linguistic through and through, and in order to establish it the subject has to empty itself, recognizing its investment in others. Thus dialogism is asserted within language, and the apparent univocity of monologistic discourse is shown to be a dissimulation.

## Political Assessments

Bakhtin's work, because it is overtly political, cannot be assessed without some degree of political evaluation. I do not want my attempt to offer such an evaluation to seem like a grudging political gesture. I believe that since language and society are inseparable in their origins, and since they are everywhere interwoven, even the most highly theorized study of language and representation is necessarily political. Bakhtin's work actually helps to bring this issue to light.

In an essay entitled 'Bakhtin and the History of Language', Tony Crowley argues that Bakhtin's ethical preference for heteroglossia is politically ambivalent, and needs to be historically relativized. If language is subject to the kind of historical development that Bakhtin suggests, 'then it is possible that in certain contexts, a preference for heteroglossia and dialogism would be politically regressive'. Gramsci is called upon to provide a counterpoint:

> If Bakhtin, faced with the increasing centralization and brutal forms of unity engendered by Stalinism, had argued for the importance of diversity and pluralism, Gramsci, faced with a divided and multi-factional national-popular mass, stressed the need for unity.[50]

The difficulty that Crowley sees with Bakhtin's work is that heteroglossia can provide no politically viable alternative to hegemonic discourse since it has no unifying theme. It is the language-image of class struggle, and, as such, is a never-ending agon of competing voices which cannot be resolved into a new order. A new order would just be a new monologism. This raises the question as to whether heteroglossia is a description of real-world social conditions, an ideal discursive situation, or a transitional phase between one monological state and another.

At one level, Bakhtin theorizes a historical development from monoglossia and monologism, via polyglossia to heteroglossia. These are three 'world-views', reflected in the attitudes of speakers of any given language, from 'absolute confidence of self-origination', to the 'acute awareness of historical roots and therefore dependence'; and then to a condition where 'both internal and external differences are uncovered'.[51] Bakhtin seems, optimistically, to be convinced that in Europe the Renaissance has 'swept away' monoglossia. Crowley is quick to decry such assertions with an appeal to 'the historical conditions which actually prevail in our world', but he goes on to point to Bakhtin's politicizing of these terms.[52] Monoglossia then becomes, not an historical epoch, but a political condition maintained by ideological exclusion. This presents a more intractable difficulty because heteroglossia is always the excluded polyphony, the cacophony of unassimilated voices that never represents a consensus, and so can never be ordered into a viable alternative to the ruling discourse.

Crowley attributes this paralysis to Bakhtin's privileging of heteroglossia and dialogism, and suggests that oppositional thinking should be just as free to adopt monoglossic, polyglossic or heteroglossic forms as are ruling forces. 'For Gramsci, unlike Bakhtin', he asserts, 'it is the historical situation which will enable the cultural activist to evaluate which are the required forms of discourse and language.' 'Unlike Bakhtin' is right. This position is more or less contrary to Bakhtin's. Crowley closes the essay with a claim which is in direct opposition to much of Bakhtin's thought, insisting that the 'political status of any particular form of discourse or representation of language cannot be decided in advance, since they depend on the historically specific forms of power which they engender'.[53]

For Bakhtin, power and discourse have a complex and mutual relationship which is expressed in the multiaccentuality of the ideological sign and the struggle for it in the concrete historical utterance. To shut down the struggle in a monological resolution, of whatever political complexion, is anathema to him. Bakhtin wants to insist upon what Crowley expressly denies: that the political status of monologism is decided in advance because it belies the real-world conflict of voices. Power is always predicated upon this exclusion.

The argument is one with particular relevance to the current political climate in Britain. Under the present electoral system, each geographical constituency is represented in Parliament by the candidate receiving the most votes, and the party which thus gains the most seats forms the government. Proponents of political reform argue that parties should gain seats in proportion to the number of votes cast for them. This debate over what has come to be called 'proportional representation' presents opponents of political reform with the opportunity to endorse the kind of argument Crowley employs: heteroglossia is debilitating; too many voices cannot be registered without arresting the decision-making process of government. The alternative is to broaden the terms of opposition so that options are narrowed until heteroglossia is translated into (what can seem like) a choice between the lesser of two evils: the so-called 'majority rule'.

The question remains: what 'historically specific form of power' could be engendered by choosing to ignore the range of diverse and conflicting opinions, other than one which becomes oppressive to some group(s) at some time? From another perspective, we might want to ask how the privileging of heteroglossia could ever proffer the political leverage to exclude the rise of Nazism, or to condemn the aim of 'ethnic cleansing'. If there is a need to be able to say, even today, that some political positions are indefensible, some opinions wrong, some practices evil, then a preference for heteroglossia can indeed be seen to be 'politically regressive', as Crowley says. But the historical relativism which delays judgement on forms of discourse until the power structures to which they give rise can be evaluated, returns interpretation, at least in its political dimension, to a backward-looking model which is incapable of illuminating the present with hope. How are we to judge, for example, what the outcome of the current debate over the freedom of the press in Britain will produce? Here and now, what determines my response to that debate?[54]

Taking this political problem into account, the principle of charity must involve some kind of response to its challenge. The very notion of a principle of charity arises out of the reciprocity between language and society, and must, therefore, acknowledge its political construction. This is a continuing concern of the remainder of this chapter. In formulating this response to the problems raised with regard to Bakhtin, it is his recognition of the intersubjectivity of linguistic creation that gives the principle of charity its explanatory force.

In hermeneutic terms the problem of power is the question of authority. A central paradox of Bakhtinian thought comes to light when he appears as the cultural champion of plurality, carnival and heterodoxy, whilst propounding a theory of language which anchors it in social reality and gives it an effective force denied it by post-humanist semiologies. This paradox is partially resolved by acknowledging that meaning is plural and eccentric, but that language is not an abstract system. The social production of meaning takes many forms, and is realized in constant conflictual engagements and discursive deference, renewing itself, piecemeal, in every encounter. Authority, legitimation in interpretation, must be re-cast as demand for language rather than command of it, an authority that is 'not within us, but between us'. Nor will this authority be absolute. It will exist in the tension between defiance and deference, having a double, Janus-like orientation towards the cardinal and the carnival, recognizing, in fact, its own status as arising in contradistinction with its other.

In an exchange with Derrida, Hans-Georg Gadamer emphasizes the importance of a dialogic principle of good will: 'both partners', he says, 'must have the good will to try and understand one another'.[55] But how can that 'must' be enforced? What empowers it as an ethical imperative? What external demand might there be that makes 'bad will' a kind of solecism, a mistake about language itself? Derrida makes clear at this point, that to call upon the will to govern interpretation is to remain within a 'metaphysics of the will', to give it power over language: precisely the state of affairs which Bakhtinian dialogism undermines:

> What is the will if, as Kant says, nothing is absolutely good except good will? Would not this determination belong to what Heidegger has rightly called 'the determination of the being of beings as will, or willing subjectivity?' Does not this way of speaking, in its very necessity, belong to a particular epoch, namely, that of a metaphysics of the will?[56]

In his response, Gadamer remains within the constraints of the will, simply disavowing any metaphysical attachments. He uses the knock-down argument that 'Derrida directs questions to me and therefore he must assume that I am willing to understand them'. This is well and good as a rhetorical gesture, but it has no force against negative will, against the will to misinterpret. Bakhtin's insistence on the social constitution of language (not as Rousseau's abandoned question of origin, but as an always already begun dialectic), affords a glimpse of the possibility of discovering a charitable dimension to language.

Monological discourse can be read as a kind of bad faith, as a dissimulation of its own dialogical construction. A paradox appears: language, as a social phenomenon, must incorporate its own principle of charity as the criterion of its operation, but the dialogism which brings it to light tends towards the breaking up of language into sociolects, even into idiolects, into heteroglossia. This approximates the double articulation of Augustine's injunction to 'love and do as you like'. Language joins the subject to the social world in which and by which its subjectivity is constituted. Language is love. But the deferential recognition of my interdependence is also the kenosis of love, the splitting of language from itself in heteroglossia. Understanding is the open-ended commitment to this process in hope, following the very impetus that gives rise to the heteroglossic diaspora. It is not now the weight of love alone that moves me; it is also 'the gravity of the other'.[57]

## 'THE GRAVITY OF THE OTHER'

### Language and Agency

A note of caution must be sounded. Magnetized by the force of a social imperative, drawn after *other* locutions, there is a risk that language may appear again in a Whorfian light. There may be a temptation to ascribe to it some kind of agency. This is not Whorfian in the sense of ascribing to any particular language a specific conceptual scheme, but in the more general sense outlined by Harpham, in his *Getting it Right* (1992).[58] There, he argues that since Edward Sapir and Benjamin Whorf's linguistic relativism, an extra-human agency has been attributed to language. This not only permits 'convenient displacements of responsibility', but also empowers 'an unaccountable and unprincipled language'.

The risks are still considerable, Harpham avers, 'even when lan-

guage is depicted as an ethically positive force'. This is so because
the assertion that language-users are bound by it to 'a particular set
of *oughts*', represses 'symmetrical, equally demonstrable cases that
language smudges or compromises distinctions; that it confuses . . .
distracts us from standards as such'.[59] Harpham's counter-claim is
that whilst language does not possess agency, language-use depends
upon ethical functions, relation and resistance, and that this recognition 'makes language itself seem to have an ethical dimension'.
But since 'language cannot be sharply distinguished from its users',
the distinction between the ascription to it of agency, and the return
of agency to the human subject is less than precise.[60] The slippage
between language and its use is evident in the definition Harpham
offers:

> Something less than an agent and more than a medium, at once
> 'nowhere' and 'everywhere', language is neither 'responsible' nor
> 'neutral', neither fully active nor entirely passive; its power is at
> best, or at least, a kind of pseudo-power to inform and shape the
> norms, values, objects, and states that acquire form and shape in
> it.[61]

This unclarity is the domain of the ethical, the locus of responsibility for interpretation, marking a subtle modulation in the language
of love. Responsibility is not to be off-loaded onto an 'unaccountable' language in the faith or hope that it will coerce its users into a
set of shared norms or values. The principle of charity must inculcate
the vicissitudes of human agency, but as modified by the 'pseudo-
power' of language. This does not undermine the claims of a sociological theory of language, since the imbrication of language and
society does not give language its own way, but actually establishes
it as Harpham's 'neither fully active nor entirely passive' 'pseudo-
power'. The paradox of charity: that it seeks both unity and difference, is the material demand for an ethical hermeneutic, responsive
to the always prior commitment seeming to have arisen with language, already there when I speak or write.

If not from language, then from where does this intimation come?
Human agency is unable to recognize itself in any other form; it is
always only as good as its word. What other form could it possibly
take? It should not be surprising that human agency seems to have
been ceded to language when there is no means of keeping them

completely separate. The third chapter of the Epistle of James expresses the interrelationship, comparing the tongue to a ship's rudder: it seems to control us: it must be controlled: 'If any man offend not in word, the same is a perfect man' (James 3:2b). Is there, then, an other-than-language which leaves the trace of responsibility in every locution? Responsibility does not arise with language. 'Language is born in responsibility', according to the French (Lithuanian, Jewish) philosopher Emmanuel Levinas (born 1906).[62]

**Reponsibility**

In *Otherwise than Being* (1974), Levinas writes:

> The oneself cannot form itself; it is already formed with absolute passivity. In this sense it is the victim of a persecution that paralyzes any assumption that could awaken in it, so that it would posit itself *for* itself. This passivity is that of an attachment that has already been made, as something irreversibly past, prior to all memory and all recall.[63]

In the enforced passivity that is prior to consciousness and to language, the latter emerges already having heard the voice of the other. Levinas' metaphor of 'a sound that would be audible only in its echo', approaches this sense of a commission or vocation which language re-cites as the trace of the other within the same or the self. Responsibility is prior to freedom, since it arrives in 'absolute passivity', in the inability of the self to form itself, or to choose being over non-being. The act of will involved in choosing is, necessarily, subsequent to being.

His notion of the 'face of the other', 'describes a self-already-in-relation: an other-in-the-same'.[64] The face arrests the ego, calling it to account in that it announces the proximity of the other and recalls the pre-conscious responsibility beyond freedom or choice. It comes as an 'extreme exposure' of defencelessness and vulnerability. This exposure is the possibility of every question asked about the world: 'the question is always *put to* someone'.[65] Language arises in this separation, but never overcomes it. It orients the subject with regard to the other, but never achieves their identity. In Walter Benjamin's words: language 'is not the abolishing of distance but the bringing of distance to life'.[66] Distance remains an ingredient of language as exchange. This is a point of divergence between Levinas and Martin Buber.

It is not that Levinas thinks of Buber as attempting to overcome the distance between 'I' and 'Thou', but as limiting its ontological importance by making the relation symmetrical and reciprocal.[67] Dialogue is the site of reciprocation, an exchange that acknowledges difference and distance. Bakhtin's dialogism, it should be noted, is modelled upon Buber's: 'I am very much indebted to him', wrote Bakhtin, 'in particular for the idea of dialogue. Of course, this is obvious to anyone who reads Buber.'[68]

For Levinas, responsibility is not reducible to reciprocation. Subjectivity is a 'hostage' relation to the other, a captivity and a substitution: 'the-one-for-the-other', that posits signification as a mode of reponsibility. Thus language repeats the relationship of subjectivity: 'My responsibility for the other is the *for* of the relationship, the very signifyingness of signification.' My responsibility exceeds the reciprocal in the constitution of subjectivity in subjection before freedom, consciousness or language, so that '[t]o be oneself, the state of being a hostage, is always to have one degree of responsibility more, the responsibility for the responsibility of the other'.[69] Constituted by this excess of answerability, the subject is other than the ego: 'It is by virtue of this supplementary responsibility that subjectivity is not the Ego, but me.'[70]

Levinas characterizes the other-in-the-same of hostage subjectivity as 'obsession': an anarchical proximity that will not yield to reason and its categories. Outside of categories the subject is 'forced to dispossess itself' in a kind of transcendental kenosis:

[D]o the being encumbered with oneself and the suffering of constriction in one's skin, better than metaphors, follow the exact trope of an alteration of essence, which inverts, or would invert, into a recurrence in which the expulsion of self outside of itself is its substitution for the other? Is not that what the self emptying itself of itself would really mean? This recurrence would be the ultimate secret of the incarnation of the subject . . .[71]

I understand this originary recurrence as the echo of the unheard, the never-present beginning of the subjectivity of the subject in absolute passivity. Passivity constitutes the otherness within the same, that obsession with the other which forces the subject into kenosis.

In his early essay on the thought of Levinas, 'Violence and Metaphysics', Derrida questions the possibility of such a leap beyond the categories of reason within philosophical language. Two of his arguments are particularly relevant here. Firstly, he shows that the dissymmetry between the self and the other necessitates thinking a prior symmetry, since the other is not reducible to *my* ego 'precisely because it is an ego . . . can speak to me, understand me, and eventually command me'. He goes on to deconstruct the distinction between the same and the other. The other can only be other in relation to me, but if it has this relation to an ego then it is no longer infinitely other. Further, the other cannot be other and yet self-identical. Therefore, it must be other than itself and not infinitely other. The other cannot, then, be wholly exterior to the same. The two poles of the opposition cannot hold themselves apart. This translates into a criticism of Levinas when Derrida points out that I am 'the other's other, and that I know I am', and that this 'is the evidence of a strange symmetry whose trace appears nowhere in Levinas' descriptions'. Furthermore, 'without this evidence, I could not desire (or) respect the other in ethical dissymmetry'.[72]

Secondly, Derrida points out that there is no bypassing the epistemological moment in ethical discourse. 'Nothing', he says, 'can appear outside the appurtenance to "my world" for an "I am".'[73] Language may arise in reponsibility, but I am only able to recognize and acknowledge this linguistically. Harpham's question of agency is apposite. My responsibility for interpretation can never be given over to language itself, but I can neither know nor discharge that responsibility outside of language. The intersubjectivity in which language involves me is a continual reminder of that responsibility, and an unavoidable challenge to follow the kenotic imperative which my investment in language repeatedly enjoins. If dialogue is unbalanced by the excessive responsibility I have before the face of the other, I am only able to take up that responsibility as I recognize the 'strange symmetry' giving rise to 'ethical dissymetry'.

The demand for language, the need of one ego to hear from another, does not come from within language itself, but from people. The problems of hermeneutics are relational, or, as Levinas puts it: 'the multiplicity of meanings is due to the multiplicity of people'.[74] He stresses that the alterity of the other cannot be assimilated, and to go beyond the assimilative drive of self-identical consciousness involves emphasizing 'the act of deference to the other in his alterity'.[75] The paradox that emerged in the discussion of Bakhtin – the social character of language involving its breaking up into anti-social factions – is here inverted. Multiaccentuality, and the tendency towards heteroglossia, raise the possibility of deference, constitute the demand for it. This is a lesson from Babel. The tower, built to approach God and establish communication that would transcend language, marks the birth of heteroglossia. The overcoming of hubristic assimilation by the resistance of multiplicity is the rise of interpretation. Babel is not just the end of monoglossia, but also the end of the world and the birth of people. It gives rise to the demand for deference, a demand that is repeated rather than negated by Pentecost.

Pentecost, of course, plays no part in Levinas' work. The antitype of Babelic confusion, it also represents another heteroglossia – a new diversity of tongues (glossolalia) that traverses and subverts the self-identical consciousness, drives heteroglossia further down to meet with the moment of kenosis. The other-within-the-same that is an obsession which overwhelms reason with an anarchic proximity. I do not mean to contradict Derrida's objection to Levinas – that within language, reason and its categories are continually re-asserted – but glossolalia takes leave of reason, if only to be re-assimilated in every discourse about it. There is a certain moment of conversion which ignites the ego, transforming it into flame, dissipating it in the open air of the social atmosphere. I have in mind here the disappearance of the voices of the preachers into the untold languages that addressed the heteroglot hearers in Jerusalem (Acts 2): 'how hear we every man in our own tongue, wherein we were born?' (v. 8). It is this multiplying of tongues, met with the self-emptying of the ego in the face of the other, that enables interpretation. This double imperative is exemplified only by Pentecost and the advent of glossolalia, appearing as tongues of fire (Acts 2:2).

## The Conversion of Conversion

The principle of charity under construction here began with the work of conversion. For Saul, on the road to Damascus, encounter with the other was not the 'face to face' of Levinas. The significance of this lies in the hermeneutical importance of conversion as a re-orientation of interpretation. Harpham has shown the process of conversion at work in interpretation, from the self-interpretation involved in any reflection in the 'infinite spiral of self-correction', to the substituting of levels of meaning, one for another, in interpreting a text. This is not a once-for-all act, but a 'continous event'. In other words, conversion is not restricted to 'sporadic, abrupt life-changes', but can include all 'ethical, i.e., self-aware, life, the transformative effect intensified at times, and continuously refashioned, but essentially constant'.[76]

If conversion is not just a matter of abrupt life changes, such changes are paradigmatic for all interpretation and ethical discourse, since, as Harpham tacitly acknowledges, the 'continuous event' is only defined in terms of the 'abrupt' change. Interpretation is a conversion of one text into another. It involves repetition of the originary text 'like an entry fee' and not a guarantee of success. Like any conversion it involves a risk of delusion, misrecognition, misrepresentation. Confronted with the text, with consciousness, with experience, there is no alternative to venturing myself in the kenotic act of coming to language.

The hidden faith, which is the subtext of each linguistic performance, already suggests the possibility of successful interpretation, and each interpretative act recalls a never-present unrepresentable moment of kenosis and of faith. In this sense the 'essentially constant' 'event' of conversion plays out over 'all of ethical, i.e., self-aware, life'. With the duration of an abruption, the 'continuous event' of conversion is never decidedly either event or process: 'The event of conversion is itself convertible into a process'.[77] The conversion of conversion is a temporal rupture and *ab-rupture*, a tearing within duration, and a tearing away from duration. The suddenness of the 'light from heaven' issued in three days of blindness for Saul. Three days without food or water, where nothing distracted from that echoing light. An abrupt moment that unwound its temporality over three days. This model of abrupt life-change, and paradigm of conversion, is also the originary conversion of conversion into a process.

Saul's conversion into Paul is not just the advent of a new hermeneutic. In terms of Levinas' notion of the face of the other, it serves to exemplify the transcendental principle of responsibility, through its refusal. Saul was the one who took the Damascus road 'yet breathing out threatenings and slaughter' (Acts 9:1), and of whom Paul wrote to the Galatians: 'beyond measure I persecuted the church of God, and wasted it' (Galatians 1:13). Turning away from the responsibility towards the other, Saul relentlessly persecuted those with whom he was at odds. Conversion, then, comes as an intervention on behalf of the persecuted other, with a moment of substitution, and a voice that questions Saul in the name of the persecuted: 'Saul, Saul, why persecutest thou me?' (Acts 9:4). This is an other whom Saul does not recognize: 'And he said, Who art thou, Lord? And the Lord said, I am Jesus whom thou persecutest.' Conversion is the arrest of denied responsibility. That which Levinas identifies as a responsibility before freedom, and the Good that is before being, requires, within the freedom of the ego, the shock of this encounter, in order to be heard.

This divergence corresponds to the epistemological moment in ethics. It can also be understood soteriologically. In *Otherwise than Being*, Levinas writes:

> The self, the persecuted one, is accused beyond his fault before freedom, and thus in an unavowable innocence. One must not conceive it to be in the state of original sin; it is, on the contrary, the original goodness of creation.[78]

'The original goodness of creation' is, for Paul, lost without trace in the fallen world pregnant with a new creation. Conversion does not permit access to 'original goodness', but to a new creation, itself burdened with longing: 'we ourselves groan within ourselves, waiting for the adoption, to wit, the redemption of our body' (Romans 8:23b). Conversion is never simply an event because it is always a conversion into hope. Hope, that transgression of presence and identity, partakes of the structure of conversion from event to process, as a birthmark. Paul's hermeneutic issues from a conversion which translated an indifference to the other into the 'labour of love' that produced the epistles.

### READING PAUL (5)

**Confronting Confrontation**

There is another kind of face-to-face encounter in Paul's work, which is made possible, if not inevitable, by his conversion – that between the Jews and the Gentile Christians. Gerd Theissen sees in this encounter the discovery of the unconscious. Paul, having become someone who stood between the two groups, observed Jews from a Gentile standpoint and vice versa. The unconscious appears when each group experiences, in the face of the other, 'something they could not have said to themselves within the framework of their previous system of convictions'.

When Paul wrote to the Corinthians, he was aware that his expectations of them were different from their own standards. This led him to suspect that, to others, his standards might fall short of some expectation(s), so he wrote: 'My conscience is clear, but that does not make me innocent' (1 Corinthians 4:4a). Thus, confrontation with an external otherness inevitably raises the question of an otherness within; a region of the self that is not subordinated to consciousness. This, of itself, is not enough to found a hermeneutic of love. Theissen writes:

> The confrontation of different cultures can also lead to heightened self-righteousness and self-defence, to, for example, the intolerant mobilization of received convictions. According to his own statements, this was the case with Paul.[79]

Witness his pre-conversion zeal in persecuting the new Christian Church. The revelation of unconscious guilt, in a light from heaven, is repeated in the socio-cultural confrontation of different systems of norms, but the repetition itself is not an arrest of self-interest. It only opens onto the dimension of responsibility for the other as it is interpreted in terms of an originary conversion – as it hears from the persecuted other, and is blinded by the encounter, rendered dependent and condemned to wait for an external intervention.

The ambivalent encounter with the other raises the necessity for the principle of charity, and directs it by means of an already moving, already directed force: 'the gravity of the other' within the same. This encounter can be experienced as confrontation or conversion, and it founds either an ego-centric, or an eccentric hermeneutic, accordingly. Paul exemplifies both – before and after his exemplary and originary conversion experience on the Damascus road. His approach to the Corinthian problem with glossolalia bears the imprint of conversion hermeneutics in confrontation with confrontation.


### Glossolalia

Glossolalia, speaking in unlearned tongues, raises precisely the questions of identity and homogeneity at stake in the encounter with the other. The problem in Corinth's Christian community was one of intra-group division. Paul decribes the situation, as he perceives it, in the opening chapter of 1 Corinthians: 'every one of you saith, I am of Paul; and I of Apollos; and I of Cephas; and I of Christ' (v. 12). The underlying sociology of these divisions is not addressed because Paul's concern is that, whatever grounds these differences, they cannot be carried over into the life of the community. 'Is Christ divided?' Paul demands (v. 13a).

Glossolalia is the issue at the centre of this divisiveness. Theissen argues that Paul 'exposes the possible ambivalent effects of glossolalia'. It can be repellant to outsiders, and put pressure on the internal cohesiveness of the community. Some glossolalic subgroups might interpret it as 'the decisive criterion for possession of the Spirit and full membership in the community'.[80] It might be interpreted as a badge of identity which actually defines the community, or as a division within the community which distinguishes between the 'haves' and the 'have nots'. Paul's response, as Theissen shows, is to relativize the importance of speaking in tongues: 'I would that ye all spake with tongues, but rather that ye prophesied' (1 Corinthians 14:5), and to shift the practice into private prayer rather than corporate worship: 'If any man speak in an unknown tongue . . . if there be no interpreter, let him keep silence in the church; and let him speak to himself, and to God' (14:27–8).

Theissen's suggestion is that Paul sought to replace tongues with prophecy, in its social function. The prophetic utterance addresses the unbeliever in such a way that 'thus are the secrets of his heart made manifest' (14:25). Speaking in unknown tongues may indeed 'serve as a sign' (14:22) that marks the Christian community out, but within the community it cannot be allowed to determine who really belongs and who does not.[81] In order to become effective as part of the social life of the community, it must be interpreted.

Into the discussion of glossolalia, and all the problems that cluster around divisiveness, Paul interposes his hymn to love, beginning with its fundamental importance to language: 'Though I speak with the tongues of men and of angels, and have not charity, I am become as sounding brass, or a tinkling cymbal' (13:1). Charity underlies meaning. Without it, even the ideal, unfallen, angelic language would become an undifferentiated cacophony. Not even the transcendent code of pre-Babelic speech escapes the fundamental movement of love. Paul's insistence on language as an engagement with the other here, casts doubt on easy assumptions that Christian discourse relies on some super-linguistic appeal to a transcendental signified. Language, for Paul, is encounter with the other; locution is interlocution. Charity is the foundation of interpretation, the condition of its possibility. Even a divinatory power, with access to some privileged realm of meaning, gains nothing except by means of this encounter: 'And though I have the gift of prophecy, and understand all mysteries, and all knowledge; and though I have all faith, so that I could remove mountains, and have not charity, I am nothing' (13:2).

The 'I am nothing' is resonant of Isaiah's 'I am undone' (Isaiah 6:5). It is the undoing of subjectivity in the encounter with the radically other. Subjectivity, here, is actually constituted in encounter. Without the charitable orientation toward the other 'I' cannot exist: 'I am nothing.' Even faith is subject to this condition. On its own, faith does not issue in meaning, but charity constructs meaning, in encounter, out of the raw material which faith provides.

At this point, faith, hope and love begin to merge in a way that aids understanding of Paul's insistence that all three are 'abiding' (1 Corinthians 13:13). It seems problematical that, even with the advent of a new kind of knowledge, which goes beyond the partial knowledge and partial prophecy of the present, faith and hope should remain. Faith, as the evidence of the unseen (Hebrews 11:1), may be presumed to become obsolete in the face-to-face encounter Paul speaks of (1 Corinthians 13:12). Similarly, why continue to hope for what is at last accessible? Paul's theme in 1 Corinthians 13, obviously, is love. More precisely it is love as an antidote to the Corinthian division (a division exemplified in the apparent quarrel over glossolalia). The charismatic emergence of unknown tongues had proved to be a linguistic event open to different interpretations. In the first two chapters Paul proceeds towards the theme of love from the starting point of the cross of Jesus as a 'multiaccentual' sign: 'unto the Jews a stumblingblock, and unto the Greeks foolishness; But unto them which are called, both Jews and Greeks, Christ the power of God, and the wisdom of God' (1:23b–24).

It is the cross that founds the unity of the Christians. They are a community inasmuch as they share the interpretation of the cross as 'the wisdom of God'. This interpretation takes place contrary to the powerful discourses of Greek and Judaic thought, between Hebraism and Hellenism. Paul considers this interpretation a powerful unifying force because it is an overturning of values derived from those cultural forces, whereby the foolish, weak and base, confound the wise, mighty and honourable (1:27–8). The very mode of being of the 'things of the world' is subjected to an apocalyptic reversal: 'God hath chosen . . . the things which are not, to bring to nought things that are' (1:28b).

The world is subjected to this upheaval through an inadequacy of language. Cognates of the word *logos* appear four times, along with 'proclamation', and 'saying' in the course of chapter 2. These are mostly with negative force: 'not with excellency of speech' (v. 1); 'not with enticing words' (v. 4); 'Eye hath not seen, nor ear heard' (v. 9); 'not in the words' (v. 13). The two positive uses of language are associated with wisdom: 'we speak wisdom among them that are perfect' (v. 6); 'we speak the wisdom of God in a mystery' (v. 7). This wisdom is the re-interpretation of the world after the cross has re-valued it. It is a wisdom which is 'spiritually discerned' (v. 14) (previous examination of the interweaving of the spiritual and the material should, at this stage, alert us to the perils of forming hasty judgements about what is meant by 'spiritual discernment' here). In the context of the overcoming of division, the social function of this discernment must be asserted. This is futher necessitated by the insight that 1 Corinthians identifies wisdom with love. It is the wisdom of the cross that unites.

Wisdom and love are further identified in the theme of maturity. Wisdom is linked with maturity in that it is a message for the 'perfect' (KJV) or 'mature' (RSV). I have already observed that although 'wisdom' and 'maturity' are self-involving categories, Paul sees them as socially determined; hence their interweaving with love. Since the wisdom of love is for the 'mature' or 'perfect', it is revealed as hope, which already involves faith. The inadequacy of language to which Paul attests, is the language that has not gone by way of the cross, that has not died to itself.[82] The central sign of the cross is the axial point for a new language because it is the uniting principle, the principle of charity. This new language is glimpsed in the community when the prophetic message reveals the 'secrets of the heart', and when the glossolalic utterance meets with an interpretation.

Paul's concern with the Corinthian practice serves to elucidate further the interweaving of love, hope and faith in the thematics of maturity. Theissen interprets Paul's attitude to glossolalia within the framework of this thematic, pointing out his appeal to the Corinthians in 14:20–1: 'be not children in understanding: howbeit in malice be ye children, but in understanding be men. In the law it is written, with men of other tongues and other lips will I speak unto this people'. In 13:11, Paul also combines these themes, reminding the Corinthians that the adult develops away from childish forms of speech: 'When I was a child, I spake as a child'.

The psychology of religion too, Theissen claims, refers to glossolalic utterance as exhibiting characteristics of childhood language. More specifically, Theissen observes that in glossolalic speech: 'The inventory of phonemes is reduced. The unity of the linguistic sign as a conventional combination of sign and what is signified disintegrates'. He goes on to argue that glossolalia is not simply reducible to a negative regression. If glossolalic behaviour can be integrated into 'the conscious life of the individual and of the group' then it can actually represent 'a broadening of psychic competence'.[83] In Pauline terms, glossolalia, to be in keeping with mature faith, requires interpretation.

It is not only in childhood language and glossolalic utterances that the disintegration of the linguistic sign causes a divisive and potentially debilitating multiplying of interpretations. Deconstruction is predicated upon such a disintegration: 'the difference between the signified and signifier *is nothing*', Derrida writes.[84] If deconstructive practice is to mature into a broadening of hermeneutic competence, it requires interpretation in line with the principle of charity. Paul does not speak of an absolute maturity in 1 Corinthians 13, but of a mediate, restricted, and proleptic vision. It is significant that progress is marked not only by encounter, as maturity is associated with love, but also by a yearning towards further encounter: 'then face to face' (v. 12). In the words of Levinas: 'The other is the future'.[85] This futurity is inseparable from language in its identity with the other. Paul's teleography or apocalyptic vision does not project an end to language. As faith, hope and love remain, language remains, repeating the kenotic gesture observed by Ricoeur: 'Speaking is the act by which language moves beyond itself as sign toward its reference and toward what it encounters. Language seeks to disappear; it seeks to die as an object.'[86] In fact, the gesture is not language's own; it is the path of the speaking subject in coming to language, and the continual renewal of my deference to the other in every linguistic act.

Language and interpretation constitute the world in its human aspect. To assert, with Paul, that faith, hope and love are the abiding traits of human intersubjectivity and interaction, is to renew the possibilities for a re-humanized language, and to agree with Levinas that humanism is not human enough, but to add that post-humanism, in its poststructuralist and postmodernist guises, is potentially antihuman and anti-social.[87] Paul's hermeneutic, with its 'work of faith, and labour of love, and patience of hope' (1 Thessalonians 1:3), represents an energy expended on behalf of others. It does not come to us in essays, monographs or theorems, but in letters addressed to particular situations, and oriented 'toward a possible answer', already bearing the internal marks of previous encounters and questioning. Its central themes are those other-involving, other-dependent proclivities: faith, hope, love: 'And now abideth faith, hope, charity, these three; but the greatest of these is charity' (1 Corinthians 13:13). Just as the teachings of the House of Hillel were said to take precedence over those of Shammai because 'they taught the teachings of the House of Shammai as well as their own . . . before they taught their own', charity is greater than both faith and hope in that it includes them: it 'believeth all things, hopeth all things' (v. 7).[88] It is that which calls forth language in the face of the other, and, in doing so, draws faith and hope through it as the possibility of meaning kept open, viable, responsive and answerable. Along with charity, language also remains. It is able to do so because charity 'endureth all things' (v. 7) – even contemporary literary theory.

# Conclusion

In proposing this Pauline hermeneutic I have remained (albeit somewhat precariously) within the rule of 'logocentrism', working towards the positing of a transcendental signified. This however, is a learned, deliberate and critical logocentrism with a deconstructive sense of its own jeopardy, but with an equally distinct appreciation of the power of faith, hope and love to disrupt deconstruction's negative semiology. The demand for interpretation which arises along with language, enforces this logocentric choice but never reduces the risk involved. It is precisely the hermeneutical risk that I take in the process of self-divestment which allows deconstruction to appear as a negative hermeneutic. I might say: 'I put my trust in the work of language, and deconstruction reveals my folly.' I can leave it at that and become a committed poststructuralist, or I can claim that the revelation of my folly is also the uncovering of the strength of my faith. The point that I am trying to make is that there is a choice to be made, not for or against deconstruction, poststructuralism or postmodernism, but for or against language, faith and understanding.

I have argued that faith is both a linguistic principle and a 'religious' one. If this is the case, then does everyone who speaks have faith, in a religious sense? To assert this would be nonsense. Language is not religion. The significance of conversion as a hermeneutic principle appears here, in that it reveals the faith already at work in language, and exposes the hiding of that faith by ideology.

The re-emergence of faith in conversion has been seen to be proleptic and profoundly hopeful. It does not seek to overcome linguistic difference by means of a recovery of some prelapsarian unmediated communication, but looks forward to the future 'face to face' encounter – to the revelation of a new kind of knowledge. Deconstruction has uncovered the Babelic distress within language, and has shown us that there is no way back beyond the tower. Whether or not there is a way *forward* is a matter of critical choice grounded in radical faith. Do I stare into the abyss of infinite signification and endlessly re-describe what I see? Or do I shift my focus and insist that the problematic of signification is only one account of language, and not necessarily the most powerful one? The latter option does not involve closing my eyes to the force of deconstruction, nor is it a peremptory dismissal of postmodern rhetorics. Rather, as I hope I have shown, it requires a difficult engagement with the texts. The process of engagement itself throws up new questions, new syntheses, new counter-strategies, new ways of reading.

Only in the context of such an engagement have the insights of divestment, deference, kenosis etc. opened up. These tropes reveal the blurring of the borders between subject and object, which makes of my investment in language a proof against both individualism and scientism. Out of this consideration has emerged the conclusion that since there is no return to the language of Eden, and no escape into either autonomous subjectivity or objective formalism, the way forward for faith cannot avoid some kind of conversion hermeneutic. I hope that I have laid a foundation for such projects by tracing the work of faith, hope and love in language, and by showing how they disrupt the assumptions and mores of contemporary modes of interpretation.

# Notes

## 1  Introduction

1.  E. Levinas, 'Revelation in the Jewish Tradition', trans. S. Richmond, in *The Levinas Reader*, ed. S. Hand (Oxford: Blackwell, 1989), pp. 190–210, pp. 192–3.
2.  M. C. Taylor, *Erring: A Postmodern A/theology*, (Chicago and London: University of Chicago Press, 1984), pp. 4–5.
3.  D. Jasper, 'The Study of Literature and Theology: Five Years On', *Literature and Theology*, 6, 1 (1992), pp. 1–10, p. 3.
4.  D. Jasper, *The Study of Literature and Religion: An Introduction* (2nd edn), (London: Macmillan, 1989, 1992), p. xv.
5.  *The Lion Handbook to the Bible*, eds D. and P. Alexander (Tring: Lion Publishing, 1973, 1983), pp. 58–9.
6.  G. Theissen, *Psychological Aspects of Pauline Theology*, trans. J. P. Galvin (Edinburgh: T. & T. Clark, 1987), p. 100.
7.  J. Derrida, *Of Grammatology*, trans. G. C. Spivak (Baltimore: Johns Hopkins University Press, 1976), pp. 144–5.
8.  R. Bultmann, *Jesus Christ and Mythology* (London: SCM, 1960), p. 38.
9.  J. Derrida, *Of Grammatology*, pp. 27–73.
10.  J. Lacan, quoted in M. Bowie, 'Jacques Lacan', in *Structuralism and Since: From Lévi-Strauss to Derrida*, ed. J. Sturrock (Oxford: Oxford University Press, 1979), pp. 116–53, p. 131.
11.  J. Derrida, 'Structure, Sign, and Play in the Discourse of the Human Sciences', in *Writing and Difference*, trans. A. Bass (London: Routledge and Kegan Paul, 1978), pp. 278–93, p. 279.
12.  S. Critchley, *The Ethics of Deconstruction* (Oxford: Blackwell, 1992), pp. 59–106, esp. pp. 68–76.
13.  J. L. Borges, 'The Library of Babel', in *Labyrinths* (Harmondsworth: Penguin, 1970), pp. 78–86. Towards the end of the piece he writes:

    > *The Library is unlimited and cyclical.* If an eternal traveller were to cross it in any direction, after centuries he would see the same volumes were repeated in the same disorder (which, thus repeated, would be an order: the Order).

    Is Borges also among the Hegelians?
14.  J.-F. Lyotard, *The Postmodern Condition: A Report on Knowledge*, trans. G. Bennington and B. Massumi (Manchester: Manchester University Press, 1984).
15.  J. Derrida, *Of Grammatology*, p. 158.
16.  J. Derrida, 'Letter to a Japanese Friend', in *Derrida and Difference*, ed. D. Wood (University of Warwick: Parousia Press, 1985), pp. 4–5.
17.  C. Norris, *Deconstruction: Theory and Practice* (London: Routledge, 1982), p. 75.

18.  K. Hart, *The Trespass of the Sign: deconstruction, theology and philosophy* (Cambridge: Cambridge University Press, 1990), pp. 167–8.

19.  Although Derrida himself is of Sephardic Jewish origin, and may well have imbibed the Arabic influences of his Algerian provenance, deconstruction's target is 'logocentrism', the desire for an all-gathering transcendental signified.

20.  F. Nietzsche, *The Twilight of the Idols*, trans. R. J. Hollingdale (Harmondsworth: Penguin, 1968, 1990), p. 121. H.-G. Gadamer, *Truth and Method*, 2nd edn, trans. and ed. G. Burden and J. Cumming (London: Sheed and Ward, 1975, 1979), pp. 235–74.

21.  S. Critchley, op. cit., p. 30.

## 2  Language, Faith, Understanding

1.  P. Ricoeur, *The Conflict of Interpretations: Essays in Hermeneutics*, ed. Don Ihde (Evanston: Northwestern University Press, 1974), p. 390.

2.  R. Browning, 'Bishop Blougram's Apology', *A Choice of Browning's Verse*, ed. E. Lucie-Smith (London: Faber, 1967), pp. 39–66.

3.  F. de Saussure, *Course in General Linguistics*, ed. C. Bally and A. Sechehaye with A. Riedlinger, trans. W. Baskin (New York: McGraw-Hill, 1966), pp. 22, 88ff.

4.  See Clark, Herbert H. and Eve V., *Psychology and Language: An Introduction to Psycholinguistics* (San Diego: Harcourt Brace Jovanovich, 1977), pp. 334–7.

5.  N. Chomsky, *Problems of Knowledge and Freedom* ( London: Fontana, 1972), p. 30.

6.  Helen Keller's life story provides an admirable example. I quote her autobiography:

> Someone was drawing water, and my teacher placed my hand under the spout. As the cool stream gushed over one hand she spelled into the other the word *water*, first slowly, then rapidly. I stood still, my whole attention fixed upon the motions of her fingers. Suddenly I felt a misty consciousness as of something forgotten – a thrill of returning thought; and somehow the mystery of language was revealed to me. I knew then that 'w-a-t-e-r' meant the wonderful cool something that was flowing over my hand.

> From: Helen Keller, *The Story of My Life* (London: Hodder and Stoughton, 1949), p. 28.

7.  F. Schleiermacher, quoted in A. Thiselton, *The Two Horizons* (Exeter: The Paternoster Press, 1980), p. 103.

8.  On the development of hermeneutic theory from Schleiermacher to Ricoeur, see Werner Jeanrond, *Theological Hermeneutics: Development and Significance* (London: Macmillan, 1991), pp. 70–7.

9.  P. Ricoeur, *The Rule of Metaphor*, trans. R. Czerny with K. McLaughlin and J. Costello (Toronto and Buffalo: University of Toronto Press, 1977), p. 4.

10.  Ibid., p. 21.

11.  J. Derrida, 'White mythology: metaphor in the text of philosophy',

   in *Margins of Philosophy*, trans. Alan Bass (Chicago: University of Chicago Press, 1982), pp. 207–71.

12. P. Ricoeur, *The Rule of Metaphor*, p. 293.

13. Ibid., p. 6.

14. J. Derrida, 'The *Retrait* of Metaphor', *Enclitic*, 2, 2 (1978), pp. 5–33.

15. P. Ricoeur, *The Rule of Metaphor*, p. 69.

16. L. Hjelmslev, *Prologomena to a Theory of Language*, trans. F. Whitfield (Madison: University of Wisconsin Press, 1969), p. 9.

17. Ibid., p. 39.

18. Ibid., pp. 39–40.

19. P. Ricoeur, *The Conflict of Interpretations*, pp. 79–96.

20. F. de Saussure, op. cit., p. 66.

21. H.-G. Gadamer, *Truth and Method*, 2nd ed., trans. and ed. G. Burden and J. Cumming (London: Sheed and Ward, 1975, 1979).

22. P. Ricoeur, *Hermeneutics and the Human Sciences*, trans. and ed. J. Thompson (Cambridge: Cambridge University Press, 1981), p. 134.

23. Ibid.

24. W. K. Wimsatt and Monroe Beardsley, 'The Intentional Fallacy', in W. K. Wimsatt, *The Verbal Icon: Studies in the Meaning of Poetry* (Lexington, Kentucky: University of Kentucky Press, 1954).

25. P. Ricoeur, *Hermeneutics and the Human Sciences*, p. 143.

26. G. Frege, 'On Sense and Reference', in *Translations from the Philosophical Writings of Gottlob Frege*, ed. M. Black and P. T. Geach (Oxford: Blackwell, 1952), pp. 56–78. On this understanding of Frege, see C. Norris, *The Contest of Faculties* (London: Methuen, 1985), pp. 47–69.

27. S. Mitchell, 'Post-Structuralism, Empiricism and Interpretation', in S. Mitchell and M. Rosen (eds), *The Need for Interpretation* (London: Athlone Press, 1983), pp. 54–89, p. 85.

28. Ibid., p. 76.

29. J. Derrida, *Of Grammatology*, p. 158.

30. Ibid., p. 50.

31. F. de Saussure, op. cit., p. 23.

32. J. Derrida, *Of Grammatology*, p. 36.

33. Ibid., p. 158. This section of Part II, chapter 2, is headed 'The Exorbitant. Question of Method'.

34. P. Ricoeur, *Hermeneutics and the Human Sciences*, p. 131.

35. S. Mitchell, op. cit., p. 80.

36. P. Ricoeur, *Hermeneutics and the Human Sciences*, pp. 131–44.

37. Ibid., p. 139.

38. A. Thiselton, 'The New Hermeneutic', in *A Guide to Contemporary Hermeneutics*, ed. D. McKim (Grand Rapids: Eerdmans, 1986), pp. 78–107, p. 78.

39. P. Ricoeur, 'Preface to Bultmann', in *The Conflict of Interpretations*, pp. 381–401, p. 389.

40. Ibid., p. 390.

41. R. Bultmann, *Jesus Christ and Mythology* (London: SCM, 1960), pp. 54–5.

42. P. Ricoeur, *The Conflict of Interpretations*, pp. 394–401.

43. R. Bultmann, *Faith and Understanding I*, ed. R. W. Funk, trans. L. P. Smith (London: SCM, 1969), p. 299.

44. R. Bultmann, 'The Concept of the Word of God in the New Testament', ibid., pp. 286–312.

45. E. P. Sanders, *Paul and Palestinian Judaism* (London: SCM, 1977), pp. 433–8.

46. G. Bornkamm, 'God's word and man's word in the New Testament', in *Early Christian Experience*, trans. P. Hammer (London: SCM, 1969), pp. 1–13, pp. 4–5.

47. P. Ricoeur, op. cit., p. 386.

48. R. Bultmann, *Existence and Faith*, selected and trans. S. M. Ogden (London: Fontana, 1973), p. 295.

49. H.-G. Gadamer, *Truth and Method*, p. 236.

50. G. Ebeling, *Word and Faith*, trans. R. G. Smith (London: Collins, 1961), pp. 318–19.

51. Ibid., p. 125.

52. Ibid., p. 318.

53. Ibid., p. 320.

54. Ibid., p. 313 n.

55. Ibid., p. 327.

56. D. Lawton, *Faith, Text and History: The Bible in English* (New York: Harvester Wheatsheaf, 1990), p. 9.

57. S. Prickett, *Words and the Word* (Cambridge: Cambridge University Press, 1986), pp. 213–14.

58. D. Lawton, op. cit., p. 12.

59. Ibid., p. 1.

60. Ibid., p. 187.

61. Ibid., p. 2.

62. Ibid., p. 57.

63. Ibid., p. 188.

64. Ibid., p. 17.

65. Ibid., p. 2.

66. Ibid., pp. 188–9.

67. Ibid., p. 190.

68. E. P. Sanders, op, cit., pp. 463–70, & 519–22.

69. See A. Thiselton, 'The New Hermeneutic', p. 83.

70. R. Barthes, 'The Death of the Author', in *Image, Music, Text*, selected and trans. S. Heath (Glasgow: Fontana, 1977), pp. 142–8, p. 147.

71. J. Derrida, *Margins of Philosophy*, trans. A. Bass (Brighton: Harvester Press, 1982), p. 6.

72. P. Ricoeur, *Interpretation Theory: Discourse and the Surplus of Meaning* (Fort Worth: Texas Christian University Press, 1976), p. 19.

73. Interpretation is seen as a particular form of understanding. Ricoeur argues that, since understanding attempts to gain access to the inner life of the author, which the autonomy of the text places at an irreducible distance, interpretation will always have taken its place (*Interpretation Theory*, ch. 4, pp. 71–88). Paul's technique here creates a similar effect.

74.   J. Derrida, *Of Grammatology*, p. 65.
75.   E. Käsemann, *Perspectives on Paul*, trans. M. Kohl (London: SCM, 1971), p. 159.
76.   J. L. Austin, 'Performative-Constative', in *The Philosophy of Language*, ed. J. R. Searle (Oxford: Oxford University Press, 1971), pp. 13–22.

## 3  Justification of Faith

1.    E. D. Hirsch, *Validity in Interpretation* (New Haven and London: Yale University Press, 1967), p. 207.
2.    J.-F. Lyotard, *The Postmodern Condition: A Report on Knowledge*, trans. G. Bennington and B. Massumi (Manchester: Manchester University Press, 1984), p. xxv.
3.    E. Dickinson, 'Those – dying then', in *A Choice of Emily Dickinson's Verse*, selected by T. Hughes (London: Faber, 1969), p. 60.
4.    J. Derrida, *Of Grammatology*, p. 158.
5.    L. Wittgenstein, quoted in A. Thiselton, *The Two Horizons*, p. 375.
6.    A. Thiselton, ibid., p. 409.
7.    Ibid.
8.    C. Norris, *Spinoza and the Origins of Modern Critical Theory* (Oxford: Basil Blackwell, 1991), p. 199.
9.    Ibid., p. 205.
10.   Ibid.
11.   F. Kermode, *The Genesis of Secrecy* (Cambridge, Mass.: Harvard University Press, 1979).
12.   C. Norris, *Spinoza and the Origins of Modern Critical Theory*, p. 197.
13.   Ibid., p. 198.
14.   P. Ricoeur, *Interpretation Theory*, pp. 71–88; E. D. Hirsch, op. cit.; J.-F. Lyotard, op. cit.
15.   MIDRASH . . . the designation of a particular genre of rabbinic literature constituting an anthology and compilation of homilies, consisting of both biblical exegesis ( . . . ) and sermons delivered in public . . . and forming a running . . . commentary on specific books of the Bible. The name Midrash derives from the root *drsh* which in the Bible means mainly 'to search', 'to seek', 'to examine', and 'to investigate' . . .
      From: *Encyclopaedia Judaica* (Jerusalem: Keter Publishing House, 1972), Vol. 11, p. 1508.
      See also: Gerald L. Bruns, 'The Hermeneutics of Midrash', in *The Book and the Text: The Bible and Literary Theory*, ed. R. Schwartz (Oxford and Cambridge, Mass.: Basil Blackwell, 1990), pp. 189–213; Roger Le Déaut, 'Apropos a Definition of Midrash', *Interpretation* XXV, 3 (1971), pp. 259–82; Michael Wadsworth, 'Making and Interpreting Scripture', in *Ways of Reading the Bible*, ed. M. Wadsworth (Brighton: Harvester Press, 1981), pp. 7–22; notes 16–18 below.
16.   G. Hartman and S. Budick (eds), *Midrash and Literature* (New Haven: Yale University Press, 1986).
17.   S. Handelman, *The Slayers of Moses: The Emergence of Rabbinic Inter-

*pretation in Modern Literary Theory* (Albany: State University of New York Press, 1982).
18.   D. Boyarin, *Intertextuality and the Reading of Midrash* (Bloomington and Indianapolis: Indiana University Press, 1990), pp. 35–6.
19.   Ibid., p. 36.
20.   Ibid., p. 37.
21.   Ibid., p. 36.
22.   Boyarin describes the Mekilta as: '[T] he earliest midrash on Exodus, having been largely compiled of materials which belong to the Tannaitic period, the time of the rabbis who produced the Mishna, from about the first to the third Christian centuries' (Ibid., p. viii).
23.   Ibid., p. 37.
24.   Ibid., p. x.
25.   Ibid., p. 37.
26.   D. Boyarin, 'The Eye in the Torah: Ocular Desire in Midrashic Hermeneutic', *Critical Inquiry* 16, 3 (1990), pp. 532–50, p. 549.
27.   J. Derrida, *Of Grammatology*, p. 49.
28.   K. Hart, *The Trespass of the Sign: Deconstruction, theology and philosophy* (Cambridge: Cambridge University Press, 1989), p. x.
29.   Ibid.
30.   Ibid., p. 75.
31.   J. Derrida, 'Letter to a Japanese Friend', in *Derrida and Difference*, ed. D. Wood (University of Warwick: Parousia Press, 1985).
32.   K. Hart, op. cit., p. 117.
33.   Ibid., p. 67.
34.   Ibid., p. 70
35.   Ibid., p. 167–8.
36.   Ibid., p. 168.
37.   Ibid., p. 170.
38.   J. Derrida, 'From Restricted to General Economy: A Hegelianism without Reserve', in *Writing and Difference*, trans. A. Bass (London: Routledge and Kegan Paul, 1978), pp. 251–77.
39.   R. Rorty, 'Two Meanings of "logocentrism": a Reply to Norris', in *Redrawing the Lines: Analytic Philosophy, Deconstruction, and Literary Theory*, ed. R. W. Dasenbrock (Minneapolis: University of Minnesota Press, 1989), pp. 204–16, p. 208.
40.   K. Hart, op. cit., p. 115.
41.   Ibid.
42.   R. Rorty, op. cit., p. 208.
43.   K. Hart, op. cit., p. 3.
44.   See also F. Nietzsche, 'On Truth and Falsity in Their Ultramoral Sense', *Early Greek Philosophy and Other Essays*, trans. M. A. Mügge (London: T. N. Foulis, 1991), pp. 173–92.
45.   P. Ricoeur, *Interpretation Theory*, p. 87.
46.   The 'non-exchange' between Gadamer and Derrida in 1981 is an interesting example of the failure of hermeneutics and deconstruction to engage with one another. See *Dialogue and Deconstruction: The Gadamer – Derrida Encounter*, ed. D. P. Michelfelder and R. E. Palmer (Albany:

State University of New York Press, 1989). I return briefly to this exchange in Chapter 6.

47. P. Ricoeur, *Interpretation Theory*, p. 74.
48. Ibid., p. 72.
49. J. Derrida, 'Structure, Sign and Play in the Discourse of the Human Sciences', in *Writing and Difference*, pp. 278–93, p. 279.
50. Ibid., p. 280.
51. J. Derrida, 'Force and Signification', ibid., pp. 3–30, p. 5.
52. J. Derrida, 'Genesis and Structure', ibid., pp. 154–68, p. 157.
53. C. Norris, *Deconstruction: Theory and Practice* (London: Routledge, 1982), p. 51.
54. P. Ricoeur, *Interpretation Theory*, p. 81.
55. S. H. Clark, *Paul Ricoeur* (London: Routledge, 1990), p. 110. He is quoting Ricoeur, *Interpretation Theory*, p. 79.
56. R. E. Palmer, *Hermeneutics: Interpretation Theory in Schleiermacher, Dilthey, Heidegger, and Gadamer* (Evanston: Northwestern University Press, 1969), p. 64.
57. E. D. Hirsch, op. cit., p. 18.
58. R. E. Palmer, op. cit., p. 65.
59. P. Ricoeur, *Interpretation Theory*, p. 87.
60. J.-F. Lyotard, op. cit., p. xxiv.
61. Ibid.
62. J.-F. Lyotard, *The Differend: Phrases in Dispute*, trans. Georges Van Den Abbeele (Manchester: Manchester University Press, 1988), p. xxi.
63. J.-F. Lyotard, *The Postmodern Condition*, p. 100, note 211.
64. B. L. Whorf, *Language, Thought, and Reality: Selected Writings*, ed. J. B. Carroll (Cambridge, Mass.: MIT Press, 1956), p. 213.
65. This is Donald Davidson's main argument against all forms of cultural relativism. See Donald Davidson, 'On the Very Idea of a Conceptual Scheme', in *Inquiries into Truth and Interpretation* (Oxford: Clarendon Press, 1984), pp. 183–98. I return to this essay in Chapter 6.
66. J.-F. Lyotard. op, cit., p. xxiii.
67. J. Baudrillard, *Selected Writings*, ed. M. Poster (Cambridge: Polity Press, 1988), p. 172.
68. Ibid., p. 173.
69. Ibid., p. 169.
70. Ibid., p. 173.
71. J. Derrida, *Of Grammatology*, pp. 141–64.
72. Ernest Gellner's Observation about epistemological theories is appropriate:

> Theories of knowledge, when treated as explanatory models, as specifications of the actually operative underlying mechanism, are rather like those wooden toys for very small children, which are 'models' of steam engines, tractors, tanks, and so forth, but only in the most elementary sense: they simulate the most obvious external movements of the objects they symbolize and resemble. They 'work' only if constantly propelled by the child's hands. The

child's imagination generously thinks away the intrusive hands, and 'sees' a steam engine or a tank . . .

E. Gellner, *Legitimation of Belief* (London: Cambridge University Press, 1974), p. 34.
He goes on to characterize dialectical thinkers (for example) as being as 'undemanding as toddlers', thinking away their 'intrusive hands'. I recognize myself in Gellner's toddler.
73. Ibid., p. 22.
74. A. Thiselton, *The Two Horizons*, p. 409.
75. J. Derrida, *Of Grammatology*, pp. 65, 93. See also 'Différance' in *Margins of Philosophy*, trans. A. Bass (Brighton: Harvester Press, 1982).

## 4  Pressing On

1. E. Bloch, *The Principle of Hope* (3 vols), trans. Neville Plaice, Stephen Plaice and Paul Knight (Oxford: Basil Blackwell, 1986), p. 204.
2. M. Edwards, 'Writing and Redemption', in *Writing the Future*, ed. D. Wood (London: Routledge, 1990), pp. 129–36, p. 134.
3. C. Norris, *Spinoza and the Origins of Modern Critical Theory*, p. 199.
4. J.-F. Lyotard, *The Differend*, pp. 179–80.
5. Ibid., p. xxi.
6. D. J. Schmidt, 'Circles – Hermeneutic and Otherwise: On Various Senses of the Future as "Not Yet"', in *Writing the Future*, pp. 67–77.
7. These are the closing words of Bloch's *The Principle of Hope* (III, p. 1376), quoted by Schmidt, ibid., p. 76.
8. Ibid., p. 75.
9. D. Wood, 'Editing the Future', introduction to *Writing the Future*, pp. 1–9, p. 9.
10. E. Bloch, op. cit., p. 7.
11. W. Hudson, *The Marxist Philosophy of Ernst Bloch* (London: Macmillan, 1982), p. 105.
12. Ibid., p. 81.
13. B. Russell, *A History of Western Philosophy* (London: Unwin, 1946, 1984), p. 182.
14. W. Hudson, op. cit., p. 77.
15. E. Bloch, *Tübinger Einleitnung in die Philosophie*, quoted in Hudson, op. cit., p. 139.
16. C. Brown, *Philosophy and the Christian Faith* (London: IVP, 1969), p. 152.
17. D. Skilton, *Defoe to the Victorians: Two Centuries of the English Novel* (Harmondsworth: Penguin, 1977), p. 152.
18. M. Arnold, 'Dover Beach', in *The Poems of Matthew Arnold*, ed. K. Allott (London: Longmans, 1965), pp. 239–43.
19. J. Macquarrie, *Christian Hope* (London: Mowbrays, 1978), pp. 97–104.
20. J. Moltmann, *Theology of Hope on the Ground and the Implications of a Christian Eschatology*, trans. J. W. Leitch (London: SCM, 1967), p. 40.
21. Ibid., p. 16.

22.    Ibid., p. 103.
23.    J. Moltmann, *The Experiment Hope*, ed. and trans. M. D. Meeks (London: SCM, 1975), p. 19.
24.    J. Moltmann, *Theology of Hope*, p. 106.
25.    Ibid., p. 165.
26.    Ibid., p. 175.
27.    C. S. Lewis, *Miracles* (Glasgow: Collins, 1947, 1974), p. 106.
28.    Ibid.
29.    J. Derrida, 'Structure, Sign and Play in the Discourse of the Human Sciences', in *Writing and Difference*, p. 291.
30.    T. W. Adorno, *Minima Moralia: Reflections from Damaged Life*, trans. E. F. N. Jephcott (London: NLB, 1974), pp. 233–4.
31.    J. Moltmann, *Theology of Hope*, p. 189.
32.    Ibid., p. 225.
33.    Ibid., p. 224.
34.    E. Bloch, quoted in J. Moltmann, *The Experiment Hope*, p. 26.
35.    J. Moltmann, *The Experiment Hope*, p. 27.
36.    Ibid., p. 33.
37.    Ibid., p. 34. See also W. Hudson, op. cit., pp. 88 & 144–5.
38.    Ibid., p. 36.
39.    D. J. Schmidt, op. cit., pp. 73–4.
40.    D. Wood, op. cit., p. 9.
41.    J. Moltmann, *The Experiment Hope*, p. 39.
42.    G. M. Hopkins, 'That Nature is a Heraclitean Fire and of the Comfort of the Resurrection', in *Gerard Manley Hopkins: Poems and Prose*, selected and ed. W. H. Gardner (Harmondsworth: Penguin, 1953, 1963), pp. 65–6.
43.    E. Bloch, *The Principle of Hope*, p. 203.
44.    P. Ricoeur, 'Freedom in the Light of Hope', in *The Conflict of Interpretations*, pp. 402–24, p. 406.
45.    Ibid., p. 403.
46.    Ibid., p. 408.
47.    Ibid., p. 409.
48.    J. Moltmann, *The Experiment Hope*, p. 37.
49.    P. Ricoeur, *The Conflict of Interpretations*, p. 409.
50.    Ibid., p. 411.
51.    W. Hudson, op. cit., p. 87.
52.    P. Ricoeur, *The Conflict of Interpretations*, p. 412.
53.    Ibid., pp. 412–13.
54.    Ibid., p. 415.
55.    Ibid., p. 420.
56.    C. Norris, 'Postmodernising History: Right-Wing Revisionism and the Uses of Theory', *Southern Review* 21, 2, 1988, pp. 123–40.
57.    P. Ricoeur, *The Conflict of Interpretations*, p. 422.
58.    J. Moltmann, *Theology of Hope*, p. 169.
59.    L. Feuerbach, quoted in ibid., p. 171.
60.    P. Ricoeur, *From Text to Action: Essays in Hermeneutics, II*, trans. K. Blamey and J. B. Thompson (London: Athlone Press, 1991).
61.    Ibid., p. 199.

62.  J.-F. Lyotard, *The Differend*, pp. 151–81. See also C. Norris, *What's Wrong With Postmodernism: Critical Theory and the Ends of Philosophy* (New York: Harvester Wheatsheaf, 1990), pp. 6–15.

63.  P. Ricoeur, *From Text to Action*, p. 204.

64.  In her *Constructions of Reason: Explorations of Kant's Practical Philosophy* (Cambridge: Cambridge University Press, 1989), Onora O'Neill offers an alternative version of the relation between practical and theoretical reason. Her contention is that Kant's Categorical Imperative is fundamental not just to his ethical philosophy but to his whole critique of reason. Reason is not algorithmic, it does not provide a set of rules or maxims for thought or action. On the contrary, O'Neill argues, it 'must . . . be seen as a *practical and collective task'*. This insight is drawn from the apparent incoherence of proposing a 'critique of reason'. How is it possible to conduct such a critique without presupposing the character of the very thing under scrutiny? O'Neill points out that Kant avoids the question of method until he has provided the material to which his method is to be applied. Once the question is engaged, he elaborates it by means of 'juridical and political metaphors'. This is because 'he sees the problems of cognitive and political order as arising in one and the same context. . . . Authority has in either case to be constructed'. Reason is not to be vindicated as some abstract generality, but:

> [T]he reasoning of those who like ourselves have no preinscribed modes of coordination, and find that their native endowment provides neither algorithm nor instinct for acting or for thinking. What can such beings do? There is no maxim of reasoning whose antecedent authority can compel them; and yet they cannot share a world if there is no cognitive order. The most then that they can do is to reject basic principles of thought and action that are barriers to cognitive order. A minimal, negative step toward any solution must be to refrain from adopting plans that others cannot adopt. . . . To act on this maxim is simply to make what Kant elsewhere calls the Categorical Imperative the fundamental principle of all reasoning and acting. It is to base action and thought only on maxims through which one can at the same time will that they be universal laws (p. 23).

There is no discontinuity, here, between the two orders of reason. Theoretical reason derives from a more fundamental practical reason. Despite this divergence in the interpretation of Kant, the implications for practical reason, in both cases, are manifestly to be sought in a critique of ideology, since both interpretations see the former as a social construct.

65.  P. Ricoeur, *From Text to Action*, p. 320.

66.  R. G. Smith, *J. G. Hamann 1730–1788: A Study in Christian Existence with selections from his writings* (London: Collins, 1960), p. 91.

67.  J. G. Hamann, ibid., pp. 235–6.

68.  P. Ricoeur, *From Text to Action*, p. 221.

69.    O. O'Neill, op. cit., pp. 24–7.
70.    J. G. Hamann, op. cit., p. 235.
71.    Ibid., p. 187.
72.    F. C. Beiser, *The Fate of Reason: German Philosophy from Kant to Fichte* (Cambridge, Mass.: Harvard University Press, 1987), pp. 16–43; I. Berlin, *The Magus of the North: J. G. Hamann and the Origins of Modern Irrationalism*, ed. H. Hardy (London: John Murray, 1993); J. C. O'Flaherty, *Unity and Language: A Study in the Philosophy of Johann Georg Hamann* (Chapel Hill, NC: University of North Carolina Studies in the Germanic Languages and Literatures 6, 1952). Henry Hardy includes a bibliography of books on Hamann in English in his edition of Berlin's book (as above), pp. 134–5.
73.    J. G. Hamann, op. cit., p. 245.
74.    F. Beiser, op. cit., p. 20.
75.    J. G. Hamann, op. cit., p. 167.
76.    Ibid., p. 214.
77.    Ibid., p. 215.
78.    J. C. O'Flaherty, op. cit., p. 86.
79.    J. G. Hamann, op. cit., p. 215.
80.    F. Beiser, op. cit., p. 41.
81.    D. Hume, quoted in ibid., p. 241.
82.    S. Kierkegaard, *Fear and Trembling*, ed. and trans. H. V. & E. H. Hong (Princeton, NJ: Princeton University Press, 1983), p. 53.
83.    Ibid., p. 122.
84.    J. Derrida, 'Cogito and the History of Madness', in *Writing and Difference*, pp. 31–63, p. 35.
85.    In this account of the debate between Kant and Hamann I am drawing heavily on Beiser's interpretation.
86.    F. Beiser, op. cit., p. 31.
87.    Ibid., p. 32.
88.    J. G. Hamann, quoted in Beiser, ibid., p. 31.
89.    J. G. Hamann, op. cit., p. 180.
90.    R. G. Smith, op. cit., p. 93.
91.    A. Thiselton, *The Two Horizons*, pp. 417–18.
92.    Bible quotations here are from the New International Version.
93.    A. Thiselton, op. cit., pp. 420–1.
94.    E. P. Sanders, op. cit., p. 449.
95.    G. Josipovici, *The Book of God: A Response to the Bible* (New Haven and London: Yale University Press, 1988), p. 245.
96.    D. E. Aune, *The New Testament in its Literary Environment* (Cambridge: James Clarke & Co, 1987), p. 207.
97.    G. Josipovici, op. cit., p. 243.
98.    C. Norris, see Chapter 3, n. 8.
99.    J. G. Hamann. op. cit., p. 241.
100.   R. G. Smith, op. cit., p. 93.

## 5  The Letter of the Spirit

1.    J. Derrida, *Of Grammatology*, pp. 34–5.
2.    Origen, *Commentary on the Song of Songs*, quoted in A. Louth, *The*

*Origins of the Christian Mystical Tradition: From Plato to Denys* (Oxford: Clarendon Press, 1981), pp. 69–70.

3. A. Louth, op. cit., p. 69.
4. I. Kant, *Critique of Pure Reason*, trans. N. Kemp Smith (London: Macmillan, 1929, 1933, p. 636 (A805/B833).
5. S. Handelman, op. cit., p. 88.
6. Ibid., p. 15.
7. J. Barr, *Old and New in Interpretation* (London: SCM, 1966), p. 104.
8. S. Handelman, op. cit., p. 95.
9. J. Barr, op. cit., p. 106.
10. G. Von Rad, 'Typological Interpretation of the Old Testament', trans. J. Bright, in *A Guide to Contemporary Hermeneutics*, ed. D. K. McKim (Grand Rapids: Eerdmans, 1986), pp. 28–46, p. 29.
11. R. P. C. Hanson, *Allegory and Event* (London: SCM, 1959), p. 31.
12. B. Smalley, *The Study of the Bible in the Middle Ages* 3rd edn (Oxford: Blackwell, 1952, 1983), p. 126.
13. Origen, *De Principiis*, trans. Rev. F. Crombie (Edinburgh: T. & T. Clark, 1869), IV, i, 11, pp. 300–1.
14. B. Smalley, op. cit., p. 41.
15. T. S. Eliot, 'Mr. Eliot's Sunday Morning Service', in *The Complete Poems and Plays of T. S. Eliot* (London: Faber and Faber, 1969), pp. 54–5. The second stanza of the poem reads:

> In the beginning was the Word.
> Superfetation of το 'εν,
> And at the mensual turn of time
> Produced enervate Origen.

16. Origen, *De Principiis*, IV, i, 19, p. 325.
17. H. Frei, *The Eclipse of Biblical Narrative: A Study in Eighteenth and Nineteenth Century Hermeneutics* (New Haven: Yale University Press, 1974), pp. 5–6.
18. E. Auerbach, *Mimesis: The Representation of Reality in Western Literature* (Princeton: Princeton University Press, 1953), p. 73.
19. Ibid., p. 74.
20. M. Reeves, 'The Bible and Literary Authorship in the Middle Ages', in *Reading the Text: Biblical Criticism and Literary Theory*, ed. S. Prickett (Oxford: Blackwell, 1991), pp. 12–63, p. 17.
21. E. Auerbach, op. cit., p. 49. S. Handelman, op. cit., p. 111.
22. C. K. Barrett, 'The Allegory of Abraham, Sarah, and Hagar in the argument of Galatians', in *Essays on Paul* (London: SPCK, 1982), pp. 154–69, p. 163.
23. Origen, *De Principiis*, IV, i, 13, p. 305.
24. P. de Man, 'The Rhetoric of Temporality', in *Blindness and Insight: Essays in the Rhetoric of Contemporary Criticism* 2nd ed. (Minneapolis: University of Minnesota Press, 1971, 1983), pp. 187–228.
25. Ibid., p. 192.
26. David Dawson reads de Man as not attending to the nuances of Coleridge's text, and employing a rhetorical strategy which turns 'what is to be the conclusion of his argument into its premise' when he claims that, in Coleridge's definition, 'the material substantiality

dissolves and becomes a mere reflection'. As Dawson points out, Coleridge speaks not of 'reflection', but of 'translucence', terms which 'seem nearly opposite in meaning'. What Dawson does not note, however, is that 'translucence' requires the same kind of 'underneath' to the text that Origen wants to maintain. So, when he appears to assert, for Coleridge, the same kind of multilateral hermeneutic that can be read in Paul, he returns to the very view of language that de Man objects to in Coleridge:

> For Coleridge, scripture is neither a literal dead letter nor an alleg-orical abstraction; instead, as symbol, scripture is a 'translucent' material form through which the eternal 'shines', so to speak, but scripture is neither organically identified nor arbitrarily associated with the eternal.

D. Dawson, 'Against the Divine Ventriloquist: Coleridge and De Man on Symbol, Allegory, and Scripture'. *Literature & Theology* 4, 3 (1990), pp. 293–310, p. 300.

In fact, there is no need to argue the case for scripture as symbol when the force of the *allegoroumena* within the hermeneutical possib-ilities of letter and spirit, body and shadow, shows a less mystifying, more dialectical approach, which has no need of romantic aesthetics.


27.  Origen, *De Principiis*, IV, i, 13, p. 306.
28.  Colossians is one of those epistles, attributed to Paul, which divides opinion with regard to its authorship. I have no case to make in this debate. I quote the passage here, as it seems to me to have influenced Origen's interpretation of interpretation, and because Handelman quotes it as a Pauline text (see below, note 39).
29.  H. G. Liddell and R. Scott, *Greek–English Lexicon* 9th edn (Oxford: Oxford University Press, 1940).
30.  M. Reeves, op. cit., p. 17.
31.  R. Zim, 'The Reformation: the Trial of God's Word', in *Reading the Text*, pp. 64–135, p. 70.
32.  S. Prickett, *Words and the Word*, pp. 124–5.
33.  S. Prickett, 'Romantics and Victorians: from Typology to Symbol-ism', in *Reading the Text*, pp. 182–224, p. 206. Prickett points out that 'conductor' is used by Coleridge 'in the newly coined electrical sense of that word'.
34.  Ibid., p. 206.
35.  B. Smalley, op. cit., p. 28.
36.  Ibid., pp. 41–2.
37.  C. Brooks, *The Well Wrought Urn: Studies in the Structure of Poetry* (New York: Harcourt, Brace & Co.. 1947); W. K. Wimsatt, *The Verbal Icon: Studies in the Meaning of Poetry* (Lexington, Kentucky: Kentucky University Press, 1954).
38.  J. Derrida, *Of Grammatology*, p. 24.
39.  S. Mitchell, op. cit., p. 85.
40.  F. Kermode, *The Genesis of Secrecy* (Cambridge, Mass.: Harvard University Press, 1979), p. 7.

41. P. Ricoeur, *The Conflict of Interpretations*, pp. 62–78.
42. J. Derrida, *Writing and Difference*, p. 292.
43. Ibid., p. 293.
44. H. Bloom, *The Anxiety of Influence: a theory of poetry* (London: Oxford University Press, 1975), pp. 14–15.
45. S. Handelman, op. cit., pp. 185–6.
46. S. Sutherland, 'Hope', in *The Philosophy in Christianity*, ed. G. Vesey (Cambridge *et al.*: Cambridge University Press, 1989), pp. 193–206, p. 197.
47. G. Harpham, *The Ascetic Imperative in Culture and Criticism* (Chicago and London: Chicago University Press, 1987), p. 61.
48. S. Sutherland, op. cit., p. 199.
49. See Chapter 3.
50. G. Harpham, *The Ascetic Imperative*, p. xvii.
51. Ibid., p. 54.
52. Ibid., p. xi.
53. L. Poland, 'Augustine, Allegory, and Conversion' *Literature & Theology* 2, 1 (1988), pp. 37–48.
54. G. Harpham, *The Ascetic Imperative*, p. 103 & p. 104.
55. L. Poland, op. cit., p. 39.
56. P. Ricoeur, *The Conflict of Interpretations*, p. 410. The *'kal ve-chomer'* is one of the thirteen 'Middot', or rules, of Rabbi Ishmael. It is 'an argument from the minor premise (*kal*) to the major (*chomer*)'. It differs from the Aristotelian syllogism in two principle ways: 'First, the element of "how much more" is lacking in the syllogism. Second, the syllogism inference concerns genus and species: All men are mortal. Socrates is a man. Therefore Socrates is mortal. Since Socrates belongs in the class "man" he must share the characteristics of that class. However, in the *kal ve-chomer* it is not suggested that the "major" belongs in the class of the "minor" but that what is true of the "minor" must be true of the "major"'.
Quotations from: *Encyclopaedia Judaica* 8, p. 367.
57. L. Poland, op. cit., p. 47.
58. G. Harpham, *The Ascetic Imperative*, pp. 128–9.
59. Quoted in Smalley, op. cit., p. 23.
60. P. Ricoeur, 'Consciousness and the Unconscious', trans. W. Domingo, in *The Conflict of Interpretations*, pp. 99–120, p. 117.
61. Ibid., pp. 101–2.
62. Ibid., p. 117.
63. Ibid., p. 120.
64. Ibid., p. 118.
65. J. Derrida, op. cit., pp. 253–4, passim.

## 6 Love and do as you like

1. R. Barthes, 'The Death of the Author', in *Image, Music, Text*, selected and trans. S. Heath (Glasgow: Fontana, 1977), pp. 142–8, p. 48.
2. T. S. Eliot, 'Tradition and the Individual Talent', in *Selected Prose*, ed. J. Hayward (Harmondsworth: Penguin, 1953), pp. 21–30.
3. M. Grene, quoted in A. Thiselton, *The Two Horizons*, p. 203.

4.    J. Derrida, *Of Grammatology*, p. 162.
5.    F. Beiser, op. cit., p. 21.
6.    I. Berlin, *Vico and Herder: Two Studies in the History of Ideas* (London: Hogarth, 1976), p. 166.
7.    G. Harpham, *The Ascetic Imperative*, p. xii.
8.    J. Derrida, *Of Grammatology*, p. 233.
9.    G. Harpham, *The Ascetic Imperative*, p. xii.
10.   Augustine, quoted in H. Chadwick, *Augustine* (Oxford: Oxford University Press, 1986), p. 82.
11.   E. Gilson, *The Christian Philosophy of Saint Augustine*, trans. L. E. M. Lynch (London: Victor Gollancz, 1961), p. 245.
12.   Ibid., p. 236.
13.   R. Barthes, 'The Pleasure of the Text', in *Selected Writings*, ed. S. Sontag (Glasgow: Fontana, 1983), pp. 404–14, p. 405. On the dialectical relationship between text and reader, see Werner Jeanrond's *Theological Hermeneutics* (op. cit.), esp. pp. 6–7 & 93–5.
14.   Augustine, *Confessions*, trans. J. G. Pilkington (Edinburgh: T. & T. Clark, 1876), IX, vi, 14, p. 218.
15.   Augustine, *The Teacher*, in *Earlier Writings*, selected and trans. J. H. S. Burleigh (London: SCM, 1953), pp. 69–101, p. 94.
16.   Ibid., pp. 96–7.
17.   Augustine, *On Christian Doctrine*, trans. J. F. Shaw (Edinburgh: T. & T. Clark, 1873), I, ii (2).
18.   A. Louth, 'Augustine on Language', *Literature & Theology* 3, 2, 1989, pp. 151–8.
19.   Augustine, *On Christian Doctrine*, II, xxiv (37).
20.   Augustine, quoted by Louth, op. cit., p. 153.
21.   A. Louth, op. cit., p. 154.
22.   Ibid., p. 156, quoting Augustine, *The Trinity* IX, vii (12).
23.   E. Gilson, op. cit., pp. 134–5.
24.   Augustine, *Confessions* XIII, ix (10).
25.   Ibid., XII, xxxi (42); XIII, xxiv (35).
26.   D. Davidson, 'On the Very Idea of a Conceptual Scheme', in *Inquiries into Truth and Interpretation* (Oxford: Clarendon Press, 1984), pp. 183–98, p. 183.
27.   Ibid., p. 197.
28.   J. Rousseau, quoted in J. Derrida, *Of Grammatology*, pp. 230–1.
29.   P. P. Giglioli, 'Introduction', *Language and Social Context*, ed. Giglioli, pp. 7–17, p. 7.
30.   Ibid., p. 8.
31.   M. Bakhtin, *The Dialogic Imagination*, ed. M. Holquist, trans. C. Emerson and M. Holquist (Austin: University of Texas Press, 1981), p. 289. In this discussion of Bakhtin, I am assuming his authorship of P. N. Medvedev and M. M. Bakhtin, *The Formal Method in Literary Scholarship*, trans. A. J. Wehrle (Baltimore and London: Johns Hopkins University Press, 1978); and V. N. Voloshinov, *Marxism and the Philosophy of Language*, trans. L. Matejka and I. R. Titunik (New York: Seminar Press, 1973). I do not wish to overlook the scholarly debate with regard to the attribution of these texts, but to use Bakhtin's

name as a collective proper noun for whoever might have been involved in their authorship. The issue illustrates the very inter-subjectivity which the texts themselves describe. The details of this debate are recounted and argued in K. Clark and M. Holquist, *Mikhail Bakhtin* (Cambridge, Mass.: Harvard University Press, 1984).

32. M. Bakhtin, *The Formal Method*, p. 124.
33. M. Bakhtin, *Marxism and the Philosophy of Language*, p. 23.
34. M. Bakhtin, *The Formal Method*, p. 8.
35. M. Bakhtin, *Marxism and the Philosophy of Language*, p. 67.
36. K. Clark and M. Holquist, op. cit., p. 10.
37. M. Bakhtin, *The Formal Method*, p. 125.
38. M. Bakhtin, *Problems of Dostoevsky's Poetics*, ed. and trans. C. Emerson (Manchester: Manchester University Press, 1984), p. 182; *The Formal Method*, p. 126.
39. M. Bakhtin, *Problems of Dostoevsky's Poetics*, p. 68.
40. M. Bakhtin, *Marxism and the Philosophy of Language*, p. 21.
41. Ibid.
42. T. Bennett, *Formalism and Marxism* (London: Methuen, 1979), pp. 91–2.
43. M. Bakhtin, *The Formal Method*, p. 14.
44. G. Myerson, *The Argumentative Imagination: Wordsworth, Dryden, religious dialogues* (Manchester: Manchester University Press, 1992), p. 6.
45. H. Fisch, 'Bakhtin's Misreadings of the Bible' *Hebrew University Studies in Literature and the Arts* 16 (1988), pp. 130–49, p. 135.
46. Ibid., p. 144.
47. M. Bakhtin, *Problems of Dostoevsky's Poetics*, p. 6.
48. K. Clark and M. Holquist, op. cit., p. 249.
49. Ibid., pp. 84–7. See also C. Lock, 'Carnival and Incarnation: Bakhtin and Orthodox Theology' *Literature & Theology* 5, 1 (1991), pp. 68–82.
50. T. Crowley, 'Bakhtin and the history of the language' (pp. 68–90), in K. Hirschkop and D. Shepherd (eds.), *Bakhtin and Cultural Theory* (Manchester: Manchester University Press, 1989), pp. 68–90, p. 84.
51. Ibid., p. 71.
52. Ibid., p. 72.
53. Ibid., p. 89.
54. As I write, the Calcutt report on press freedom has just been published. The question of Government control over what appears in newspapers is what is at stake. This seems particularly relevant to any consideration of monologism in our time.
55. H.-G. Gadamer, *Dialogue and Deconstruction* (op. cit.), p. 33.
56. J. Derrida, ibid., pp. 52–3.
57. E. Levinas, 'Substitution', trans. A. Lingis, in *The Levinas Reader*, ed. S. Hand (Oxford: Blackwell, 1989), pp. 88–125, p. 108.
58. G. Harpham, *Getting it Right: Language, Literature, and Ethics* (Chicago and London: University of Chicago Press, 1992).
59. Ibid., p. 69.
60. Ibid., p. 4.
61. Ibid., p. 73.

62.	E. Levinas, 'Ethics as First Philosophy', trans. S. Hand and M. Temple, in op. cit., pp. 75–87, p. 82.
63.	E. Levinas, 'Substitution', p. 94.
64.	S. Handelman, 'Parodic Play and Prophetic Reason: Two Interpretations of Interpretation' *Poetics Today* 9, 2 (1988), pp. 395–423, p. 404.
65.	S. Handelman, 'Parodic Play and Prophetic Reason', p. 404.
66.	W. Benjamin, quoted in G. Josipovici, 'The Bible: Dialogue and Distance', in *Ways of Reading the Bible*, ed. M. Wadsworth (Brighton: Harvester, 1981), pp. 133–53, p. 136.
67.	See J. Derrida, *Writing and Difference*, p. 314, note 37; and S. Handelman, 'Parodic Play and Prophetic Reason', p. 403.
68.	M. Bakhtin, quoted in S. Handelman, ibid., p. 403.
69.	E. Levinas, 'Substitution', p. 107.
70.	E. Levinas, quoted in F. Ciaramelli, 'Levinas's Ethical Discourse Between Individuation and Universality', in *Re-Reading Levinas*, eds. R. Bernasconi and S. Critchley (London: Athlone, 1991), pp. 83–105, p. 88.
71.	E. Levinas, 'Substitution', p. 100.
72.	J. Derrida, 'Violence and Metaphysics: An Essay on the Thought of Emmanuel Levinas', in *Writing and Difference*, pp. 79–153, p. 128.
73.	Ibid., p. 131.
74.	E. Levinas, 'Revelation in the Jewish Tradition', trans. S. Richmond, in *The Levinas Reader*, pp. 190–210, p. 195.
75.	Ibid., p. 209.
76.	G. Harpham, *Getting it Right*, pp. 109 & 110.
77.	Ibid., p. 110.
78.	E. Levinas, 'Substitution', p. 111.
79.	G. Theissen, *Psychological Aspects of Pauline Theology*, trans. J. P. Galvin (Edinburgh: T. & T. Clark, 1987), p. 98.
80.	Ibid., p. 303.
81.	Ibid., pp. 74–9.
82.	C.f.: '. . . the ideal meaning is a void and an absence which demand to be fulfilled. By such fulfilling, language comes into its own, that is to say, *dies to itself*' P. Ricoeur, *The Conflict of Interpretations*, p. 87 (my emphasis).
83.	G. Theissen, op. cit., p. 314.
84.	J. Derrida, *Of Grammatology*, p. 23.
85.	E. Levinas, 'Time and the Other', trans. R. A. Cohen, in *The Levinas Reader*, pp. 37–58, p. 44.
86.	P. Ricoeur, *The Conflict of Interpretations*, p. 85.
87.	E. Levinas, 'Substitution', p. 117.
88.	R. Schwartz, 'Introduction' to *The Book and the Text*, ed. R. Schwartz (Oxford: Blackwell, 1990), p. 5.

# Bibliography


Adorno, Theodor, *Minima Moralia*. Trans. E. F. N. Jephcott. London: NLB, 1974.

Alexander, David and Pat (eds), *The Lion Handbook to the Bible* (2nd ed.), Tring: Lion Publishing, 1973, 1983.

Alexander, Philip S. (ed. and trans.), *Textual Sources for the Study of Judaism*. Manchester: Manchester University Press, 1984.

Arnold, Matthew, *The Poems of Matthew Arnold*. Ed. Kenneth Allott. London: Longmans, 1965.

Auerbach, Erich, *Mimesis: The Representation of Reality in Western Literature*. Princeton: Princeton University Press, 1953.

Augustine, *Confessions*. Trans. J. G. Pilkington. Edinburgh: T. & T. Clark, 1876.

*On Christian Doctrine*. Trans. J. F. Shaw. Edinburgh: T. & T. Clark, 1873.

'The Teacher', in *Augustine: Earlier Writings*. Selected and trans. John H. S. Burleigh. London: SCM, 1953.

'The Spirit and the Letter', in *Augustine: Later Works*. Selected and trans. John Burnaby. London: SCM, 1955.

Aune, David E., *The New Testament in Its Literary Environment*. Cambridge: James Clarke & Co., 1988.

Bakhtin, Mikhail, (see also Medvedev, P. N., and Voloshinov, V. N.) *The Dialogic Imagination*. Ed. Michael Holquist; trans. Caryl Emerson and Michael Holquist. Austin: University of Texas Press, 1981.

*Problems of Dostoevsky's Poetics*. Ed. and trans. Caryl Emerson. Manchester: Manchester University Press, 1984.

*Rabelais and His World*. Trans. Hélène Iswolsky. Bloomington: Indiana University Press, 1984.

Barr, James, *The Semantics of Biblical Language*. London: Oxford University Press, 1961.

*Old and New in Interpretation*. London: SCM, 1966.

Barrett, C. K., *Essays on Paul*. London: SPCK, 1982.

Barthes, Roland, *Image, Music, Text*. Selected and trans. Stephen Heath. Glasgow: Fontana, 1977.

*Selected Writings*. Ed. Susan Sontag. Glasgow: Fontana, 1983.

Baylor, Michael (ed. and trans.), *The Radical Reformation*. Cambridge: Cambridge University Press, 1991.

Beiser, Frederick C., *The Fate of Reason: German Philosophy from Kant to Fichte*. Cambridge, Mass.: Harvard University Press, 1987.

Bennett, Tony, *Formalism and Marxism*. London: Methuen, 1979.

Berggren, Douglas, 'The Use and Abuse of Metaphor', in *Review of Metaphysics*. Part 1: Dec. 1962 (pp. 237–58); Part 2: March 1963 (pp. 450–72).

Berlin, Isaiah, *Vico and Herder: Two Studies in the History of Ideas*. London: Hogarth, 1976.

Bernasconi, Robert and Critchley, Simon (eds), *Re-Reading Levinas*. London: Athlone, 1991.

Bloch, Ernst, *The Principle of Hope*. (3 vols) Trans. Neville Plaice, Stephen Plaice and Paul Knight. Oxford: Basil Balckwell, 1986.

    *Heritage of Our Times*. Trans. Neville Plaice and Stephen Plaice. Cambridge: Polity Press, 1991.

Bloom, Harold, *A Map of Misreading*. New York: Oxford University Press, 1975.

    *Kabbalah and Criticism*. New York: Seabury Press, 1976.

Bonhoeffer, Dietrich, *Letters and Papers from Prison*. Ed. Eberhard Bethge. Glasgow: Collins, 1959.

Bornkamm, Günther, *Early Christian Experience*. Trans. Paul L. Hammer. London: SCM, 1969.

Boyarin, Daniel, *Intertextuality and the Reading of Midrash*. Bloomington and Indianapolis: Indiana University Press, 1990.

    'The Eye in the Torah: Ocular Desire in Midrashic Hermeneutic.' *Critical Inquiry* 16 (1990), pp. 532–50.

Brown, Colin, *Philosophy and the Christian Faith*. London: IVP, 1969.

Brown, David, *Continental Philosophy and Modern Theology: An Engagement*. Oxford: Basil Blackwell, 1987.

Buber, Martin, *I and Thou*. Trans. Walter Kaufmann. Edinburgh: T. & T. Clark, 1970.

Bultmann, Rudolf, *Jesus Christ and Mythology*. London: SCM, 1960.

    *Faith and Understanding I*. Ed. Robert W. Funk; trans. Louise Pettibone Smith. London: SCM, 1969.

    *Existence and Faith: Shorter Writings of Rudolf Bultmann*. Selected and trans. Schubert M. Ogden. London: Fontana, 1973.

Bultmann, Rudolf and Rengstorf, Karl Heinrich, *Hope*. Trans. Dorothea M. Barton. London: Adam & Charles Black, 1963.

Buren, Paul M. van, *The Edges of Language: An Essay in the Logic of a Religion*. London: SCM, 1972.

Chadwick, Henry, *The Early Church*. Harmondsworth: Penguin, 1967.

    *Augustine*. Oxford: Oxford University Press, 1986.

Chomsky, Noam, *Selected Readings*. Ed. J. P. B. Allen and Paul van Buren. London: Oxford University Press, 1971.

Clark, Herbert H. and Eve V., *Psychology and Language: An Introduction to Psycholinguistics*. San Diego *et al.*: Harcourt Brace Jovanovich, 1977.

Clark, Katerina and Holquist, Michael, *Mikhail Bakhtin*. Cambridge, Mass.: Harvard University Press, 1984.

Clark, S. H., *Paul Ricoeur*. London: Routledge, 1990.

Critchley, Simon, 'The Chiasmus: Levinas, Derrida and the ethical demand for deconstruction.' *Textual Practice* 3, 1 (1989), pp. 91–106.

    *The Ethics of Deconstruction: Derrida and Levinas*. Oxford: Blackwell, 1992.

Culler, Jonathan, *The Pursuit of Signs: Semiotics, Literature Deconstruction*. London: Routledge and Kegan Paul, 1981.

    *Framing the Sign: Criticism and its Institutions*. Oxford: Blackwell, 1988.

Davidson, Donald, *Inquiries into Truth and Interpretation*. Oxford: Clarendon Press, 1984.

Dawson, David, 'Against the Divine Ventriloquist: Coleridge and De Man on Symbol, Allegory, and Scripture.' *Literature & Theology* 4, 3 (1990), pp. 293–310.

Day, J. P., 'Hope.' *American Philosophical Quarterly* 6, 2 (1969), pp. 89–102.

Déaut, Roger Le, 'Apropos a Definition of Midrash.' *Interpretation* XXV, 3 (1971), pp. 259–82.

De Man, Paul, *Blindness and Insight: Essays in the Rhetoric of Contemporary Criticism.* (2nd, rev.) Minneapolis: University of Minnesota Press, 1971, 1983.

Derrida, Jacques, (See also Michelfelder and Palmer, eds) *Of Grammatology.* Trans. Gayatri Chakravorty Spivak. Baltimore: Johns Hopkins University Press, 1976.

*Writing and Difference.* Trans. Alan Bass. London: Routledge & Kegan Paul, 1978.

'The *Retrait* of Metaphor.' *Enclitic* 2, 2 (1978), pp. 5–33.

*Margins of Philosophy.* Trans. Alan Bass. Brighton: Harvester Press, 1982.

'Of an Apocalyptic Tone Recently Adopted in Philosophy.' Trans. John P. Leavey, Jr. *Oxford Literary Review* 6, 2 (1984), pp. 3–37.

'Letter to a Japanese Friend.' *Derrida and Difference.* Ed. David Wood. University of Warwick: Parousia Press, 1985.

Dilthey, Wilhelm, *Selected Writings.* Ed. and trans. H. P. Rickman. Cambridge: Cambridge University Press, 1976.

Dorsch, T. S. (trans.), *Aristotle, Horace, Longinus: Classical Literary Criticism.* Harmondsworth: Penguin, 1965.

Ebeling, Gerhard, *The Nature of Faith.* Trans. R. G. Smith. London: Collins, 1961.

*Word and Faith.* Trans. James W. Leitch. London: SCM, 1963.

Eliot, T. S., *Selected Prose.* Ed. John Hayward. Harmondsworth: Penguin, 1953.

*The Complete Poems and Plays of T. S. Eliot.* London: Faber and Faber, 1969.

Ellis, E. Earle, *Paul and His Recent Interpreters.* Grand Rapids, Michigan: Eerdmans, 1961.

'Soma in First Corinthians.' *Interpretation* XLIV, 2 (1990), pp. 132–44.

Enright, D. J. and Chickera, Ernst de (eds), *English Critical Texts.* Oxford: Clarendon Press, 1962.

Fawcett, Robin P., *Language as a Semiological System: A Re-interpretation of Saussure.* Offprint from *The Ninth LACUS Forum 1982.* Ed. J. Morreall. Columbia: Hornbeam Press, 1983.

Foucault, Michel, 'The Order of Discourse.' *Untying the Text.* Ed. Robert Young. Boston: Routledge and Kegan Paul, 1981.

Fisch, Harold, 'Bakhtin's Misreadings of the Bible.' *Hebrew University Studies in Literature and the Arts* 16 (1988), pp. 130–49.

Frege, Gottlob, 'On Sense and Reference.' *Translations from the Philosophical Writings of Gottlob Frege.* Ed. Max Black and P. T. Geach. Oxford: Blackwell, 1952.

Frei, Hans W., *The Eclipse of Biblical Narrative: A Study in Eighteenth and Nineteenth Century Hermeneutics.* New Haven: Yale University Press, 1974.

Frye, Northrop, *The Great Code.* London: Routledge & Kegan Paul, 1982.

Funk, Robert W., *Language, Hermeneutic, and Word of God*. New York: Harper and Row, 1966.

Gadamer, Hans-Georg, (see also Michelfelder and Palmer, eds) *Truth and Method* (2nd edn). Trans. and ed. Garrett Burden and John Cumming. London: Sheed & Ward, 1975, 1979.

Gardiner, Michael, *The Dialogics of Critique: M. M. Bakhtin and the Theory of Ideology*. London: Routledge, 1992.

Gasché, Rodolphe, 'Deconstruction as Criticism.' *Glyph* 6 (1979), pp. 177–215.

Gellner, Ernest, *Legitimation of Belief*. London: Cambridge University Press, 1974.

Giglioli, Pier Paolo (ed.), *Language and Social Context*. Harmondsworth: Penguin, 1972.

Gilson, Étienne, *The Christian Philosophy of Saint Augustine*. Trans. L. E. M. Lynch. London: Victor Gollancz, 1961.

Grant, Robert M. and Tracy, David, *A Short History of the Interpretation of the Bible*. (2nd, rev.). London: SCM, 1963, 1964.

Hamann, Johann Georg (see Smith, Ronald Gregor).

Handelman, Susan A., *The Slayers of Moses: The Emergence of Rabbinic Interpretation in Modern Literary Theory*. Albany: State University of New York Press, 1982.

   'Parodic Play and Prophetic Reason: Two Interpretations of Interpretation'. *Poetics Today* 9, 2 (1988), pp. 395–423.

Hanson, R. P. C., *Allegory and Event*. London: SCM, 1959.

Harpham, Geoffrey Galt, *The Ascetic Imperative in Culture and Criticism*. Chicago and London: The University of Chicago Press, 1987.

   *Getting It Right: Language, Literature, and Ethics*. Chicago and London: The University of Chicago Press, 1992.

Hart, Kevin, *The Trespass of the Sign: Deconstruction, theology and philosophy*. Cambridge: Cambridge University Press, 1990.

   'The ins and outs of mysticism.' *Sophia* 30, 1 (1991), pp. 8–15.

Hartman, Geoffrey H., and Budick, Sanford (eds), *Midrash and Literature*. New Haven: Yale University Press, 1986.

Heidegger, Martin, *Basic Writings*. Ed. David Farrell Krell (2nd, rev.). London: Routledge, 1978, 1993.

Hirsch, E. D., *Validity in Interpretation*. New Haven and London: Yale University Press, 1967.

Hirschkop, Ken, and Shepherd, David (eds), *Bakhtin and Cultural Theory*. Manchester: Manchester University Press, 1989.

Hjelmslev, Louis, *Prologomena to a Theory of Language*. Trans. Francis J. Whitfield. Madison: The University of Wisconsin Press, 1969.

Hofstadter, Albert and Kuhns, Richard (eds), *Philosophies of Art and Beauty: Selected Readings in Aesthetics from Plato to Heidegger*. Chicago and London: University of Chicago Press, 1964.

Hopkins, Gerard Manley, *Selected Poems and Prose*. Ed. W. H. Gardner. Harmondsworth: Penguin, 1953, 1963.

Hudson, Wayne, *The Marxist Philosophy of Ernst Bloch*. London: Macmillan, 1982.

Jasper, David, *The Study of Literature and Religion: An Introduction* (2nd edn). London: Macmillan, 1989, 1992.

 'The Study of Literature and Theology: Five Years On.' *Literature & Theology* 6, 1 (1992), pp. 1–10.

Jeanrond, Werner G., 'Hermeneutics and Christian Praxis: Some Reflections on the History of Hermeneutics.' *Literature & Theology* 2, 2 (1988), pp. 174–88.

 *Theological Hermeneutics: Development and Significance.* London: Macmillan, 1991.

Josipovici, Gabriel, *The Book of God: A Response to the Bible.* New Haven and London: Yale University Press, 1988.

Kant, Immanuel, *Critique of Pure Reason.* Trans. Norman Kemp Smith (2nd, rev.). London: Macmillan, 1929, 1933.

Käsemann, Ernst, *Perspectives on Paul.* Trans. Margaret Kohl. London: SCM, 1971.

Keller, Helen, *The Story of My Life.* London: Hodder & Stoughton, 1949.

Kermode, Frank, *The Genesis of Secrecy.* Cambridge, Mass.: Harvard University Press, 1979.

Kierkegaard, Søren, *Fear and Trembling*, in *Kierkegaard's Writings, VI.* Ed. and trans. Howard V. Hong and Edna H. Hong. Princeton, NJ: Princeton University Press, 1983.

Kirwan, Christopher, *Augustine.* London: Routledge, 1989.

Lampe, Peter, 'Theological Wisdom and "The Word About the Cross": the Rhetorical Scheme in 1 Corinthians 1–4.' *Interpretation* XLIV, 2 (1990), pp. 117–31.

Lash, Nicholas, *A Matter of Hope: A Theologian's Reflections on the Thought of Karl Marx.* London: Darton, Longman and Todd, 1981.

Lawson, Hilary, *Reflexivity: The Postmodern Predicament.* London: Hutchinson, 1985.

Lawton, David, *Faith, Text and History: The Bible in English.* New York: Harvester Wheatsheaf, 1990.

Leach, Edmund, *Culture and Communication: The logic by which symbols are connected.* Cambridge: Cambridge University Press, 1976.

Levinas, Emmanuel, *The Levinas Reader.* Ed. Seán Hand. Oxford: Blackwell, 1989.

Lewis, C. S., *Miracles.* Glasgow: Collins, 1960.

Liddell, H. G. and Scott, R., *Greek–English Lexicon* (9th ed.). Oxford: Oxford University Press, 1940.

Lock, Charles, 'Carnival and Incarnation: Bakhtin and Orthodox Theology.' *Literature & Theology* 5, 1 (1991), pp. 68–82.

Louth, Andrew, *The Origins of the Christian Mystical Tradition: From Plato to Denys.* Oxford: Clarendon Press, 1981.

 'Augustine on Language.' *Literature & Theology* 3, 2 (1989), pp. 151–8.

Lyotard, Jean-François, *The Postmodern Condition: A Report on Knowledge.* Trans. Geoff Bennington and Brian Massumi. Manchester: Manchester University Press, 1984.

 'Notes on Legitimation.' Trans. Cecile Lindsay. *Oxford Literary Review* 9, 1–2 (1987), pp. 106–18.

*The Differend: Phrases in Dispute*. Trans. Georges Van Den Abbeele. Manchester: Manchester University Press, 1988.

Macleod, C. W., 'Allegory and Mysticism in Origen and Gregory of Nyssa.' *Journal of Theological Studies* XXII, 2 (1971), pp. 362–79.

Macquarrie, John, *Christian Hope*. London and Oxford: Mowbrays, 1978.

Medvedev, P. N. and Bakhtin, Mikhail, *The Formal Method in Literary Scholarship*. Trans. Albert J. Wehrle. Baltimore and London: The Johns Hopkins University Press, 1978.

Michelfelder, Diane P., and Palmer, Richard E. (eds), *Dialogue and Deconstruction: The Gadamer-Derrida Encounter*. Albany: State University of New York Press, 1989.

Mitchell, Sollace, 'Post-structuralism, empiricism and interpretation.' *The Need for Interpretation*. Ed. Sollace Mitchell and Michael Rosen. London: Athlone Press, 1983, pp. 54–89.

Moltmann, Jürgen, *Theology of Hope on the Ground and Implications of a Christian Eschatology*. Trans. James W. Leitch. London: SCM, 1967.

*The Experiment Hope*. Ed. and trans. M. Douglas Meeks. London: SCM, 1975.

'Has Modern Society any Future?' Trans. Margaret Kohl. *Concilium* special issue (1990–1), pp. 54–65. 'On the Threshold of the Third Millenium'. Ed. the Foundation.

Myerson, George, *The Argumentative Imagination: Wordsworth. Dryden, religious dialogues*. Manchester and New York: Manchester University Press, 1992.

Nietzsche, Friedrich, *Twilight of the Idols and The Anti-Christ*. Trans. R. J. Hollingdale. Harmondsworth: Penguin, 1968, 1990.

Norris, Christopher, *Deconstruction: Theory and Practice*. London and New York: Routledge, 1982.

*The Contest of Faculties: Philosophy and Theory after Deconstruction*. London: Methuen, 1985.

*Derrida*. London: Fontana, 1987.

'Postmodernising History: Right-Wing Revisionism and the Uses of Theory.' *Southern Review* 21, 2 (1988), pp. 123–40.

'Philosophy as *Not* Just a "Kind of Writing": Derrida and the Claim of Reason.' *Re-Drawing the Lines: Analytic Philosophy. Deconstruction and Literary Theory*. Ed. R. W. Dasenbrock. Minneapolis: University of Minnesota Press, 1989, pp. 189–203.

*What's Wrong With Postmodernism: Critical Theory and the Ends of Philosophy*. New York: Harvester Wheatsheaf, 1990.

*Spinoza and the Origins of Modern Critical Theory*. Oxford: Basil Blackwell, 1991.

O'Flaherty, James C., *Unity and Language: A Study in the Philosophy of Johann Georg Hamann*. Chapel Hill, NC: University of North Carolina, 1952.

O'Neill, Onora, *Constructions of Reason: Explorations of Kant's Practical Philosophy*. Cambridge: Cambridge University Press, 1989.

Ong, Walter J., *Orality and Literacy: The Technologizing of the Word*. London and New York: Methuen, 1982.

Origen, *De Principiis* in *The Writings of Origen I*. Trans. Rev. Frederick Crombie. Edinburgh: T. & T. Clark, 1869.

Palmer, Richard E., *Hermeneutics: Interpretation Theory in Schleiermacher.*

Dilthey. Heidegger, and Gadamer. Evanston: Northwestern University Press, 1969.

Peirce, Charles S., *The Philosophy of Peirce: Selected Writings*. Ed. Justus Buchler. London: Routledge & Kegan Paul, 1940.

Poland, Lynn M., 'Augustine, Allegory, and Conversion.' *Literature and Theology* 2, 1 (1988), pp. 37–48.

Prickett, Stephen, *Words and The Word: Language. Poetics and Biblical Interpretation*. Cambridge: Cambridge University Press, 1986.

Prickett, Stephen (ed.), *Reading the Text: Biblical Criticism and Literary Theory*. Oxford: Basil Blackwell, 1991.

Rad, Gerhard von, 'Typological Interpretation of the Old Testament.' *A Guide to Contemporary Hermeneutics*. Ed. Donald K. McKim. Grand Rapids: Eerdmans, 1986.

Ricoeur, Paul, *The Conflict of Interpretations*. Ed. Don Ihde. Evanston: Northwestern University Press, 1974.

*Interpretation Theory: Discourse and the Surplus of Meaning*. Fort Worth: Texas Christian University Press, 1976.

*The Rule of Metaphor: Multi-Disciplinary Studies of the Creation of Meaning in Language*. Trans. R. Czerny with K. McLaughlin and J. Costello. Toronto and Buffalo: University of Toronto Press, 1977.

*Essays on Biblical Interpretation*. Ed. Lewis S. Mudge. London: SPCK, 1981.

*Hermeneutics and the Human Sciences*. Ed. and trans. John B. Thompson. Cambridge: Cambridge University Press, 1981.

*From Text to Action: Essays in Hermeneutics II*. Trans. Kathleen Blamey and John B. Thompson. London: Athlone Press, 1991.

Robinson, James M. (ed.), *The Future of Our Religious Past*. Trans. Charles E. Carlston and Robert P. Scharlemann. London: SCM, 1971.

Rorty, Richard, 'Two Meanings of "Logocentrism": A Reply to Norris.' *Re-Drawing the Lines: Analytic Philosophy. Deconstruction and Literary Theory*. Ed. R. W. Dasenbrock. Minneapolis: University of Minnesota Press, 1989, pp. 204–16.

Russell, Bertrand, *A History of Western Philosophy*. London: Unwin, 1946, 1979.

Salusinszky, Imre, *Criticism in Society*. London: Methuen, 1987.

Sanders, E. P., *Paul and Palestinian Judaism: A Comparison of Patterns of Religion*. London: SCM, 1977.

Saussure, Ferdinand de, *Course in General Linguistics*. Ed. Charles Bally and Albert Sechehaye with Albert Riedlinger, trans. Wade Baskin. New York: McGraw-Hill, 1966.

Schwartz, Regina (ed.), *The Book and the Text: The Bible and Literary Theory*. Oxford and Cambridge, Mass.: Basil Blackwell, 1990.

Scruton, Roger, *Kant*. Oxford: Oxford University Press, 1982.

Searle, J. R. (ed.), *The Philosophy of Language*. Oxford: Oxford University Press, 1971.

Skilton, David, *Defoe to the Victorians: Two Centuries of the English Novel*. Harmondsworth: Penguin, 1985.

Smalley, Beryl, *The Study of the Bible in the Middle Ages* (3rd, rev.). Oxford: Basil Blackwell, 1952, 1983.

Smith, Ronald Gregor, *J. G. Hamann 1730–1787: A Study in Christian Existence with Selections from His Writings*. London: Collins, 1960.

Spinoza, Benedict de, *Tractatus Theologico-Politicus*. London: Trübner & Co., 1862.

Steiner, George, *After Babel: Aspects of Language and Translation*. Oxford: Oxford University Press, 1975.

Sturrock, John (ed.), *Structuralism and Since*. Oxford: Oxford University Press, 1979.

Taylor, Mark C., *Erring: A Postmodern A/theology*. Chicago and London: University of Chicago Press, 1984.

Theissen, Gerd, *Psychological Aspects of Pauline Theology*. Trans. John P. Galvin. Edinburgh: T. & T. Clark, 1987.

Thiselton, A. C., 'The New Hermeneutic.' *A Guide to Contemporary Hermeneutics*. Ed. Donald K. McKim. Grand Rapids: Eerdmans, 1986, pp. 78–107.

*The Two Horizons*. Exeter: Paternoster, 1980.

Tracy, David, 'Metaphor and Religion: The Test Case of Christian Texts.' *Critical Inquiry* (Autumn 1978), pp. 91–106.

Vesey, Godfrey (ed.), *The Philosophy in Christianity*. Cambridge: Cambridge University Press, 1989.

Voloshinov, V. N., *Marxism and the Philosophy of Language*. Trans. Ladislav Matejka and I. R. Titunik. New York: Seminar Press, 1973.

Wadsworth, Michael (ed.), *Ways of Reading the Bible*. Brighton: Harvester Press, 1981.

Warner, Martin (ed.), *The Bible as Rhetoric: Studies in Biblical Persuasion and Credibility*. London: Routledge, 1990.

Wellek, René, and Warren, Austin, *Theory of Literature* (3rd ed.). Harmondsworth: Penguin, 1949, 1954, 1963.

Whorf, Benjamin Lee, *Language, Thought, and Reality: Selected Writings*. Ed. John B. Carroll. Cambridge, Mass.: MIT Press, 1956.

Wiederkehr, Dietrich, *Belief in Redemption: Concepts of Salvation from the New Testament to the Present Time*. Trans. Jeremy Moiser. London: SPCK, 1979.

Wimsatt, W. K., *The Verbal Icon: Studies in the Meaning of Poetry*. Lexington, Kentucky: University of Kentucky Press, 1954.

Wood, David (ed.), *Writing The Future*. London: Routledge, 1990.

Wright, T. R., *Theology and Literature*. Oxford: Basil Blackwell, 1988.

<h1 style="text-align:center">Name Index</h1>

# Subject Index